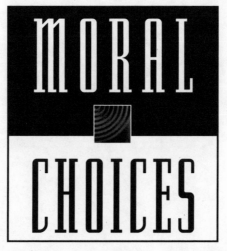

MORAL CHOICES

An Introduction To Ethics

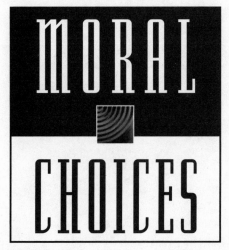

An Introduction To Ethics

Scott B. Rae

ZondervanPublishingHouse
Grand Rapids, Michigan

A Division of HarperCollinsPublishers

Moral Choices
Copyright © 1995 by Scott B. Rae

Requests for information should be addressed to:

 ZondervanPublishingHouse
Grand Rapids, Michigan 49530

Library of Congress Cataloging-in-Publication Data

Rae, Scott B.
    Moral choices : an introduction to ethics / Scott B. Rae.
       p. cm.
    Includes bibliographical references and index.
    ISBN: 0-310-20013-X (hardcover : alk. paper)
    1. Ethics. I. Title.
BJ1012.R32 1995
170—dc20   95-9393
                                                    CIP

This edition printed on acid-free paper and meets the American National Standards Institute Z39.48 standard.

All Scripture quotations, unless otherwise indicated, are taken from the *Holy Bible: New International Version*®. NIV®. Copyright © 1973, 1978, 1984 by International Bible Society. Used by permission of Zondervan Publishing House. All rights reserved.

Edited by Gary L. Knapp
Interior design by Susan A. Koppenol

Printed in the United States of America

97 98 99 00 01 02/❖ DH 10 9 8 7 6 5 4

CONTENTS

ACKNOWLEDGMENTS

Special thanks are in order for a number of people who helped make this book a reality. My colleagues at Talbot School of Theology, Biola University—particularly Drs. Walt Russell, J. P. Moreland, Klaus Issler, Paul Cox, and Doug Geivett and Professor Kenman L. Wong—all provided encouragement, support, and intellectual stimulation, which have helped keep me sharp and motivated to be the most competent ethicist I can be. My former dean, Dr. Bing Hunter, was instrumental in helping introduce me to the editors at Zondervan and convincing them to allow me to write this book. My mentors, Drs. William W. May and Dallas Willard of the University of Southern California, offered further encouragement to Zondervan in this area. My current dean, Dr. Dennis Dirks, allowed me the time off from teaching to devote myself to the book and complete it on time.

Many of my associates on the Ethics Committee at Holy Cross Medical Center in Mission Hills, California, read parts of the manuscript and offered insightful critiques. I appreciate their taking time out of their busy schedules in the health care profession to carefully read and comment on the book. My editors at Zondervan have been a delight to work with and have helped make my work much more readable. I am very appreciative of their painstaking efforts in making the book accessible to a nontechnical audience.

Finally, my wife, Sally, and my sons, Taylor and Cameron, bore most of the burden of my writing this book. I deeply appreciate their patience with me and their willingness to enable me to finish the book. It is gratefully dedicated to them.

1

INTRODUCTION: WHY STUDY ETHICS?

In Plato's classic work *The Republic*, the myth of Gyges sets out the question, Why be moral? Gyges was given the opportunity to live life as an invisible entity, able to do anything he wanted to do with no one ever discovering what he had done. That is, he could do whatever he wanted and would be assured of getting away with it. Given the chance to live life like this, the question Plato raises is, Would a person want to be moral?[1] After a good deal of dialogue, Plato concluded that being moral was inherently valuable, apart from any additional benefits it produced or harm that it enabled a person to avoid.

How would you respond to the question, Why be moral? Since the moral life and moral decision making are the focal points of this book, this question is foundational. If you decide that being moral is not that important, then you probably will not spend much time reading this or any other book on ethics. But if being moral is important to you, then the content of this book will hopefully be helpful in shaping how you view morality.

Most people, when they are genuinely honest with themselves, still associate doing well in life with being a good person. Having moral character is still essential to most people's conceptions of what makes a person flourish in his or her life. For example, it is difficult to imagine a person being considered a success in life if he has gained his wealth dishonestly. It is equally difficult to call a person a success who is at the top of his profession, but cheats on his wife, abuses his children, and drinks too much. On the other hand, we rightly hold up a person like Mother Teresa as a model of living a good life, even though she lacks most material goods that society values. One of the principal reasons for being moral is that it is central to most concepts of human fulfillment. For the Christian, being moral is critical to a life that seeks to honor God. We could say that being moral is inherently good because it is foundational to a person's flourishing in life, since doing well in life and being a good person still go together for most people.

The same holds true for society as a whole. Most people would not want to live in a society in which morality was unimportant, in which conceptions of right and wrong carried little weight. In fact, it is unlikely that any sort of civilized society could continue unless it had concern for important moral values such as fairness, justice, truthfulness, and compassion. Ethics are important because they give direction to people and societies, who have some sense that they cannot flourish without being moral.

Ethics are important because moral questions are at the heart of life's most important issues. Morality is primarily concerned with questions of right and wrong, the ability to distinguish between the two, and the justification of the distinction. Closely related are questions like, What is a good person? What things are morally praiseworthy? What constitutes a good life? and What would a good society look like? These are fundamental to your view of the world. You cannot formulate an adequate worldview without providing answers to these moral questions. A wide variety of professions, whether or not they realize it, actually deal with moral questions. For example, morality is fundamental to politics, since politics and the law concern the way in which people order their lives together in society.

Ethics are also important because you face moral choices every day. Every so often you will face emotionally wrenching moral dilemmas that have no easy answers. Many decisions you will make on a day-to-day basis also involve questions of right and wrong. Ethics provide the basis on which you make those decisions. Most people have some kind of an idea of what sorts of things are right and wrong. Explaining why you think something is right or wrong or whether a particular person is good or evil, however, is altogether another question. The basis on which you make moral choices is often as important as the choices themselves. Yet, few people have thought through the way in which they justify their conceptions of right and wrong.

Finally, ethics are important in facing a number of issues, including abortion, euthanasia, homosexuality, war, and capital punishment. Debates on issues such as these seem endless and irreconcilable, and they promise to continue far into the future. What many of these issues share is a fundamental disagreement over the ultimate source of moral authority. Some individuals hold that moral authority is ultimately a human construction, while others insist that moral authority comes from some transcendent source that is beyond human beings, such as a revelation from God or nature.[2] As you read the newspaper and various newsmagazines and listen to television news, you will be increasingly aware of the importance of these issues. You will also notice that, apart from legal intervention, these issues are no closer to being resolved today than they were ten years ago.

Not only does intractable debate characterize these issues, but society has a general sense of bewilderment over a number of other issues. Many of these involve matters of science and technology that have run far ahead of ethical reflection. For example, genetic engineering, various reproductive technologies, and the use of human fetal tissue in the treatment of certain diseases all involve moral dilemmas that are just beginning to be substantively discussed. Most observers in these areas acknowledge that technology has outpaced society's ability to determine the moral parameters for its use. There is a general sense that ethics are necessary for dealing with our increasingly technological society.

More people have an interest in ethics today than at any other time in the recent past. Some of that interest is due to the complex issues spawned by technology, while others have an alarming sense of a general moral decline in society. With the consistent increase in teenage pregnancies, drug abuse, child abuse, violent crime, and sexually transmitted diseases, many are wondering if the moral fabric of society is coming unraveled. In addition, the numerous scandals that have rocked the business community and other professions have left some to ask if "business ethics" and "professional ethics" are indeed oxymorons. Some people are aware of the need to stress values in various educational arenas, including public schools. Many are also realizing that the value-neutral approach to education at all levels is not working, and some even suggest that such value neutrality is impossible.

OVERVIEW OF THE BOOK

As you read this book, you will be exposed both to foundations in ethics and to the application of those foundations to the most pressing moral issues of the day. Believing that morality ultimately issues from the character of God, I find the most critical and foundational element of ethics to be the direction that God provides, both in his Word (i.e., special revelation), and outside his Word (i.e., general revelation). Chapter 2 will outline the distinctive elements of Christian ethics. This entire book could be about Christian ethics. Indeed, some works are entirely devoted to this subject. Here, however, you will simply get a synthesis of the main parameters of biblical ethics.

Throughout the ages, many philosophers, even some whose inquiries predate the written Scriptures, have wrestled with the questions of right and wrong and arrived at somewhat different answers.

Recognizing, then, that the Bible is not the only source of ethical inquiry, chapters 3 and 4 endeavor to provide an honest look at alternative ethical systems, such as relativism, utilitarianism, and ethical egoism. We will also examine the major figures who systematized them, including Plato, Aristotle, Augustine, Aquinas, and Kant. These must be brief, but I have included resources, especially original sources, should you wish to study any of these individuals or systems further. For each alternative approach to ethics, I will offer a description of the system and its major advocate, a presentation of the strong points of the system, a comparison of it with Scripture, and a critique of the system, both from within the system itself and from the perspective of Christian ethics. In order to be able to converse with an increasingly secular world about ethics and morality, students need exposure to the ways in which other people have done ethics. Some of these approaches contain truth that ultimately comes from God, even if the people formulating the alternative are unaware of it. Also, for the sake of clarity, I have tried to use terms in a manner consistent with their use in secular works on ethics.

Chapter 5 contains a model for making moral decisions and illustrates its use on some particularly knotty moral dilemmas. This model can be used in virtually any setting and does not require any particular worldview commitment for its profitable use. I offer this model not as a type of computer program for generating correct moral decisions, but as a guideline to insure that all the important bases are covered when you make moral decisions. This chapter begins to build the bridge from theory to application that will be more clearly defined in subsequent chapters.

Chapters 6 through 12 deal with some of the current issues that are hotly debated both among individuals and in society. Discussion in these chapters will recognize the way these issues affect people individually (personal ethics) as well as how they affect social policy (social ethics). Since medical ethics contains some of the most frequently debated and complex issues, chapters 6 through 8 begin with such issues as abortion, euthanasia, and reproductive technologies. Staying within the arena of ethics pertaining to life and death, chapter 9 addresses the issue of capital punishment. Chapter 10 addresses the subject of sexual ethics, including a discussion of homosexuality. Chapter 11 takes up the issue that has been debated longer than any other, the morality of war, which is still a significant issue even after the end of the Cold War. The book concludes with some guidelines for legislating morality, a subject important for Christians who are becoming actively and aggressively involved in politics and public policy.

INTRODUCING KEY TERMS AND DISTINCTIONS IN ETHICS

One of the difficult aspects of studying a subject like ethics is that you are introduced to many terms with which you are unfamiliar. For example, new members of the hospital ethics committee with whom I consult are often unfamiliar with terminology customarily used by ethicists. So, to keep you from the initial shock of jumping headfirst into a new subject, this section will introduce you to some of the key terms that you will often see as you read this book.

Most people use the terms *morality* and *ethics* interchangeably. Technically, morality refers to the actual content of right and wrong, and ethics refers to the process of determining right and wrong. Ethics is both an art and a science. It does involve some precision like the sciences, but like art, it is an inexact and sometimes intuitive discipline. Morality is the end result of ethical deliberation, the substance of right and wrong.

Major Categories

Four broad categories have traditionally fallen under the heading of ethics. They include (1) *descriptive ethics*, (2) *normative ethics*, (3) *metaethics*, and (4) *aretaic ethics*. Normative ethics will be the primary concern in this book.

First, *descriptive ethics* is a sociological discipline that attempts to describe the morals of society, often by studying other cultures. Anthropologists often use it in their fieldwork to describe the distinctives of other cultures.

Second, *normative ethics* refers to the discipline that produces moral norms or rules as its end product. Most systems of ethics are designed to tell you what is normative for individual and social behavior, or what is right and wrong, both generally and in specific circumstances. Normative ethics *prescribes* moral behavior, whereas descriptive ethics *describes* moral behavior. When we examine important moral issues in later chapters, we will be trying to establish a norm to apply to that particular issue. When most people debate about ethics, they are debating normative ethics, or what the moral norm should be.

Of course, ethics is not the only normative discipline.[3] For example, the law produces legal norms, but not necessarily moral ones, although law and morality probably overlap significantly. We will pick this up again in chapter 12 when we discuss the subject of legislating morality. In addition, there are norms of good taste and social acceptability, which we call etiquette. Further, religion produces behavioral norms, often defined by a religious authority such as a pastor or other church official, that govern a person's relationship to God. In chapter 2 we will see that Christian ethics includes a substantial overlap between duties with respect to a person's relationship to God and duties with respect to the people around him or her.

Third, *metaethics* is an area of ethics that investigates the meaning of moral language, or the epistemology of ethics, and also considers the justification of ethical theories and judgments. For example, it focuses on the meaning of the major terms used in ethics, such as *right, good,* and *just.* The primary focus of technical philosophers, metaethics has been receiving more attention from a popular audience today since more people are insisting that the language of right and wrong is nothing more than an expression of personal preferences. Accordingly, some will argue that the judgment that homosexuality is wrong is not a statement about right and wrong but simply a personal distaste for homosexuality. Morality is thus reduced to matters of taste and preference and has little to do with right and wrong. We will look at this later in chapter 4 when we discuss "emotivism."

Fourth, *aretaic ethics* is a category of ethics that focuses on the virtues produced in the people, not the morality of specific acts. Also known as *virtue theory*, it is growing in popularity today. The term *aretaic* is taken from a Greek term that is translated "virtue." Recognizing that there is more to the moral life than simply making right decisions, many people believe that matters of virtue and character are equally, if not more, important than the way in which we resolve moral dilemmas.

When discussing whether someone or something is moral, it helps to be very specific. Normally, making a moral judgment involves at least four specific considerations.[4] First, you should consider the *action* itself. This is usually the focus of a moral judgment, but hardly the only aspect of moral evaluation. Second, you should evaluate the *motive* of the person (called the "moral actor") performing the action. In some cases the motive is the only difference between two otherwise identical actions. For example, your motive in giving something to someone is often the only difference between a gift and a bribe. Third, you should evaluate the *consequences* of your actions and decisions. Bear in mind, however, that actions may be inherently right or wrong, regardless of the consequences. For example, slavery in the pre-Civil War South was wrong regardless of how slavery benefited the Southern economy, because human beings are not objects that should be bought and sold. Fourth, although a bit more difficult to do than the previous three considerations, you should attempt to evaluate the *character* of the moral actor. Character is the tendency of a person to act in predictable ways over time. Virtue theorists have led the way in insisting that any ethic that does not concern itself with character and virtue is incomplete and reduces ethics to merely a preoccupation with actions, specifically moral dilemmas that people do not often face.

Ethical Systems

Ethical systems may be classified as either *action-oriented* systems or *virtue-based* systems. Under these two major divisions are three subcategories by which ethical systems may be further classified. These three subcategories are *deontological* systems, *teleological* systems, and *relativism*. Most of the technical terms have to do with the action-oriented systems.

First, *deontological* systems are systems that are based on principles in which actions (or character, or even intentions) are inherently right or wrong. There are three primary deontological systems: (1) *divine command theory*, (2) *natural law,* and (3) *ethical rationalism*. The Christian will tend to be more deontologically oriented because of the emphasis in Christian ethics on the commands of God as moral absolutes. _end_

Second, *teleological* systems are systems that are based on the end result produced by an action. Since the consequences rather than principles determine right actions for teleological systems, no action is inherently right or wrong. Whether an action is right or wrong depends on the consequences produced by that action. If it produces more beneficial consequences than harmful consequences, then it is moral. If not, then it is immoral. The primary form of teleological ethics is called *utilitarianism*, which holds that the action that produces the greatest good for the greatest number is the moral choice. Another form of teleological ethics is called *ethical egoism*, which maintains that the right thing to do is whatever is in a person's self-interest. Thus, for the ethical egoist the only consequence that matters is whether it advances his or her own self-interest.

Third, *relativism* refers to an ethical system in which right and wrong are not absolute and unchanging but relative to one's culture (cultural relativism) or one's own personal preferences (moral subjectivism). Both forms of relativism are widely embraced today. With the current emphasis on multiculturalism and appreciation for the cultural diversity that exists in much of the world, and the importance of a culture's values in its self-definition, it should not surprise us that there is a movement toward accepting all cultures' values as equally valid, which is the equivalent of cultural relativism. Moral subjectivism is advocated every time someone says, "Whatever is right for you is OK, but don't force your view on me!" This statement implies that each individual's choice is right, reducing morality to merely individual preference. One of the primary arguments in favor of abortion rights involves moral subjectivism about the moral status of the unborn child. Pro-choice advocates recognize that if a woman views the fetus as a person, then abortion is not a moral option for her. But if she views the fetus as not yet a person, then she can obviously justify abortion. Thus, pro-choice advocates object to the pro-life movement's desire to pass restrictive abortion laws that would impose a view of the fetus that should be decided only by each individual pregnant woman.

You will undoubtedly be introduced to other new terms and ideas as you read this book. But don't let the terminology intimidate you. Every thoughtful person should be concerned about and interested in ethics, since it addresses the ultimate questions about the good life, the good person, and the good society. As Socrates said in Plato's *Republic*, "We are discussing no small matter, but how we ought to live."

NOTES

[1]Technically, the *Republic* is concerned with the question of justice. In Gyges case, would a person still desire to be just. But for Plato, justice for an individual was closely associated with virtue, so the illustration still fits the question, Why be moral?

[2]For further detail on the issues currently being endlessly debated and the two sources of moral authority, see James Davison Hunter, *Culture Wars* (New York: Basic Books, 1992), and his most recent, *Before the Shooting Begins: Searching for Democracy in America's Culture War* (New York: Free Press, 1994).

[3]See Louis Pojman, *Ethics: Discovering Right and Wrong* (Belmont, Calif.: Wadsworth, 1990), 4–5.

[4]Ibid., 7–10.

2

CHRISTIAN ETHICS

Despite modern departures from it, the Judeo-Christian system of morality has had a profound impact on society from its inception. In this chapter we will put forth the various emphases in Christian ethics and address some of the criticisms of Christian ethics. Initially, we will establish a scriptural foundation by examining various points of ethical emphasis in both Old and New Testaments. Although both Old and New Testament ethics are vast subjects on which entire volumes have been written, a synthesis of the major emphases in biblical ethics is all that space here will allow.

Much of biblical ethics revolves around God's specially revealed commands. For many people, therefore, the divine command theory of ethics has become synonymous with biblical ethics. Such a theory of ethics, however, raises questions about whether something is good because God commanded it or whether God commands something because it is good. This is known as the "Euthyphro dilemma," since the question was first raised by Plato in his dialogue *Euthyphro*. This dilemma cannot be adequately addressed without a consideration of what is called natural law. Previously emphasized primarily by Roman Catholics and at times treated with scorn by Protestants, this concept is important for a fully developed biblical ethic. Its definition and biblical justification will be explored toward the end of this chapter.

OLD TESTAMENT ETHICS

Just as the Old Testament is not a systematic theology but a mixture of different theological emphases presented in a variety of literary styles, so too, the Old Testament is not a carefully arranged system of ethics, but a mixture of different types of moral reasoning. The Old Testament reflects great diversity in methods of moral reasoning. With the Mosaic Law providing the ethical principles by which Israel ordered its life, it is not surprising that deontology, or an appeal to principles, is strongly emphasized in the Old Testament. In their appeal to the Law as the basis of their prophetic message, the prophets depend heavily on deontology. But there is more to morality in the Old Testament than the simple appeal to principles and commands. The Wisdom Literature contains a measure of utilitarian reasoning. For example, many of the Proverbs contain explicit descriptions of the consequences of certain actions and character traits. The writers of the Proverbs appear to praise wisdom because of the good consequences it produces, while they warn against folly because of the harmful consequences that it produces. To be sure, the Wisdom Literature is ultimately grounded in the Law, and thus ultimately grounded in principles. The Wisdom Literature, then, does not attempt to use utilitarianism as a self-sufficient system for discovering morality, but the appeal to principles is supplemented by appeal to consequences, a use of both utilitarian and deontological methods.

The Old Testament also appeals to egoism and self-interest, specifically in the covenant blessings and cursings in Deuteronomy 27–30. Here God reveals to Moses that Israel's agriculture and national security face certain consequences dependent on her obedience to the covenant. Thus her loyalty to the covenant will result in certain blessings, while her disobedience will lead to certain cursings. Accordingly, Israel would have a high degree of self-interest to obey the Law. The prophets repeatedly refer to the blessings and cursings of the covenant in their attempts to call Israel back to faithfulness to God, suggesting that the covenant cursings and blessings form a significant aspect of Old Testament ethics. Again, this is not to say that Scripture uses egoism as a self-sufficient ethical system, but rather, that the appeal to principles is supplemented by an appeal to self-interest.

Finally, the Old Testament also appeals to natural law. For example, the book of Proverbs defines right and wrong (wisdom and folly) by observations drawn from nature (Prov. 6:6–11; see also Ps. 19:1–6) and human relationships (Prov. 24:30–34). Natural law is not strictly limited to observations from nature, however. It refers to universal moral principles that are not specifically derived from special revelation. The oracles to the nations (e.g., see Isa. 13–23; Jer. 46–51; Ezek. 25–32) are good examples of biblical appeal to natural law. Unlike Israel who had the Mosaic Law, these nations lacked the Law and are still condemned for many of the same transgressions as Israel, including injustice, violence, and oppression of the poor. We can conclude, therefore, that these nations were somehow aware of their crimes, otherwise God could not be just in holding them accountable for their crimes. The means by which God made them aware of these moral obligations is general revelation, or natural law. Thus in the Old Testament natural law supplements the ethics provided by special revelation.[1]

The Law as the Core of Old Testament Ethics

The foundation of Old Testament ethics is the Law. Some scholars use the term *Law* more narrowly to refer to the Ten Commandments (Ex. 20:1–17; Deut. 5:1–21). We will use it more broadly to refer to the first five books of the Old Testament, the Pentateuch, but especially to the material found in Exodus 20–40, Leviticus, and Deuteronomy 5–30. The Law sets out the fundamental principles and commands for Israel and consists of three primary parts: (1) the moral law, or the Ten Commandments; (2) the civil law, which governed social relations and institutions; and (3) the ceremonial law, which governed Israel's worship of God. When referring to Old Testament ethics, most scholars use the moral and civil law as the foundation. The ceremonial law is often considered a part of Israel's religious ritual, and not strictly related to ethics.

Much of the remainder of the Old Testament ethics can be seen in relation to the Law. In the Poetic Literature, especially Psalms, worship is often presented as a response to the revelation of God in the Law. The Wisdom Literature attempts to take the general demands of the Law and make them persuasive to an international audience, without any of the features directly related to Israel, such as the sacrificial system, the Promised Land, the covenants, and the tabernacle or temple. The Prophets appeal to the Law as their primary point of reference in making their indictments against Israel.

One major difference between the Law and the Prophets is that the Prophets make a general appeal to the broad overarching principles in the Law, namely, avoiding idolatry and maintaining justice, in contrast to the detailed specifics in the Law. These are key concepts for Old Testament ethics, reflecting the emphasis of the Ten Commandments on both worship and social relations, or on one's relationship with God and with other people in the community. Rarely do the Prophets address the people with the specifics contained in the Law. Essentially they are preaching the general principles contained in the Law, and they frequently direct attention to the cause and effect relationship between obedience and agricultural prosperity in the covenant blessings and cursings of Deuteronomy 27–30.

In the Old Testament, Israel was a theocracy,[2] a nation in which the law of God was automatically the law of the land. Accordingly, all morality was legislated. No distinction was made between law and morality, as one could find in a pluralistic society. The church today, however, is not under the civil and ceremonial aspects of the Law as was Israel. Even though this distinguishes Old Testament Israel from modern, nontheocratic Western nations, a case can be made for Israel as a model for a biblical social ethic. This assertion is based on the premise that the principles underlying the Law are still valid and applicable for the church today.

The Overlap of Personal and Social Ethics

Being a theocracy, Israel made no distinction between personal and social ethics. Today ethicists usually separate ethics into personal ethics (concerning individual ethical decisions), and social ethics (concerning morality for groups, namely, the broader society). A social ethic mandates morality for the society at large, or the degree to which individual moral positions should also be moral obligations for society at large.

The abortion debate effectively illustrates the distinction between personal and social ethics. Many people argue that while it may be valid to be personally opposed to abortion, it is not necessarily valid to say that abortion is wrong for the rest of society. This type of reasoning has also been applied to the subjects of adultery and homosexual behavior. In the case of murder, however, everyone—regardless of background, culture, or religious tradition—believes that it is wrong and should be wrong for everyone in society. In this case there is an overlap of personal and social ethics. In the Old Testament, personal and social ethics were virtually indistinguishable. What was moral for the individual (personal ethics) was also moral for the society (social ethics).

The emphasis on individual morality occurs most frequently in the Wisdom Literature. Perhaps this is because the wisdom books are intended universally in a way that the Law was not. The Wisdom Literature was written more for a international audience and the Law was addressed to the covenant community of Israel. Thus personal and social ethics overlap more in the Wisdom Literature because the bonds of community are not emphasized as much as they are in the parts of the Old Testament addressed directly to Israel.

Holiness as the Unifying Theme of Old Testament Ethics

The central concept that unifies Old Testament ethics is the idea of holiness.[3] The Hebrew term for "holy" derives from the Hebrew word *qadosh,* which means "set apart." This is the root concept of the New Testament idea of sanctification.[4] Israel is set apart as a nation to reflect the character of God in their worship, their social relations, and their institutions. One of the primary reasons that God issues his commands is to set Israel apart from its pagan neighbors. This is what Exodus 19:6 means when it refers to Israel as a "holy nation" and a "kingdom of priests." Vivid examples of how God desired Israel to be set apart occur in the specific commands in Deuteronomy that are aimed at producing a contrast between Israel's practices and those of the other nations in the ancient Near East. The following examples will illustrate this.

First, Deuteronomy 17:16–17 places limitations on the person who would eventually occupy the office of king in Israel. He must not acquire great wealth, military might, or national security alliances (through intermarriage with foreign women), since these would undercut his dependence on God for personal and national security. Throughout the ancient world at this time, the king was virtually deified, and limits on his sovereignty were rare. The king of Israel, however, was to bow before the sovereignty of God. Due to these limitations placed on Israel's king, the surrounding nations knew that he was not a god, but only a servant of the living God.

Second, the treatment of women captured in the course of warfare illustrates how the Law set Israel apart from its neighbors. In much of the ancient world, women who were taken captive by a victorious army were subject to a wide variety of sexual offenses. Israel, however, was obligated to treat them humanely and with respect. If an Israelite wanted to marry her, he could do so. But the Law strictly prohibited Israelites from selling these women as slaves, either for domestic or sexual purposes (Deut. 21:10–14).

Third, the treatment of other slaves was also to be humane, in contrast to much of the ancient world. After six years of service, slaves were to be released (unless they wanted to remain with the family), and upon their departure their master was to provide for them liberally, rather than leave them destitute (Deut. 15:12–18). The treatment of the poor in the land was similar (Lev. 25:25–29, 35–43; Deut. 15:1–11).

The primary way in which Israel was to be set apart for God was in its worship. The Law repeatedly prohibited Israel from worship rituals that contained any compromise with the Canaanite religious practices of their neighbors. For example, sorcery, spiritism, witchcraft, and divination, all of which were associated with Canaanite idolatry, were forbidden in an effort to distance Israel from the worship patterns of their neighbors (Deut. 18:9–13).

The first two commandments explicitly prohibit worshiping false gods (Ex. 20:1–6). Other prohibitions contained in the Law may forbid certain practices simply because the practices resembled the worship practices of Israel's pagan neighbors. For example, when Aaron's sons offered "unauthorized fire" in the tabernacle, God took their lives (Lev. 10:1–5). Although this passage has various interpretations, the one that is most consistent with God's harsh treatment of the priests is that perhaps they introduced a pagan religious ritual into the worship of God in the tabernacle. Likewise, the prohibition in Exodus 23:19 ("Do not cook a young goat in its mother's milk") may have nothing to do with kosher laws or good health practices. Instead, the practice may be prohibited because it resembled a pagan religious ritual. In addition, because the worship of the Canaanite god Baal frequently involved sexual immorality, illicit sexual relations are prohibited (Lev. 18; Num. 25:1–3). God's desire for Israel to be set apart for him was central to Old Testament ethics. This is the reason why Israel's request to have a king like all the other nations (1 Sam. 8) undercut God's purpose for Israel to be a "kingdom of priests" and a "holy nation."

Obedience as Personal Loyalty to God

Even though obedience to the precepts of the Law was strongly emphasized as one of the means by which Israel was to be set apart, obedience was not seen as an end in itself. Rather, obedience to the Law was seen primarily as loyalty to God. This emphasis made Old Testament ethics different from the other legal codes of the ancient world. Although the Law shares some similarities with other codes of the ancient world, such as the Babylonian Code of Hammurabi, it is also quite distinct from them in that it is person-centered. A critical emphasis in Old Testament ethics is that God is a person who stands behind the precepts, a concept that is expanded by Jesus in the Gospels in his repudiation of Pharisaic legalism. The emphasis is on obedience to a Person, not just to a command. For example, even the first line of the Ten Commandments refers to God as the One who delivered the Hebrews from slavery in Egypt. Accordingly, this summary statement of what God had already done on their behalf provides a motive for the people of God to remain loyal to him (Ex. 20:2–3).

Exodus and Deuteronomy, two of the primary books of the Law, clearly demonstrate that God's provision for the people precedes the giving of his precepts for them to obey. Exodus 1–18 details the story of God's miraculous provision to remove his people from bondage in Egypt and make them into a nation. Only after the Exodus and the provision of God for his people are recorded does he outline the nation's responsibility to obey him. God presents himself as supremely loyal to his people and then asks for their obedience. In other words, Israel sees the person of God before seeing his precepts. Similarly, Deuteronomy 1–4 functions as an historical prologue, chronicling God's provision for his people and affording them a clearer view of him as a person devoted to them. The remainder of the book lays out his precepts, which follow from his devotion to Israel. Again, we observe the link between obedience to his precepts and personal loyalty to him.

The overall structure of Deuteronomy also illustrates the relationship between obedience and loyalty. The structure is based upon the format of the suzerainty treaty, which was used consistently throughout the ancient world at this time.[5] This treaty form first lays out the commitment of the king to his subjects, and then stipulates what he expects of the people. Inherent in the treaty is the connection between loyalty to the king and obedience to his precepts. Perhaps one reason this type of treaty form was used to structure Deuteronomy was to strengthen the link between obedience to God's commands and loyalty to the person of God.

The Social Dimension of Old Testament Ethics

God's design for Israel as a kingdom of priests and a holy nation was to be an ideal society. The Law mandated individual behavior and in doing so, it structured the society. The very structure of Israel's society was to reflect their relationship with God. It was assumed that the Law addressed the structures of both society and individuals. Consequently, much of the Law comes under the heading of civil law, which governed social relationships and established institutions that would ensure a proper ordering of society and maintain justice within the society (see, e.g., Ex. 21–23, esp. 20:12–17; Lev. 18–20, 25; Deut. 19–25). Since the economic aspects of life in the Promised Land presented great challenges to the Israelites in their attempt to be obedient to God, much of the civil law addressed issues concerning property and economics. The ceremonial part of the Law was also well-developed (see Ex. 24–40; Lev. 1–10, 22–23; Deut. 5–16).

The prophets also develop the social dimension of Old Testament ethics. They frequently accuse Israel of violating the social aspects of the Law. Charges of oppression, perversion of justice, and exploitation of the poor were all reminders that the people had both personally sinned and set up structures in their society that violated the Law (see, e.g., Amos 4:1; 5:11–13; Mic. 2:2; Hab. 1:4). Not only do the prophets look back to the Law, but they also look forward to the consummation of the kingdom for the social dimension of Old Testament ethics. In most of their visions of the kingdom of God, the prophets emphasize a rightly ordered society as well as a people who worship God properly. Perhaps the clearest examples of this are the Servant Songs of Isaiah (chaps. 42, 49, 50, and 53), especially in 42:1–4 where the Servant-Messiah (Jesus) will bring about justice or a proper ordering of society. Whereas Israel failed in the ordering of society, the Servant-Messiah will succeed.

Leviticus 25, where much of Old Testament real estate law is codified, provides several examples of the way in which the civil law structured social relations in Israel. Since the land was central to the Old Testament agricultural economy, this section of the Law is very important. This passage establishes several important institutions, including the sabbatical year (Lev. 25:1–7), the Year of Jubilee (25:8–24, 35–46), and the law of redemption (25:25–34, 47–55). The sabbatical year legislation mandated that the Israelites were to let the land rest every seventh year by not planting crops on it. This was a visible means by which the Israelites demonstrated to their neighbors their trust in God to provide food for them in the years in which they did not harvest crops.

The Year of Jubilee (25:8–24, 35–46) was an even more radical institution established by the Law. Every fiftieth year, all land was returned to its original owners and all slaves were released. Leases on land were priced according to the proximity to the Jubilee, that is, more expensive if the Jubilee was far off, less expensive if the Jubilee was near. The purpose of the Jubilee was to regularly redistribute the land. This prevented the inordinate accumulation of land and provided an opportunity for a person to make a living from the land, the primary means by which people supported themselves in an agricultural society.[6] This institution also demonstrated that the land belonged to God and thus could not be permanently bought and sold (25:23).

The law of redemption (25:25–34, 47–55) functioned like the Jubilee, only more regularly and not quite as radically. This law required that if a person became so impoverished that he had to sell his land or sell himself into slavery in order to survive, the nearest relative had the legal obligation to buy the land or the person, and return the land to the individual or allow the person to avoid slavery and work independently. In addition, if at some point after he had sold his land or himself, he obtained the means to buy his land back or buy himself out of slavery, he had the right to do so and could not be refused. As a last resort, at the Jubilee, his land automatically reverted back to him, as would his status as a free man. The law of redemption is applied in the book of Ruth, as Boaz not only redeems Ruth (a different law of redemption, in which the nearest relative was required to marry a childless widow to carry on the lineage of her deceased husband and provide for her support) as well as the property that belonged to her husband prior to his death.

Another real estate law that structured a type of welfare system was the law of gleaning (Lev. 19:9–10), which mandated that when harvesting one's field, the owner was to leave the perimeter of the field unharvested and only go through the field one time to gather the crops. The unharvested edges and the crops that were dropped or missed on the first pass were to be left for the poor and the immigrant to harvest for themselves. This set up a kind of "workfare," providing for the needs of the poor but also requiring that they take initiative and work for it. This too is applied in the book of Ruth when Ruth as a widow seeking support is allowed to glean in Boaz's field.

Other examples of laws which structured Israelite society include prohibitions of usury (Ex. 22:25; Lev. 25:35–37), moving boundary stones that delineated a person's property (Deut. 19:14; 27:17), and perverting the legal system by showing bias, accepting bribes, or committing perjury (Ex. 23:1–2; Deut. 18–20; see also the Ninth Commandment in Exodus 20:16, which prohibited bearing false witness). The Law regulated both individual behavior and societal structures, producing institutions that were based on Israel's covenant relationship with God for the purpose of developing an ideal society that would bear corporate witness to the reality of God in Israel's midst.

NEW TESTAMENT ETHICS

In the New Testament the emphasis is not as much on institutional morality and social ethics as it is on a morality for the church. With the coming of Christ, the people of God are no longer under the Law. The ceremonial law has been superseded by the death of Christ and the civil law no longer applies directly because the primary agent of God's work in the world is the multinational, multiracial church, as opposed to the theocratic nation of Israel.[7] Thus, for the church, not only has the way that a person relates to God changed, but the way in which God views the mission of his people has also changed. Although the broad objective—to glorify God by bearing witness to his rule over the earth—

is the same in both testaments, the way in which it is achieved is different. Under the Law, Israel was literally "one nation under God." The church, however, is a multiethnic body of believers for whom national boundaries are irrelevant. The church is to bear witness to the reality of God by the type of community that is experienced in it, as was the case in Old Testament Israel. But the commands of the New Testament do not provide the same institutional framework to the church as the Law did for Israel. That does not mean that the gospel has no social element, but rather that the New Testament did not attempt to structure institutions for the church or society in the same way that the Old Testament did.

This does not mean that the church should not attempt to effect institutional change in society today. That, in fact, is an aspect of the kingdom of God. The kingdom in the Old Testament clearly had both an individual and a social dimension. When Jesus preached that "the kingdom of heaven is at hand," he did not indicate that he was changing the Old Testament concept of the kingdom in any significant way. The disciples and others who heard his message seemed to understand the kingdom in its Old Testament context. When the kingdom is fulfilled in its entirety, it will have both an individual and social dimension.

Most of the Old Testament texts that prophesy the coming kingdom envision a kingdom with a social aspect, one in which the resulting society is rightly ordered, being free from injustice, oppression, and exploitation of the poor. The institutions that reinforced an unjust society would be dismantled. If the kingdom had a social dimension at its inception and has a social dimension at its culmination, then it seems logical to assume that in the interim, a social dimension will be important, too.

Even though the New Testament does not emphasize a social dimension as much as the Old Testament, it does not follow that the gospel completely lacks a social aspect. Many things that the New Testament church did not overtly endorse or encourage are openly supported in the church today. For example, the fact that the early church did not build hospitals, orphanages, or other similar institutions (not to mention church buildings or seminaries) does not mean that later church support of these was inappropriate. Just because the New Testament church did not focus on institutional social change does not imply that it is an illegitimate action for the church today.

As was the case with Old Testament ethics, entire books have been written on New Testament ethics. In this section, therefore, we will attempt to synthesize the main emphases in the New Testament's description of the moral life. Constructing any kind of system of New Testament ethics is difficult because so little of Jesus' teaching on ethics is developed systematically.[8] Also, Paul's and the other apostles' contributions on ethics are often given in response to specific problems in the churches and are not necessarily universally applicable or binding. Just as it is difficult to systematize the theology of the New Testament, so it is with New Testament ethics. The following is offerred as the main emphases of New Testament ethics.

A Reinterpreted Deontology

The deontological system of ethics, which emphasizes principles in which actions (or character, or even intentions) are inherently right or wrong, dominates New Testament ethics. Jesus essentially reinterprets and reapplies the principles of the Law that were misused by the Pharisees. For example, in the Sermon on the Mount (Matt. 5–7), he does not nullify the Law. Rather he critiques the Pharisees for their misinterpretation and misapplication of it. He deepens the requirements of the Law and promotes to both the religious leaders and general population a deontology that is both action and intent oriented. The Pharisees exemplify some of the abuses of an unbalanced deontology with their system of rigid rules and insensitivity to both the people involved and the consequences of such strict attention to rules.

For example, when Jesus is criticized in Matthew 12:1–14 for healing a man with a withered hand on the Sabbath, he was grieved at their blind adherence to rules and resulting lack of compassion for the man. Jesus makes it clear that he is rejecting not the Sabbath command, but the Pharisee's misreading of it. In addition, when Jesus is criticized in Mark 7:1–20 for not following the religious traditions of the Jews, he responds with an example of how that tradition can actually produce harm. Mark 7:11 refers to the tradition of "Corban," a term that translates a Hebrew word that literally means "offering." In Jesus' day "Corban" referred to something devoted to God, and, in this case, it involved money. Since the money was devoted to God, it could not be used for anything else, including financial assistance for one's own needy parents. In rebuking the Pharisees for their rigid misapplication of the Law, Jesus sought a radical change in the primary perspective of ethics among first-century Jews. He rejected a rigid and callous commitment to principles that were not consistent with the Law. He aimed for a deontology that accurately applied the Law, combining a commitment to principles with a compassion for people.

For Paul and the apostles who wrote the Epistles, the emphasis on principles is much the same. It emerges not in confrontations with the Pharisees, but in conflicts with other heretical deviations from the gospel. For example, when Paul confronts the adherents of Jewish-Christian legalism (the Judaizers) in Romans and Galatians, he affirms a primary principle of the Christian ethical life—sanctification cannot be accomplished by one's individual effort alone. Rather, it happens by grace through faith, in the same way a person originally came to saving faith (Gal. 3:1–3). Also, in Colossians Paul confronts the heresy of Gnosticism, or the glorification of knowledge as the means by which the spiritual elite achieve spiritual perfection. He affirms the principle that spiritual growth takes place not by knowledge alone but by the working of "Christ in you" (Col. 1:27). Even in areas in which there are no clear-cut moral rules, the "doubtful things" or morally gray areas (Rom. 14–15; 1 Cor. 8–10), Paul appeals to the principle of not offending one's weaker brother. There is no backing away from deontological reasoning on the part of the apostles, since it was such a clear emphasis in Jesus' ministry. The apostles' primary ethical goal was to accurately represent Jesus' teaching and apply it to relevant problems in the church.

This is perhaps seen most clearly in 1 Corinthians, where Paul addresses specific problems by appeal to principles. To their divisiveness (chaps. 1–4), he applies the principle of the unity of the body of Christ. To their immorality, he applies the principle of maintaining sexual purity in the church (chaps. 5–6). To the question of marriage and singleness (chap. 7), he applies the principle of being content in whatever state one is in. To the question of meat offered to idols (chaps. 8–10), he applies the principle of not offending the weaker brother. To the question of worship in the church and spiritual gifts (chaps. 12–14), Paul applies the principle that things in the church are to be done in an orderly fashion so that the entire church is built up. Paul appeals to the church to practice principles that they already know, thus living life consistently with the principles established by Christ.

For Members Only

In the New Testament, ethics follows from what membership in the kingdom demands. Ethics and discipleship overlap significantly. Little distinction is made between the moral and the spiritual life, except that the former deals mainly with the believer's responsibility to the church and the world, while the latter relates to one's worship of God. A consistent pattern emerges in the New Testament in that Jesus and the apostles would initially preach the message of the kingdom, and then its ethical implications. But the ethical implications are addressed quickly, since it was inconceivable to the early church that someone would profess Christ and not adhere to the moral demands of life in the kingdom.

A good example of this occurs in the gospel of Matthew. After the events of Jesus' birth and preparation for ministry (Matt. 1:1–4:11), Jesus comes boldly proclaiming that "the kingdom of heaven is near" (4:17). The first disciples are gathered (4:18–22), then large crowds begin to follow him (4:23–25). Shortly after crowds gather and his message gains popularity, he preaches the Sermon on the Mount (chaps. 5–7), where he presents the ethical demands of life in the kingdom. Likewise, the material on sanctification, or the spiritual life, in the book of Romans (chaps. 6–8; see also chaps. 12–15, which address more practical moral problems in the church) is not presented until after the doctrine of justification by faith is outlined and defended (chaps. 1–5). Paul taught that the attempts of unregenerate people to be moral fell far short of what God required. Such attempts were never viewed by either Jesus or Paul as substitutes for membership in the kingdom.

An Ethic of Love

Any account of New Testament ethics that does not include love as the central focus is surely incomplete. Jesus and the apostles take the central command of the Law, "Love the LORD your God with all your heart and with all your soul and with all your strength" (Deut. 6:5), and develop an ethic of love for God and one's neighbor. The parable of the good Samaritan (Luke 10:25–37) defines one's neighbor as anyone who has a need that you can meet, and applies the principle to those outside the church as well as fellow believers. When an astute young lawyer asked Jesus about ethical and spiritual priorities in life, he replied that a person's chief duties were to love God and one's neighbor as oneself (Luke 10:25–29; see also Matt. 22:34–40, where Jesus similarly answers the question of the hostile religious leaders). Paul summarizes the entire Law under the heading of love, suggesting that love fulfills the Law (Rom. 13:8–10; Gal. 5:14).[9]

New Testament Ethics: A Special Place for the Poor

The preferential place of the poor is a particular emphasis in Jesus' teaching. The poor and others outside the social mainstream are some of the people with whom Jesus spent most of his time (other than time with his disciples). Thus, he modeled as well as verbally taught this ethical imperative. This emphasis surely reflects the Old Testament stress on the institutions of the Law that were designed to take care of the poor in the land of Israel.[10] He realizes that the poor will always exist in society (Matt. 26:11), but the implication is to take care of them, not ignore them. The poor are singled out as the special recipients of the gospel (Matt. 11:5; Luke 4:18) and are blessed (Luke 6:20), perhaps because the materially poor most easily grasped the notion of spiritual poverty (Matt. 5:3). The Epistles encourage caring for the poor, especially the poor in the church, being sensitive to their vulnerability, and treating them with esteem, not contempt (Rom. 15:26; 2 Cor. 8:1–7; 9:1–15; James 2:1–13).

Jesus captures the importance of caring for the poor in Luke 14:12–14. When one gives a banquet, the poor and the marginal members of society should be invited instead of one's friends, because a person's friends will inevitably repay the invitation, whereas the poor lack the material means to repay. Thus, one is to invite the poor since they cannot repay, trusting God for a reward in heaven (14:14). Doing this forces the host to show unconditional grace toward the poor and models the unconditional love with which God loves each believer. The church's concern for the poor is one of the clearest illustrations of God's unconditional care for the individual person, and perhaps is one of the reasons why such care for the poor is mandated.

The Dynamic: The Indwelling Holy Spirit

This emphasis stands in sharp contrast with the prevailing opinion in the world of the New Testament. The Jewish religious leaders relied on spiritual discipline to develop holiness and the Greeks depended on education to produce morality. The New Testament assumes that both are insufficient. Instead it provides an internal source that assists in decision making and enables one to mature spiritually. This theme is introduced in the Gospels (John 13–17) and developed in the Epistles, particularly those of Paul. For example, Romans 8 discusses the role of the Holy Spirit in producing sanctification in the individual believer. The person without the Spirit is not able to welcome spiritual things into his or her life (1 Cor. 2:14). The process of being transformed from one stage of glory to the next comes ultimately from the Spirit (2 Cor. 3:18). Believers who "walk by the Spirit" will produce the fruit of the Spirit (Gal. 5:16, 22–23), and will not satisfy their innate inclination to sin. Clearly, the New Testament envisions moral and spiritual maturity only in connection with the internal ministry of the Spirit who transforms a person from the inside out.

An Ethic of Virtue

Although the New Testament greatly emphasizes deontology, it also places high value on virtue.[11] The Gospels and Epistles never envision the moral life as simply doing the right thing—as the religious leaders emphasized—apart from developing character and virtue. The virtues centered around those of Christ, and the development of character was synonymous with becoming more like Christ.

In terms of virtue theory, the ideal person will model Christ. The fruit of the Spirit (Gal. 5:22–23) and the deeds of the flesh (Gal. 5:19–21) provide an initial list of the virtues and their opposing vices. The vices are expanded in Mark 7:20–23 and 1 Corinthians 6:9–10. Perhaps the reason why there is no systematic discussion of the virtues is because they are illustrated so well in the Gospel accounts of the life of Christ. The apostles did not need to describe much further what was already so well depicted in the narrative accounts of Jesus' life. Whatever the reason, it is clear that any ethic that claims consistency with the New Testament must include its emphasis on cultivating virtue, namely, the virtues exemplified in Jesus' life.

DIVINE COMMAND THEORY

Given the high place in biblical ethics for God's commands, and the assumption throughout Scripture that his commands are to be obeyed, we can reasonably assert that a divine command theory of ethics in some form is an integral part of Christian ethics. A divine command theory of ethics is one in which the ultimate foundation for morality is the revealed will of God, or the commands of God found in Scripture.

Why Are Things Good? Two Views

Of course, Christian ethics is not the only religious moral system with an emphasis on divine commands. Judaism, Islam, neo-orthodox Christianity (as represented by Karl Barth and Emil Brunner), and many of the ancient polytheistic religions place great importance on divine commands for their ethics. In fact, the original philosophical tensions raised by divine command ethics came from the classical Greeks during the time of Plato. In his well-known dialogue, the *Euthyphro*, Plato asks the question that must be addressed by every adherent of divine command theory. Does God (in Plato's case, the gods) command things because they are good, or are things good because God commands them? In other words, Do God's commands make something right or indicate that it is right? If one answers that God commands things because they are good, it would seem to make God's commands redundant, simply reinforcing what is already obvious and available to everyone. But if one answers that things are good because God commands them, then God appears arbitrary, and he would be free to command anything, even those things that violate society's widely held moral principles.

For example, if things are good because God commands them, then he could command that we torture babies, and that would be good, simply because he commanded it. But that seems strongly counterintuitive for most people, and the average person would have great difficulty worshiping that kind of God. This view is known as ethical voluntarism, and when critics attack divine command morality, they usually target ethical voluntarism.

Islamic ethics is considered to be the best example of ethical voluntarism. Muslims hold very strongly to the sovereignty of Allah, and, consequently, they believe that he cannot be accountable to anyone or anything. Because of this understanding of Allah, it is consistent for Muslims to hold that such a sovereign being can command whatever he desires, and that, in and of itself, makes it good. Critics of Islamic ethics insist that this makes Allah arbitrary and gives him freedom to be even capricious in his commands. To see the God of the Bible in this way makes most Christians uncomfortable, because the Scripture portrays God as bound by his character, which makes him unable to command certain things. Thus there are questions about the degree to which ethical voluntarism is consistent with the biblical portrait of God.

The other side of the question posed in the *Euthyphro* is to insist that God commands things because they are good. This is the view of historic, rabbinic Judaism and of Roman Catholic ethics as developed by Thomas Aquinas.[12] God is not free to command anything he so desires, but is restricted by his character. This does not undermine God's sovereignty, but prevents him from acting in a way inconsistent with his own character. Thus, morality is not grounded ultimately in God's commands, but in his character, which then expresses itself in his commands. Another way to state this is that whatever a loving God commands is good. In other words, anything that God commanded that was consistent with his character, which is love, would be good. Should God hypothetically command that we were to torture babies, it would not be good and believers would not be accountable for obedience to it.[13] This solution avoids the charge of ethical voluntarism.

Goodness and General Revelation

Another way to approach this problem as presented in the *Euthyphro* is to see God's commands in Scripture (special revelation) in conjunction with his moral values expressed outside of Scripture (general revelation). This aspect of Christian morality is commonly called natural law and will be outlined in more detail below. Natural law posits that moral precepts exist prior to God's commands, and that objective moral values exist outside of special revelation. These concepts are logically independent of Scripture, and are thus indirectly revealed by God in creation. The Christian notion of goodness includes more than just what is revealed in the Bible. It also includes what God has revealed by general revelation, too. Just as God has revealed truths about the sciences outside of Scripture, he has also revealed truths about morality outside of Scripture.

Natural law is simply general revelation in the area of moral values. This idea is important for developing a divine command theory that does not make God an arbitrary commander. Not only must his commands be consistent with his character, they must also be consistent with the values he has revealed in general revelation. If it is not unreasonable to believe in a God who can reveal himself in special revelation in the Bible, then neither is it unreasonable to believe in a divine command theory in which God's commands must be compatible with general revelation. To take this view, one would obey a divine commander, without being a strict divine command theorist or ethical voluntarist.[14]

Problems with Divine Command Ethics

Even if one accepts this as the way to resolve the *Euthyphro* dilemma, there are still two problems with divine command ethics that must be addressed. First is the problem raised by many critics of Christian ethics that calling God "good" presupposes a prior notion of goodness that must be independent of God and religion.[15] However, this criticism confuses two different philosophical categories, namely, *epistemology*, or one's knowledge of something, and *ontology*, or the essential nature of a thing. Just because a person must know something about what is good before calling God good, it does not follow that goodness is essentially independent of God. If I am traveling to San Francisco from my home near Los Angeles, I must look on a road map to find it before I arrive there. But surely it does not follow that the road map is logically prior to the city of San Francisco. My knowledge of San Francisco is not logically prior to the existence of that city. In the same way, just because I must know something about goodness before I can tell that God is good does not mean that morality is independent of God.

A second problem with divine command theories arises when there is an apparent conflict between two commands in Scripture. For example, during World War II, when Corrie Ten Boom gave sanctuary to Jews in her native country of the Netherlands, she was often asked by the authorities if she was hiding

Jews in her home. If she told the truth, the Jews would have been taken to extermination camps. But if she lied, they would have been saved. Here she was faced with a genuine moral dilemma, or a conflict of commands. She had a moral duty to tell the truth, but she was also responsible for preventing harm when it was in her power to do so, especially when it involved saving life. What was she morally obligated to do?

Consider the example of Rahab in Joshua 2. Here Rahab the prostitute was commended for her faith in sheltering the Israelite spies sent out on a reconnaissance mission to the Promised Land. She was directly asked by the authorities if she knew the location of any Israelite spies. Not only did she tell them that she did not know where the spies were, but she also sent them after the Israelite spies in the wrong direction. She was actually hiding them in her attic. She is included in God's "hall of faith" in Hebrews 11, and though she is never directly commended for her lie, she is praised for her act of faith in providing a safe refuge for the spies. Clearly, part of providing that refuge was deceiving the authorities who were after the spies.

When divine commands genuinely conflict, there are usually three ways to resolve the conflict.[16] In using these alternatives, one must recognize that a true moral conflict exists and not rationalize away a clear command of Scripture that one simply does not want to obey.

The first alternative is to maintain that no conflict actually faces the believer. The person who holds this position reasons as follows: since an infallible God inspired his inerrant Word, no such conflict of commands is possible. To admit to a conflict would compromise the character of God by admitting that he is capable of giving commands that conflict. The way out of moral "dilemmas" would be to appeal to God's providence to open the way out. According to this view, Corrie Ten Boom should have told the truth and trusted God to work out his will for the Jews she was hiding. Critics of this view cite the example of Rahab mentioned above as an example of a moral conflict that invalidates this view.

A second alternative is to admit that real moral conflicts do exist, but sin is still sin, even when a person is faced with competing obligations. Advocates of this view hold that because we live in a fallen world, real moral conflicts can and do occur. Moral dilemmas are due not to any flaw in God's character or commands, but to the existence of sin and depravity in the world in which the commands are to be applied. God's law is absolute, moral conflicts are inevitable in a fallen world, and people have the duty to do the lesser evil. But it is still evil, for which forgiveness is available for the Christian. Thus, Corrie Ten Boom should have lied to protect the Jews, the lie being the lesser of two evils facing her. Then she should have immediately bowed at the foot of the cross and asked God for forgiveness for lying. The problem that is often raised against this view is that having a duty to sin in certain situations is morally problematic. It is hard to imagine that a person can be morally culpable for something that could not be avoided and about which the person had no choice.

A third alternative is similar to the second. Like the second view, this alternative also holds that moral conflicts are real due to life in a fallen world. When the lesser evil is chosen, however, it holds that it is not sin but a morally justifiable option. A person has the obligation to do the greater good and is not morally culpable for doing what could not be avoided. This view recognizes that God's laws are absolute, yet there are higher and lower laws, or a hierarchy, within God's laws. For example, God's command to the apostles to preach the gospel was over his command to be in submission to the state (Acts 4:13–20). Jesus makes reference to the "weightier matters of the law" (Matt. 23:23–24), a reference to the greater importance of justice, mercy, and compassion over the law of tithing. This view attempts to combine the nature of God's commands, the reality of life in a fallen world, and a proper understanding of moral accountability. Thus, in this view, Corrie Ten Boom would have been morally justified in lying to protect the lives of the Jews she was harboring.

NATURAL LAW IN CHRISTIAN ETHICS

Among all the unusual occurrences that took place in the 1992 confirmation hearings of United States Supreme Court Justice Clarence Thomas was his belief in a concept called *natural law*. Once he mentioned it in the course of answering a question, many members of the Senate Judiciary Committee expressed immediate concern, and protests went up from numerous special interests groups, namely, feminist groups. Why did his reference to natural law raise so much concern? We mention three possibilities below.

First, natural law refers to an ethic that is transcendent rather than an ethic that is a human creation. The mind-set of the modern world, however, is an immanent one. Modern people tend to treat matters of metaphysics with skepticism, probably because they get nervous when they think about being accountable to some divine being such as God. This admission, however, would undoubtedly be slow in coming from any of the critics of Clarence Thomas or natural law.

Second, the concept of "nature" has been used historically to oppress women and minorities. In the Middle Ages "nature" was used to maintain a static social order in which everyone had their place, especially women. It is likely that the feminist and gay rights groups that opposed Judge Thomas had this in mind.

Third, the term *natural* is a widely debated term today, subject to all sorts of misapplications. Perhaps the claim about what is natural implies a "God's eye view" of morality, considered hopelessly out of date by modern philosophers. This may be what many people objected to about Thomas's use of the term. Whatever the reasons for the objections, it is clear that the concept of natural law is still debated today.

There has been much disagreement within Christian circles about the validity of natural law. The Reformers and their predecessors were very skeptical of natural law for two reasons. First, they believed that sin made it difficult to discover morality apart from the clear revelation of God in Scripture. Second, they believed that the Bible was the central source of moral and spiritual authority. The Reformers held that the Catholic view of natural law undercut both of those crucial doctrines. A second group of critics were the twentieth century Protestant neo-orthodox theologians (e.g., Karl Barth, Emil Brunner) who argued that natural law undercut the centrality of Christ for the moral life.

Critical Issues Concerning Natural Law

For Christian ethics, natural law is an important concept at the heart of the debate over several crucial questions:

1. To what degree do moral values exist apart from special revelation? What is the relationship between reason and revelation in ethics? If one holds to a concept of natural law, then objective moral values do exist apart from Scripture, and reason works together with revelation to discover moral values. If one denies the existence of natural law, then all legitimate moral values are derived from Scripture, and reason functions only to interpret revelation.
2. To what degree can a person be good without the special grace of God? For adherents of natural law, people can be good without saving grace, but for those who deny its legitimacy, the only way people can be called good is if they are believers who have received God's redeeming grace.
3. To what degree is Christian ethics distinctive from nonreligious ethical systems? To what degree is there common ground between Christian and non-Christian morality? For those who hold to some form of natural law, Christian ethics has substantial overlap with non-Christian ethical systems. There is little distinctive content to Christian ethics, since the nonbeliever is called to most of the same acts and character attributes to which the Christian is called. The distinctiveness of Christian ethics has more to do with the motive for ethics and the way that one's ethic is justified than the actual content of moral behavior. For the person who minimizes the role of natural law, Christian ethics constitutes a different and higher standard of morality than any secular morality.

Ultimately, the degree to which one holds to natural law will determine the way in which one can try to persuade the world to adopt Christian ethics. If natural law is not a viable concept, then the believer can only talk to the world with the gospel, and would likely hold that the social mission of the church is unimportant, or to be accomplished by a community that produces social change indirectly, by the witness of its life together in community.[17] But if natural law is viable, then the church can engage in a legitimate social mission and Christian activism on moral issues that can complement the proclamation of the gospel.

Defining Natural Law

One of the most difficult aspects of natural law is defining it. The term is used in two primary ways today. First, it refers to general, objective, and widely shared moral values that are not specifically tied to the special revelation of Scripture. Values such as justice, fairness, respect for an individual's dignity, the obligation not to harm another, truth telling, and the respect for life in prohibitions against killing are some examples of virtually universal values whose origins predate Scripture.[18] Oxford University theologian John Macquarrie has put it this way: "In fact the very term 'natural law' is misleading if it is taken to mean some kind of code. The natural law is not another code or system of laws in addition to all the actual systems, but is simply our rather inaccurate way of referring to those most general moral principles against which particular rules or codes have to be measured."[19] These values are a consensus that comes out of the observations and conclusions of mankind over the centuries. In the same way that God has revealed truth about the sciences in creation, and revealed truth in the observations of mankind in the social sciences, natural law refers to God's revelation of morality from all sources outside of Scripture. In this sense, natural law is general revelation applied to moral values.

A more specific form of natural law in which specific moral rules are codified is used predominantly in Roman Catholic circles. For example, the Catholic view of reproductive ethics, especially contraception and the use of reproductive technologies to alleviate infertility, uses natural law reasoning to reach conclusions about their validity. Here natural law is tied to what is natural in creation. For example, since the natural process of reproduction that God ordained in creation begins with sexual relations and progresses from conception to pregnancy to birth, anything that interferes, interrupts, or replaces this natural process is morally wrong. This explains why Catholic teaching prohibits contraception, abortion, and most reproductive technologies.

This specific form of reasoning should be evaluated on a case-by-case basis. Most Protestants tend to reject this form of reasoning when applied to contraception or reproductive technologies, but embrace it when dealing with issues like genetic engineering, in which medical researchers are cautioned against "playing God" and interfering with his created order. In particular, evangelicals use natural law reasoning in voicing opposition to homosexuality. According to many evangelical groups, homosexual relationships are not legitimate, because they are unnatural, that is, they are against the created order that God ordained. Thus, before dismissing this more specific form of natural law, evangelicals need to recognize how frequently they invoke it in their arguments on different social issues.

The Biblical Basis for Natural Law

Perhaps the central passage in the Bible that affirms natural law in the broad sense is Romans 2:1–16. After Paul appeals to creation to point out the sin of the nonreligious, and, interestingly, to oppose homosexuality, he proves that the moralistic person is also condemned before God because of his sin (Rom. 1:18–32). As it applies to natural law, the heart of this passage is in Romans 2:14–15, where Paul states,

> Indeed, when Gentiles, who do not have the law, do by nature things required by the law, they are a law for themselves, even they do not have the law, since they show that the requirements of the law are written on their hearts, their consciences also bearing witness, and their thoughts now accusing, now even defending them.

God appears to hold those without the Law accountable for their sin in the same way that he holds the Jews accountable (Rom. 2:17–29). For God to legitimately hold the world accountable for sin, they must have access to God's standard of morality, even if they lack special revelation. This would be natural law, or general revelation applied to morality. God has revealed these values outside of Scripture and made them accessible to those who lack the Scriptures. Paul's teaching in Romans 2 parallels the oracles to the nations (Isa. 13–27; Jer. 46–51; Ezek. 25–32; Amos 1–2) in which the prophets condemn Israel's pagan neighbors, who did not have the Law, for many of the same things he condemned Israel, who did have the Law.[20] Unless the nations have access to God's law apart from the written Law, it is hard to see how God can be just in holding them accountable for that which they have no knowledge.[21]

In the Old Testament, the concept of wisdom opens the door for at least the more general form of natural law.* The Wisdom Literature suggests two sources of wisdom: natural and revealed. Although revealed wisdom (God's wisdom in the Scripture) claims authority by being God's Word and natural wisdom (God's wisdom revealed outside of Scripture) appeals to empirical evidence for its authority, both are legitimate and authoritative.

Scripture affirms that there is a fixed order that governs the natural physical world (Jer. 31:35–36; 33:20–21, 25–26). This is also known as the laws of nature and have been discovered by physics, astronomy, chemistry, and biology. Creation psalms like Psalm 19, which praises God for the way he has revealed himself in creation, reflect this idea. In Proverbs 8:22–31, it is clear that God's wisdom was intimately bound up with creation (see also Prov. 3:19–20). The Hebrew term translated "fixed order" in Jeremiah 33:25 derives from a term that means "cut in, inscribe, or decree." This same Hebrew word is elsewhere translated as "law" (e.g., Lev. 18:4). In other words, what is "cut in" the cosmos is one

---

*I am indebted to a colleague, Dr. John H. Coe, for his insights on this matter.

source of what is "cut in" the commands of God. God's wisdom is expanded in Proverbs 8:32–36 to include interpersonal and especially moral knowledge. It is "inscribed" in nature and can be discovered by reason. The writer draws conclusions about one's character and morality based on adherence to God's wisdom that is "inscribed" in creation, suggesting that God's wisdom in creation includes moral knowledge.

The message of the Proverbs is that living in harmony with this order brings peace (shalom) and well-being, but living at odds with this order is folly and brings self-destruction. Proverbs 8:32–36, which personifies wisdom and refers to it in the first person, puts it this way:

> Now then, my sons, listen to me [wisdom];
>   blessed are those who keep my [wisdom's] ways.
> Listen to my instruction and be wise;
>   do not ignore it.
> Blessed is the man who listens to me,
>   watching daily at my doors,
>   waiting at my doorway.
> For whoever finds me finds life
>   and receives favor from the LORD.
> But whoever fails to find me harms himself;
>   all who hate me love death.

Since this passage directly follows Proverbs 8:22–31, which links God's wisdom and the creation, it is the moral and spiritual conclusion drawn from the reality of God's natural wisdom. Notice that all of the references to God's wisdom in creation precede the existence of any special revelation of Scripture. The concept of wisdom then suggests that God has revealed objective moral values outside of Scripture, or natural law.

Thus, Scripture and God's natural wisdom are two sides to God's wisdom. Although the wise sage responsible for Proverbs was under inspiration, this does not negate the fact that the sage gained these insights from his own observations. Two specific proverbs make the link between the sage's observations and moral conclusions drawn from them. In Proverbs 6:6–11, the sage observes the diligence and forethought of the ant, and draws a conclusion about diligence and laziness. Likewise, Proverbs 24:30–34 draws the identical conclusion, repeated verbatim, from observation of a lazy person and the consequences of laziness. Thus, observations drawn from the physical and interpersonal worlds are some of the sources for gleaning God's natural wisdom and drawing appropriate moral conclusions. The goal of the sages was to discover and transmit those values embedded in creation through God's cosmic wisdom. They discovered them by observations of nature (what Roman Catholics call the "order of nature") and by reason (what they call the "order of reason").[22]

	Ultimate Source	Immediate Source	Primary Interpreter	Basis Of Authority
Special Revelation	God	Scripture	Priest	"Thus says the LORD!"
Natural Wisdom	God	World	Wise Sage	"It works!"

The Limits of Natural Law

Many of the criticisms of natural law relate not to its existence, but to how it can be reliably known. With their strong view of sin and depravity, the Reformers held that natural law was virtually useless, since the capacity of fallen human beings to discern it apart from Scripture was so flawed that no separate moral principles could be confidently known. Certainly, the ability of fallen human beings to discover natural law has been corrupted by the Fall, particularly their ability to use morality to mask self-interest.[23]

Special revelation is needed because it is not always clear if something is natural because of sin or creation. In addition, many aspects of the spiritual life do require special revelation, such as those that relate to salvation and eternity. Although natural law does help reveal some moral obligations, the proper motive, the context, and the justification of Christian morality depend on further insights gained from Scripture. Certainly, what some might refer to as natural law can and frequently does conflict with Scripture. In these cases, Scripture is the final arbiter. All of natural law is consistent with Scripture, but not all of it is contained in Scripture, although some of it is clarified by Scripture.

Natural Law and Jurisprudence

Much of the contemporary debate and redefinition of natural law is being done by lawyers. Specifically, they are asking, What makes a law just? and On what basis are human rights to be protected? There are two schools of thought on the relation between natural law and the law.[24]

First, the legal positivists hold that there is no essential relationship between law and morality. Laws are valid simply because they are creations of recognized institutions. Perhaps legal positivists are motivated by the fear that if there were too close a link between law and morality, then certain groups might impose their morality with the force of law.

Second, the school of moral realism is committed to the idea that laws that do not correspond to objective values are nonlaws, or invalid laws. For law on any level to be accepted as valid, it must relate to objective moral truths. Ultimately, for the Christian there are objective values that are grounded in the creative activity of God, revealed in general revelation, deduced by reason and experience. They are also substantially revealed in Scripture, which is the final authority in cases of conflict. Of course, the clearer revelation is found in Scripture, but it is supplemented by natural law which provides a common ground between Christian and non-Christian ethics. This enables effective dialogue with the world about the substance of Christian ethics. Natural law provides the means by which Christian ethics are made persuasive to a secular world.

FOR FURTHER READING

Curran, Charles E., and Richard C. McCormick, eds. *Readings in Moral Theology, Vol. 7: Natural Law and Theology*. New York: Paulist Press, 1992.

Helm, Paul. *The Divine Command Theory of Ethics*. New York: Oxford University Press, 1979.

Kaiser, Walter C., Jr. *Toward Old Testament Ethics*. Grand Rapids: Zondervan, 1983.

Longenecker, Richard. *New Testament Social Ethics for Today*. Grand Rapids: Eerdmans, 1984.

Quinn, Philip. *Divine Commands and Morality*. New York: Oxford University Press, 1981.

Wright, Christopher J. H. *An Eye for an Eye: The Place of Old Testament Ethics Today*. Downers Grove, Ill.: InterVarsity Press, 1983.

NOTES

[1]This will be developed later in this chapter.

[2]Most contemporary examples of theocracies are in the Islamic world. Nations such as Iran and Saudi Arabia derive their constitutions and their judicial systems from the Koran.

[3]For further discussion of this, see Walter C. Kaiser, Jr., *Toward Old Testament Ethics* (Grand Rapids: Zondervan, 1983).

[4]The Greek term used in the New Testament for sanctification, *hagiazo,* is derived from the Hebrew term *qadosh.*

[5]For further reading on this treaty form, see Meredith Kline, *The Structure of the Biblical Authority* (Grand Rapids: Eerdmans, 1972).

[6]Contrary to the suggestions of many liberation theologians and evangelicals of a more liberal political and economic persuasion, the Jubilee does not necessarily provide a redistribution of income, only opportunity.

[7]This is not to say that the law has no relevance for the church today, or that it must be applied in terms of broader principles. It is still applicable to the church, although it is no longer directly addressed to the church.

[8]The exceptions to this are in the Sermon on the Mount (Matt. 5–7).

[9]Interestingly, in these two passages, Paul uses the command to love one's neighbor as oneself as the fulfillment of the law, not the command to love God. Perhaps this is to suggest that one's moral and spiritual priorities are not to be viewed hierarchically, but

as simultaneous responsibilities. For further discussion, see J. Grant Howard, *Balancing Life's Demands* (Portland, Ore.: Multnomah Press, 1983).

[10]See the above discussion of the Jubilee, law of redemption, and gleaning.

[11]For a more complete discussion of virtue theory, see chapter 3.

[12]For more discussion of the ethics of Thomas Aquinas, the dominant theologian and philosopher of the Middle Ages, see chapter 3.

[13]For further development of this view, see Robert Merrihew Adams, "A Modified Divine Command Theory of Ethical Wrongness," in Gene Outka and John P. Reeder, eds., *Religion and Morality* (New York: Anchor Books, 1973), 318–47.

[14]Most critics of religious morality assume that if divine commands are an important component of one's ethical system, one must be an ethical voluntarist. But that is not necessarily the case, as the above discussion has shown. Thus, when Christians encounter criticism of their ethics, they must be sure that the critic has not set up the straw man of the ethical voluntarist.

[15]For example, see Kai Nielsen, *Ethics Without God* (New York: Prometheus Press, 1985), particulary chapter 2, for a larger description of this criticism of Christian ethics.

[16]Adapted from Norman L. Geisler, *Christian Ethics* (Grand Rapids: Baker, 1989), 86–110.

[17]See, for example, the work of John Howard Yoder, in *The Politics of Jesus* (Grand Rapids: Eerdmans, 1972), and *The Priestly Kingdom* (Notre Dame, Ind.: University of Notre Dame Press, 1984).

[18]For a catalog of these values traced historically, see the appendix in C. S. Lewis, *The Abolition of Man* (New York: Macmillan, 1947).

[19]John Macquarrie, "Rethinking Natural Law," in Charles E. Curran and Richard A. McCormick, eds., *Readings in Moral Theology, Vol. 7: Natural Law and Theology* (New York: Paulist Press, 1991), 239.

[20]See the above discussion of the oracles to the nations.

[21]For further exegetical study on the biblical basis for natural law, see Alan F. Johnson, "Is There Biblical Warrant for Natural Law Theories?" *Journal of the Evangelical Theological Society* 27 (June 1982): 185–99.

[22]For further detail on this distinction, see Richard Gula, *Reason Informed by Faith* (New York: Paulist Press, 1989).

[23]For more on this, see Reinhold Niebuhr, *Moral Man and Immoral Society* (New York: Scribner's, 1932).

[24]The classic debate between the positivists and realists took place in the pages of the *Harvard Law Review*, between Oxford Professor H. L. A. Hart and Harvard Law Professor Lon Fuller. See Hart, "Positivism and the Separation of Law and Morals," *Harvard Law Review* 71 (1958): 593–629; and Fuller, "Positivism and Fidelity to Law: A Response to Hart," *Harvard Law Review* 71 (1958): 630–72.

3

MAJOR FIGURES IN THE HISTORY OF ETHICS

Christian ethics was never intended to exist in a vacuum, isolated from other relevant ideas about right and wrong. Regardless of its specific emphasis, Christian ethics has been forced historically to interact with competing versions of morality. Like the gospel, Christian ethics has been the most vital and powerful when it has opposed other moral systems, influencing the discipline of ethics by providing a compelling account of its definition of and grounding for morality. Christian ethical thinkers have traditionally critiqued rival accounts of morality as a part of the overall effort to make the gospel message relevant to the world.

Throughout intellectual history, Christian moral philosophers have made significant contributions to the history of ethics and have dominated the moral landscape during some time periods. For example, Augustine was the dominant figure during the beginning of the Dark Ages, as was Thomas Aquinas during the Middle Ages. However, with the decline of the influence of religion and the rise of secularism that characterized the Renaissance and Enlightenment, Christian ethics suffered a similar loss of influence. During this latter period, many other moral philosophers devised ethical systems to replace Christian ethics as the moral system of the masses. Competing versions of morality proliferated during this period. Many of these secular thinkers sought to undermine Christian ethics by providing an account of morality independent of God's special revelation in the Bible. Other philosophers simply attempted to bypass any specifically religious input for morality. They essentially ignored the claims of religious ethicists, and developed their respective moral system without any reference to metaphysics, leaving open questions about one's worldview.

Nevertheless, many ethical systems not specifically grounded in Scripture have much to offer to the Christian ethicist. Historically, many systems of theological ethics have borrowed explicitly from the best of nonreligious ethical thought. For example, Thomas Aquinas, the principal architect of medieval Roman Catholic morality, sought to bring together the philosophy of Aristotle with the theology of Augustine. He produced a Christian ethic that was strongly influenced by Aristotle's secular ethics. Many would suggest that Aristotle's contribution was significant and consistent with theology and the Bible. Many of the Reformers, however, disagreed, suggesting that Aristotle's contribution had actually watered down the distinctive Christian content of Aquinas's ethical system.[1] Christians were not the only ones who tried to blend Aristotle's ethics with their theology. Muslims and Jews who were contemporaries of Aquinas engaged in a similar project. Debate continues in both of those religious traditions about the value of Aristotle's contribution.

Thus, any Christian ethic that is serious about being heard and having an influence in a secular world must interact with the other major figures in the history of ethics. We have much to learn from the great minds that have given their lives to the study of ethics. This is consistent with the theological notion of general revelation. If all truth is God's truth, then the source is ultimately God, and the intermediate source is not relevant to a determination of its validity. If Aristotle discovered truth about ethics, then it should be recognized as truth ultimately derived from God. This is true even for truth discovered by ethicists who consciously sought to undermine Christian ethics. If in their attempt to do so, they discover things that are truth, then the Christian ethicist must recognize them as such. Of course, if their truth claims violate logic or the teaching of Scripture, then Scripture must be the final judge. But simply the fact that valid propositions about ethics do not come from explicitly Christian sources is no reason to dismiss them as unimportant.

On the other hand, ethical theories that undermine a Christian ethic must be addressed and answered with a coherent account of Christian ethics as an alternative to secular accounts of morality. This cannot be done without giving attention to the individuals who shaped the history of ethics. Just as the apostle Paul was familiar with the writings and ideas of his philosophical opponents on Mars Hill (Acts 17), one who desires to give a rational account of Christian ethics must be familiar with those whose systems were designed to supplant Christian ethics. This is the reason why this treatment of ethics includes a survey of some of the major thinkers who have influenced the development of ethical theory.

The figures surveyed in this chapter include both Christian and non-Christian contributors. The survey will proceed chronologically and will include representatives of classical Greek ethics, such as Plato and Aristotle, and their Greek and Roman successors, the Stoics and Epicureans. The two primary Christian figures, Augustine and Thomas Aquinas, follow chronologically. Then the representatives of the Renaissance and Enlightenment, including Thomas Hobbes, David Hume, and Immanuel Kant, will be examined. The focus of this chapter is the original work of these major figures. Some overlap will occur with the next chapter, "Ethical Systems and Ways of Moral Reasoning," which will emphasize the contemporary expressions of what was started by these major figures. Since many of these thinkers developed influential ethical systems, some overlap is to be expected. In addition, some ethical systems, such as ethical relativism, are not widely attributed to any one particular thinker. These will also be addressed in the next chapter. Between these two chapters, you will be exposed to the major systems of ethics, most of which are still widely in use in the popular culture, as well as the major thinkers who contributed to their development.

The major figures in the history of ethics can be grouped roughly into two primary categories. The first includes those who see morality as essentially a human creation, that is, morality that is *created* by human beings. For example, Aristotle, Hobbes, Hume, and even the later utilitarians Jeremy Bentham and John Stuart Mill would be considered representatives of this group. A second group includes those who see morality as something that *transcends* human nature (Plato, Augustine, Aquinas, and Kant), that is, morality that is not a human creation but that is *discovered* by a variety of means (e.g., reason, intuition, and divine revelation).

The difference between these two groups may at times appear slight, but the way in which each group approaches morality in general is very different. The essential difference is the way each group views the notion of moral authority. For the first group, moral authority is immanent; that is, human beings have the authority to create their own moral rules and systems. For the second group, moral authority is transcendent; that is, the authority exists outside of ordinary human experience. In the latter case, moral rules are discerned by human beings who recognize that the source of these rules is someone or something that is "above" them.

Basic conflict between these two groups over current moral issues still exists today. In fact, the issue that separates the different sides in the current conflict is still the ultimate source of moral authority.

In the abortion debate, the pro-choice side holds to the right of a woman to terminate her pregnancy because the fetus is a part of her body. This principle is purported to be rooted in the right to privacy afforded by the United States Constitution, a human creation.[2] The pro-life movement holds to their position against abortion based on a fundamental right to life, and the principle of protecting life is grounded either in religious morality or in some form of natural law, both transcendent forms of moral authority.

The euthanasia debate can be similarly framed. Most of the arguments in favor of euthanasia are called *utilitarian*, that is, they justify the morality of an action by focusing on the consequences produced by it. Although not exclusively so, the argument against euthanasia is premised on the responsibility of physicians not to take an innocent life. This principle is grounded in either religious morality or natural law. Thus, our contemporary cultural conflict has deep roots that go back to the conflict between Plato and Aristotle, a conflict over the source of moral authority that continues even to this day.

Each of these major figures must be understood against the backdrop of his time period. One must recognize the sociological roots of their moral theories, and see how their view of morality may have been shaped by the cultural context in which they lived. For example, one of the reasons that Enlightenment thinkers sought to divorce morality from religion was the intolerance, persecution, and religious wars that often accompanied religiously-based visions of morality and the good society. Due to the adverse social consequences produced by religious intolerance in the period before the Enlightenment, people were skeptical, if not hostile, toward any moral system that claimed to have the sanction of a religious group.

Similarly, a major difference exists in the outlooks of Augustine and Aquinas. On the one hand, Augustine emphasized sin and grace in his theology, which reflected the mood of the period in which he lived, the Dark Ages. On the other hand, Aquinas developed his moral system during the more optimistic conditions of the thirteenth century, which was reflected in his much more optimistic view of human nature and human possibilities. There is a similar contrast between the optimism of classical Greek ethics and the spirit of resignation that characterized Stoicism, a movement that developed during later periods while the Greek empire was disintegrating internally.

Of course, any ethical system involves both a personal and intellectual commitment to follow its dictates. Any particular view of morality commits a person, whether he or she knows it, to a certain view of the world. It commits a person to a certain view of *metaphysics*, or the nature of reality, of which moral values are a part, especially those which claim to have a transcendent source. It also commits a person to a certain view of *epistemology*, or theory of knowledge, because moral responsibility is linked to a person's knowledge of the rules of morality produced or discovered by a particular system. Questions of epistemology are especially important for moral systems that appeal to a transcendent source of moral authority, because how a person discovers moral values is critical to the viability of such a moral system. Support of a particular moral system also commits a person to a certain view of *anthropology*, or view of human nature, because of the connection between one's ethics and a person's ability to live up to that ethical standard. Thus, it is important to consider the questions of metaphysics, epistemology, and anthropology when examining the major figures in the history of ethics.

Several other important questions need to be asked as we examine and summarize the major points of each major figure. They are as follows:

1. How does this particular thinker define what is morally good?
2. What are the criteria used for determining what is good?
3. How are good persons, institutions, actions, and traits produced and maintained?

These are key elements of any moral theory, and any moral theory will try to answer each of these questions.*

PRE-PHILOSOPHICAL ETHICS

The term *pre-philosophical ethics* refers to the way ethics was done prior to the advent of more formal ethical theory around 500 B.C. In the pre-philosophical period there was no structured moral theory, and no developed discussion of the basis for making moral decisions. Without any implication that these ancient cultures were inferior, labeling this period "pre-philosophical" means only that those persons who were concerned with morality during this period did not give attention to some of the foundational questions that concerned some later thinkers. Most ethics were contained in straightforward law codes such as the Code of Hammurabi, the Pentateuch, and other law codes from Egypt and Mesopotamia, rather than in formal philosophical treatises. The people who received these codes considered them to be of divine origin. Thus it should not be surprising that they do not contain a great deal of justification for the laws they prescribe, other than the implicit, and often explicit, mention of their divine source. These cultures had many laws that were similar, as well as many that differed.[3] For the most part, these various law codes consisted of making distinctions between right and wrong, and prescribing rewards for right and penalties for wrong.

A representative example of the kinds of moral distinctions that were made in the pre-philosophical period is contained in Job 31. This passage is significant because it was probably from the patriarchal era (ca. 2000 B.C.) and preceded the Old Testament law. It is characteristic of the way that morality was treated in the ancient world. In this passage Job asserts his integrity against the charges of his three friends, who believe that somehow Job deserves the calamities which have befallen him. In reminding them of his character, Job outlines many of the moral distinctions and areas of moral evaluation that characterized the pre-philosophical era. While some of the contrasts explicitly express only one of the aspects, its

---

*I am indebted to Dr. Dallas Willard for his contribution to my thinking in the history of ethics.

opposing moral quality can easily be inferred from the context. Here are some of the contrasting moral distinctions addressed in this passage:

- Falsehood/deceit as opposed to verbal integrity (Job 31:5–6)
- Covetousness as opposed to generosity (vv. 7–8)
- Adultery as opposed to marital fidelity (vv. 9–12)
- Exploitation of servants, as opposed to treating them justly (vv. 13–15)
- Greediness toward the poor, as opposed to generosity (vv. 16–23)
- Wealth-driven arrogance as opposed to humility (vv. 24–25)
- Idolatry as opposed to true worship of God (vv. 26–28)
- Vengeance as opposed to forgiveness (vv. 29–30)
- Hospitality as opposed to greed (vv. 31–32)
- Hypocrisy as opposed to truthfulness about one's life (vv. 33–37)
- Theft as opposed to honestly earning one's living (vv. 38–40)

Particularly notice the sets of character attributes with their opposing traits. It is important to note that it is not merely actions that are described and contrasted, but also character traits and virtues applied in specific situations. What Job 31 and other pre-philosophical parallels describe is a series of distinctions between dispositions, which are tendencies to act in specific ways, rather than specific actions in specific cases. Morality was more about developing specific character traits than resolving moral dilemmas. It was more about cultivating virtue than about making the right moral decision in difficult cases.

In pre-philosophical ethics a relationship exists between ethics and the ethnic. In early ethics a social group would emphasize propriety. In many cases doing what was proper was critical to the survival of the community, since impropriety meant offending the gods of that particular culture. Although most moral codes had many moral elements in common, there was some diversity in the specifics. Some of that diversity had to do with the differences in religious practices and differences in the way each culture applied general principles that were held in common.

Today most discussion about morality revolves around resolving difficult cases, or what is known as casuistry. The pre-philosophical and the classical Greek approach differs greatly from the approach of today's university and secular culture. The emphasis today is on determining what is the right thing to do, and justifying the way in which that determination is made. It is *act-oriented*. In the pre-philosophical and classical periods, morality was bound up with the kind of person one is becoming. The approach of these periods asked what does being a good person involve. Ethics was primarily *character-oriented*.

Around 500 B.C. classical Greek thinkers generated much in the area of ethical theory. One reason for this is that the Greeks came into contact with other cultures within their empire and became aware of a great deal of moral diversity among these other cultures. As a result, they began to ask questions about the differences in conceptions of right and wrong. They began to ask important questions that are at the heart of moral theory: *What constitutes a good person/action?* and *On what basis do we make these judgments?*

CLASSICAL GREEK ETHICS: PLATO AND ARISTOTLE

Plato and Aristotle dominated the classical period not only in ethics, but also in most major areas of philosophy. Their lives overlapped and Aristotle spent approximately twenty years at the Academy that Plato founded. Their influence in shaping not just classical ethics but ethics in general is difficult to overstate. Ethical traditions based on their thought and writings have survived to this day. The influence of Aristotle has been especially significant, since each of the major religious traditions of the Middle Ages (Catholicism, Islam, and Judaism) attempted to understand his philosophy with their particular theological perspectives.[4] Some prominent modern moral philosophers still recognize the value of classical ethics and continue the attempt to apply that tradition today.[5]

Plato

Plato lived from roughly 426–347 B.C. He came from a wealthy, aristocratic family that allowed him the luxury of study. His background likely contributed to his somewhat negative appraisal of democracy. He was a close associate of Socrates. Accordingly, Socrates plays a role in most of Plato's writings, and a most prominent one in some of Plato's writings on ethics. At some time during the 370s he founded the Academy, a place of higher education where he taught through his well-known method of dialogue and questioning. Aristotle was a member of the Academy during the last twenty years of Plato's life.

Most of Plato's writings consist of his "dialogues," which actually bear more resemblance to monologues. He wrote roughly twenty-five of these dialogues, and the most well-known and widely read of these is *The Republic*. In this work he presented much of his ethical theory, although many of the other dialogues contain material that deals with ethics. For example, the *Laws*, written toward the end of his life, spell out in more detail the implications of principles outlined in *The Republic*.

The emphasis in Plato's thought is not on rights, moral principles, or consequences, but on questions of the soul. His moral philosophy is not concerned with whether certain actions are right or wrong, but with whether or not one is a good person. As a result, one notices little distinction between philosophy and psychology in his thought. What is today called *virtue theory* dominated classical ethics, and Plato was the consummate virtue theorist. He and other Greek moral theorists thought that they could know the good person, that is, the right way to live one's life in general. They were more concerned with one's character and virtue than with any action-based theory of ethics.

For Plato life was parallel to a craft or skill, that is, the right way to live life was parallel to a right way to perform a craft or skill.[6] Each craft or skill has something built into it, an end that defines it. The function of a thing is to do that which can be done by means of it. Thus, function accounts for something's being and being what it is. A thing is virtuous or excellent if it performs its function well and the evaluation of a thing depends on how well it performs its function. Life is also parallel to a craft in that to live well one must have training and focus in one's function. One faces two key questions: How should I live? How do I find out how to live? Underlying both of those questions was the more fundamental question, What kind of a thing am I?

The title of Plato's work *The Republic* reflects both his method and his answer to the question, What kind of a thing is a human being? The essence of a human being that makes him unique is the presence of the soul. The method used in *The Republic* is the drawing of a parallel between the soul and the city. According to Plato, the city illustrated the soul on a large scale. The reason he used this analogy is that you can see the parts of the city functioning in ways that you cannot see in the soul. The use of this analogy may also imply that morality is not an individual enterprise, but is dependent on a person being in the right kind of society. There is a strong connection between producing a good society and producing good people.

The central place of the soul is why *The Republic* places so much emphasis on the idea of justice. For Plato, justice was not so much a moral principle as a state of well-being in one's soul. It is parallel to the Hebrew concept of *shalom*, which means more than simply peace, but refers to a sense of wholeness or well-being that one experiences personally and internally. Justice in the soul is parallel with justice in the city, with all the parts doing their function well. For Plato, the soul, the source of change and emotion, had three major parts: (1) the *vegetative*, from which comes desire and the appetites, such as nutrition and procreation; (2) the *passionate*, from which comes the emotions (what Plato called "the spirited part"), such as anger, shame, and love; and (3) the *rational*, from which comes knowledge and thinking. The well-being of the soul depends on the parts working together harmoniously. Even though the parts are different dispositions that act differently, they are not contradictory. The function of the soul comes from its inherent properties. The function of the soul is to have reason control the appetites and passions. One's obligations in life emerged out of the answer to questions of the soul.

If the central element of a human being is the soul, then justice would be one of the primary virtues, since it is defined as a proper harmony between the parts of the soul. Justice is found not in external acts but in internal harmony, with all the parts functioning in proper balance. Similarly, the just society is the one in which each person performed his or her function with excellence. The just act is the act that produces or maintains justice in the soul. Justice is produced by training that gets one in the habit of doing them, or those things that a person would characteristically do.[7] Plato thought that you could tell whether a person had a just soul simply by observing them.

The idea of "the good" cannot be defined as precisely as justice. According to Plato, what people saw on earth were manifestations of the form of the good, but that was as close to defining the good as was possible. For Plato, good meant resemblance to the ideal model of the good, which he called the form of the good. This is the standard which guides all moral evaluations and conformity to the ideal model and determines the degree to which actions and people are virtuous. Plato's chief concern in *The Republic* appears to be identification of what can be clearly defined, which is justice, not necessarily the form of the good. One of the most significant contributions of Aristotle was further development of Plato's thought and more clear definition of what for Plato could not be defined.

Plato's moral philosophy does not sound similar to many modern systems of moral philosophy or similar to the modern thinkers that are described later in this chapter for a good reason. Plato approached ethics with a very different set of questions than later thinkers. His concern was becoming a good or virtuous person, and he presented a more holistic view than the action-oriented ethics of later thinkers.

Aristotle

Aristotle continued in the Platonic tradition of the virtuous person but spelled out the specific virtues and a psychology of moral behavior in much more detail. He spent much of his life (384–322 B.C.) in the political world, since his father was the physician to Amyntas II, King of Macedon. Aristotle assumed leadership in the Academy of Plato after Plato's forced suicide and remained there until 342 B.C., when he accepted the invitation to become the personal mentor for Alexander the Great. After this three-year assignment, he established schools in the different areas of Greece in which he resided.

Aristotle wrote voluminously, both on the popular level and the more sophisticated scientific and philosophical level. He wrote on a wide variety of subjects, including logic, physics, psychology, natural history, and philosophy. The core of his philosophical writings included works on metaphysics, ethics, and politics. He considered ethics and political philosophy to be inseparable, and thus his *Politics* is a logical extension of his three works on ethics, namely, the *Nicomachean Ethics*, the most well-developed ethical treatise; the *Eudemian Ethics;* and the *Magna Moralia*. The discussion here of Aristotle's ethics will center on the *Nicomachean Ethics* since it is his most thorough and systematic treatment of ethics.

Aristotle extended Plato's thought in two important ways. First, he provided the connection between knowing the form of the good and producing it in a concrete context. Aristotle realized that one needed to know not only the form of the good, but also what human goodness is. Second, he viewed the function of man as a whole. Plato had no view of the function of man as a whole, only the parts of the soul. According to Aristotle, the function of a human being as a whole was to guide action by reason. Thus, while he retained much of Plato's virtue theory, he also built on it.

One of the major differences between Plato and Aristotle is their metaphysics. Plato's ethic is a transcendent ethic, whereas Aristotle's is a human construct. Plato's aim was to conform human behavior to the transcendent ideal notion of the good, the form of the good. Aristotle's goal was to create an ethic that was tailored to the demands and ends of human nature. Aristotle developed more of the psychology of virtuous behavior, and a psychology of reason, especially with regard to how reason works in governing feelings and actions. For Aristotle, sufficient material goods were needed to be happy as well as virtuous. In other words, virtue alone did not make for happiness. But for Plato, having justice in the soul was better than having all the world's goods and not having justice. For Plato, having justice in the soul gives people all they need.

Aristotle's ethical theory has two primary lines of thought. To put it another way, what is morally good has a two-fold meaning. First, it is understood in terms of the Greek word *telos*, the end or goal. In other words, goodness is the end toward which all of life aims. Goodness is self-sufficient and complete in itself and not desired as a means to something else. But goodness is also defined in terms of the function of a human being. That is, goodness is defined in terms of what is unique or fitting for human beings. To be more specific, for Aristotle, happiness is the end,[8] and virtue revolves around the function of a human being. The primary function of a human being in Aristotle's ethics is to guide action and feeling by reason. That function manifests itself in the specific virtues that he presented in his later discussion of the "golden mean."

Thus his moral theory moves from the concept of well-being (the end, or happiness) to being a good person (the function, or virtue). He assumed that virtue is the means to happiness, yet he never logically brought the two primary lines (the end and the function of a human being) of his thought together. He maintained that one could be virtuous and not be happy, because it takes adequate external goods to insure happiness. This means that something else must help him define the good life. The good life involves the combination of virtue and sufficient external goods so that one has the "luxury" of being virtuous. Happiness is not totally dependent on virtue (function) but a significant part of it involves virtue, since goodness is defined in terms of function. Virtuous acts are not measured by their consequences, but by their intrinsic value.

Virtue is defined in two separate aspects. Intellectual virtue, which is obtained by speculative reason, governs the realm of thought and speculative philosophy.

Moral virtue governs the realm of character, which is obtained by the exercise of practical reason. Moral virtue, the type of virtue that is emphasized in the *Nicomachean Ethics,* is a learned feeling and capacity for discernment about what is good. Acquiring moral virtue requires rigorous training and proper habit patterns. Aristotle recognized that there is no inherent connection between happiness and pleasure. Rather the key connection is between happiness and virtue. One can have pain and still be happy if one responds to pain in a virtuous manner.

Aristotle's specific virtues derive from his concept of the *mean*. He is perhaps best known for this way of describing the virtues, popularly known as the "golden mean." A virtue is the mean between two extremes of behavior or emotion, usually between the extremes of excess and deficiency. For example, courage is described as the mean between rashness (an excess) and cowardice (a deficiency). Temperance is the mean between overindulgence (an excess) and self-denial (a deficiency). Other virtues include liberality, honor, gentleness, friendliness, and truthfulness. The ethic of the mean is an ethic of moderation that produces happiness in a human being. The mean is not merely the middle, but a mean that is relative to a person's circumstances.

An important aspect of Aristotle's theory is his view of the interaction between feeling and action, guided by reason. His view of the individual is more specific than Plato's and the interaction of the various parts of the person provides a more specific psychology than Plato. The key is the interaction between thought and reason, passion and desire, and action. He picked up a key question that Plato only assumed, namely, How does reason work? Plato held that reason worked effectively as it was educated, but Aristotle deepened that view of reason.

Aristotle held to the same three parts of the soul that Plato held to: (1) the *rational,* the area he called theoretical reason and intellectual virtue; (2) the *emotion,* which is subject to what he called practical reason as it directs action and feeling; that is, the emotions hear the rational as the voice of a friend and obeys, thus producing moral virtue; and (3) the *appetite*, which does not hear or obey the rational, but can only be trained. He distinguished between the appetites and the emotion.

With his emphasis on happiness, Aristotle needed to explain how the notion of pleasure related to it. Pleasure and happiness are not equated, but pleasure completes an activity. It is a by-product of that activity, not an inherent part of it, and not inherently a value for Aristotle. Although pleasure does complete an activity but is not its end, it can be used as a means to an end to train people. The place given to friendship helps fill out the concept of happiness. One of the greatest pleasures was that of a friendship that enabled one to share life with another. This emphasis on friendship assumes that ethics was done in a community of one's friends, and not in isolation. He described self-love as a necessary feature of friendship. Interestingly, the idea of benevolence appears here, but is not a virtue per se.

Aristotle's ethic is an ethic of confidence. He shared the classical Greek notion of optimism by means of reason. By the proper use of reason and with correct training, human beings could live well and be good people, a notion parallel to the faith in reason that characterized the Enlightenment period. Yet Greece fell due to the different city-states warring against each other. This can be seen as a failure of reason to provide the kind of good person that could make the city, or republic, work.

THE EPICUREANS AND THE STOICS

Out of these ruins came an entirely different ethical emphasis produced by two groups popular among both Greeks and Romans, the Epicureans and the Stoics. They constructed moral systems in which well-being was defined apart from one's circumstances. Instead, a person's well-being was based on an inner state of mind, so that the disintegrating circumstances around a person would not be able to affect the person. These new theories were clearly influenced by the difficult circumstances that followed the fall of the Greek empire. Their ethics were mainly concerned with a world that seemed incapable of rational control. Their aims were to understand, to change oneself, and to comfort oneself by changing attitudes. Both of these new approaches were ethics of withdrawal. Like the classical Greeks, the Epicureans and Stoics were still asking questions about what makes a good person and a good life.

Both Epicureanism and Stoicism began with the Greeks. Later, during the times of Christ and the apostles, we discover that both of these systems still had followers among the Romans. Also, both of these systems are based on "nature," that is, the way things are. Their concepts of nature did not require belief in God as the creator of nature. Rather, they began with the world as it was, which they called "nature." The goal of their moral systems was to produce a good life that was in accord with the way things were.

The Epicureans

The Epicurean school derives its name from Epicurus (341–270 B.C.), whose teachings were later adopted by the Roman Lucretius (99–55 B.C.). The Epicurean ethic has been widely misunderstood. Many people have understood the maxim, "Eat, drink and be merry, for tomorrow we die," to be the heart of Epicureanism, but only the second half of that maxim is part of their philosophy. Thus, it is an ethic of survival, not of pleasure, at least not in the normal sense of the word. The Epicureans defined pleasure as simply the absence of pain. It would perhaps be more accurate to call it an ascetic ethic, or an ethic of self-denial. The Epicurean goal was to live outside the city in a simple life with friends, that is, living life according to nature or according to the way things were. In other words, they did not demand more out of life than it could give. It is a pessimistic ethic, based on withdrawal from the world in order to survive it.

Their definition of goodness and virtue centers on the end of pleasure, which for them means freedom from pain in both body and mind. The virtuous person was able to live this way, in freedom from physical and mental pain. Pleasure is defined as "freedom from pain in the body and trouble in the mind," and is not just the negative avoidance of pain and trouble, but can also be positive, that which is in accord with one's desires. The Epicureans did not completely eliminate desire like the Stoics did. But one can be in bondage to those desires. Pleasure is inseparable from virtue. Epicurus stated that "the virtues are by nature bound up with the pleasant life, and the pleasant life is inseparable from them."[9] The key for the Epicureans is to live within the limits of what pleasure can provide. Nature sets those limits and they are discerned by reason and observation. The primary subordinate virtue is prudence, which is the ability to discern what makes for pleasure according to the Epicurean definition of pleasure. There is still a high place for reason, since unreasoned opinions produce trouble in the mind.

The Epicureans were later eclipsed by a school called the neo-Platonists, who scorned the world and found it senseless to locate value in the material world. One can argue that the neo-Platonists were an even more extreme response to a world gone even more mad during the Dark Ages. It may be that the Christian emphasis on the afterlife, and the postponement of pleasure until then, as well as the concept of adversity producing maturity, was parallel to this general ethic of withdrawal. To be sure, the Great Commission mandated that the church win the world for Christ, which meant participation in it, but the church also became a counterculture community, living outside the city, claiming to be aliens and strangers, waiting for the consummation of the kingdom, their true home.

The Stoics

The Stoics were founded by Zeno (ca. 336–264 B.C.), whose teachings later found adherents among the Romans, including notable figures such as Seneca (4 B.C.–A.D. 65), Epictetus (ca. A.D. 50–130), and Marcus Aurelius (121–180). The Stoic ethical system is even more ascetic than the Epicureans. While the Epicureans continued to give a legitimate place to desire, the Stoics discouraged the expression of one's desires until they could be brought under control and ordered according to nature. The key element in the Stoic ethic is to not will that which is not in accord with nature. Regardless of what happens, says the Stoic, accept it and order one's life accordingly in order to survive, and do not expect more from the world than it can give you.

The primary assumption underlying Stoic ethics is that some things in our lives we can control, and some we cannot. The teachings of Stoicism clearly emphasize those things that are not within a person's power to control. The Stoic endeavored to live according to nature, that is, according to those things that are within one's power. The crucial factor is one's attitude toward those things that are not in one's control. The mark of the virtuous person is that one is not dependent on others for one's well-being. The ultimate goal was to destroy desire and to be without feeling until one's desires could be controlled adequately. Reason still had a high place in Stoic ethics. Reason was used both to determine what accords with nature and to alter one's state of mind in accordance with nature.

A major consideration for Stoic ethics was determining what was according to nature. To prevent the theory from becoming subjective and to help them discern what things were in accord with nature, they suggested the following guidelines. First, they suggested that a person look at what is invariable or unchangeable from person to person. This was a view of nature that was actually based on human nature, and they held that it was reasonable to expect that which is a part of human nature. Second, they suggested that a person look at one's own actions to determine what was according to nature. For example, to compete in the Olympics, one must practice rigorously. That was simply how things were. Thus one's actions could be a guide to determining what was according to nature. Third, they suggested that what was within a person's power to do within relationships would guide the person toward right action. Things not within our power are morally neutral. Fourth, they suggested that a person choose the mind over the body when they conflicted.

Thus, happiness involved living according to nature. The virtuous person was the one who was able to control his or her desires and not desire things that the world could not provide. The highest virtue for the Stoics was contentment. For them the emphasis was on controlling one's life and desires from within. It was a reaction to a world gone out of control.

For both the Epicureans and Stoics, morality became a private matter for the individual. Given the times in which they lived, it should not surprise us that ethics was solely personal. The classical connection between personal and social ethics, or between virtuous individuals and a just society was minimal. Since the Epicureans and Stoics had resigned themselves to surviving, rather than shaping, their world, virtually no connection existed between ethics and politics, as had been the case for Plato and Aristotle.

ST. AUGUSTINE

St. Augustine (354–430) is widely considered to be the dominant contributor to ethical theory during the transition between the ancient world and the Middle Ages. He attempted to formulate an explicitly Christian ethic for a world that was just beginning to experience Christianity.

After searching for a worldview that would hold together for him, he converted to Christianity from a life of hedonism in 386. For the first few years of his spiritual life, however, he was strongly influenced by the heresies known as Manicheanism, a system characterized by a dualism between good and evil. The Manichean view of the world was quite negative. Consequently, their ethical system was rigidly ascetic, denying the flesh and the world as evil. Ultimately, Augustine rejected this influence, although he held onto a disdain for the world, based on his strong view of sin and the doctrine of eternal life. His pessimistic view of the world was colored both by the times in which he lived and by his personal experience of guilt and worthlessness prior to becoming a Christian.

He wrote a wide variety of works, both philosophical and theological. As he grew older, his interest turned more toward the Scriptures and pastoral work and away from more technical philosophy, although his ministry in the church was always strongly influenced by his background in philosophy. From about 390 until the end of his life, he worked as a priest and later served as a bishop in North Africa. Perhaps his two best known works are the *Confessions* and his work in social ethics, *The City of God*. He was the first Christian to systematically develop Christian ethics.

As Christian ethics were more systematically developed and the traditions were being formed, a significant shift in emphasis from well-being to "well doing" took place. The emphasis on being a good person was not lost, as a concern for developing virtue continued. But the believer's well-being was assumed since the believer was under the care of a sovereign God. Thus the stress was more on well doing, or on conforming to God's directions, embodied in Christ. Although Augustine's system emphasized eternal life and could be viewed as a continuation of the Epicurean and Stoic ethic of withdrawal, his development of it departed significantly from that of the Stoics and Epicureans. For him right action and virtue were understood in terms of relationship to others and to God, not in retreat from the world.

One of the major questions in ethics to this point was how to acquire virtue. Plato and Aristotle assumed that it was acquired by education and training, yet the failure of the Greek city-state illustrated the weakness of this view. The Stoics and Epicureans believed that one acquired virtue by reason and contemplation. Augustine addressed this question directly. Due to his view of the effect of sin upon mankind and a lack of confidence in man's ability to acquire virtue through his own resources, he believed in the necessity of God's grace to develop virtue. He suggested that virtue was acquired by means of God's grace through the gospel, the sacraments, and the ministry of the Holy Spirit within the soul of the believer. This emphasis upon the necessity of the grace of God replaced the Stoic and Epicurean solution of contemplation as the route to blessedness. Although Augustine's approach somewhat overlapped the neo-Platonism of his day, his was a thoroughgoing Christian ethic.

Augustine held that all being is good, because it is created by a good God. He stated that "all things that exist, therefore, seeing that the Creator of them all is supremely good, are themselves good."[10] Evil as an independent entity does not exist, but is only the privation of good. The notion that all being is good likely comes from two sources: (1) a classical Greek source, that says that nature has purpose embedded within it; and (2) a Hebrew source, that maintains that creation reflects a good act by a good God. Evil, then, is the absence of good. The evil will that an individual has within himself or herself has no cause, since it is not a positive reality, but rather only a diminishment of good and a perversion of nature. This is particularly emphasized in Augustine in part due to his "conversion" to Manicheanism prior to coming to Christ. On the other hand, the good will remains so by the "helpful operation" of God. The virtues that were central to Stoicism are for Augustine ultimately grounded in one's relationship to God. In addition, given the weakness of human nature, any attempt to develop these virtues apart from grace is futile.

Happiness, or "blessedness," to use Augustine's term, consists in community and fellowship in the kingdom of God. The supreme good for a human being is eternal life, that is, the perfect enjoyment of God for eternity. Clearly, this is not attainable in this life. In contrast, eternal death is the supreme evil. Realization of man's supreme good depends on his living rightly, empowered by the grace of God. Righteousness, or virtue, is defined in relation to the ultimate good, that is, a relationship with God. It is submission to God, or choosing the ultimate blessedness. Preferring or choosing anything else is unrighteousness.

In addition to his more personal ethic, Augustine also developed a social ethic that has had a pervasive influence throughout the history of political philosophy. For example, the realism about human beings in Augustine's thought had a significant influence on Martin Luther, John Calvin, Thomas Hobbes, and John Locke, who in turn exercised a substantial influence on the American founding fathers, and Reinhold Niebuhr, the most recent advocate of Christian political realism. In his social ethic, Augustine conceives of two radically different communities with two different ideas of what is good, the city of God and the city of man. Believers are the residents of the city of God and the world apart from God's grace inhabits the city of man. His view of the effects of sin on institutions prompted his pessimism about the state doing anything other than keeping the world safe for the proclamation of the gospel. Thus he recommended a minimal role for the state, namely, to maintain order and keep human beings from killing or otherwise hurting each other. Given the depravity both of leaders and citizens, Augustine was seriously suspicious regarding the possibility for development of public virtue, a theme very important to Plato and Aristotle.

Augustine's vision of society was highly individualistic, with society composed of individuals seeking to maximize their self-interest. Augustine attributed this individualism and self-interest to the effects of sin. He viewed society through the lens of conflicting pursuits of self-interest. This is called a conflict model of society, in which the social world is disordered and full of lustful self-interest. Sin has corrupted the cosmos, and God has sovereignly saved some from this corruption by his grace. God has permitted the establishment of government to maintain minimal peace and harmony. Augustine compared this minimal peace to a "peace among robbers." However, the ability of people in society to create government indicates that society does not entirely revolve around conflict. They still have some ability to cooperate, which is part of the image of God in man. This place for government within a conflict model of society was further developed by Hobbes, Locke, and Rousseau in their notion of the social contract.

This view of society affected how Augustine envisioned the role of reason in determining what is good. In his view, the human understanding about what is good for society is not objectively rational, but is self-interested and self-deceptive. According to Augustine, moral reason cloaks self-interest and is a weapon in social conflict. Thus his social ethic is not about social progress but about a balance of power and the achievement of a rough justice. In other words, we must do the best we can to maintain order in society, and rescue as many people as possible from the city of man, knowing that perfect justice in social arrangements is found only in eternal life.

In Augustine's social ethic, the city of God coexists with the city of man. Augustine did not see the church as an agent of social change, but instead looked to the state to protect the church and even to prosecute heresy. In other words, the church could legitimately use the state to advance its interests.

ST. THOMAS AQUINAS

Thomas Aquinas (1224–1274) was born and raised in Italy, studied under Benedictine monks as a child, and attended the University of Naples before joining the Dominicans, the order of preachers in the Catholic church. His advanced study in philosophy and theology took place primarily at the University of Paris. After receiving his doctorate there, he began a twenty-year period as an active teacher (1252–1273). He was invited to remain on the faculty at Paris for the next two years. Following his tenure at Paris, he lectured for the next decade at various Dominican monasteries in Italy, then returned for his second assignment at Paris, a period of roughly four years. Called back to Italy in 1272, his health began to fail, and he died in 1274.

Most of his voluminous writing was accomplished during his time as a teacher, particularly during his second stint in Paris. Most of his work consists of lengthy theological and philosophical works in the form of disputations, or debates, on a wide variety of topics. The best known of his works is the multivolume *Summa Theologica*. Most agree that this work is representative of his overall philosophy, and his work on ethics is only a part of this massive work. Thomas's method of debate differs from Plato's in *The Republic*, since the debating partner or questioner is never explicitly mentioned. He organizes his work by answering objections to the central question he raises in each section.

From the time of Augustine to Aquinas, the world changed dramatically. After the chaos of the Dark Ages, stability emerged in the medieval period as people again started effecting positive change in the world. This period was marked by a revival of economic activity and numerous agricultural innovations. As a result, the world generally became a more peaceful and secure place to live. At the height of the Middle Ages during the eleventh and twelfth centuries, people were generally more optimistic about the world than they were during the time of Augustine. Against this sociological background and a newfound optimism, St. Thomas Aquinas began to address himself to theology and social philosophy.

The need for law, particularly law properly grounded in theology, to govern this new activity was central to the ethical writings of Aquinas. In order to maintain the Catholic Church's status as a universal church whose message was relevant to the world in a climate strikingly similar to that surrounding the Greek city-states of Plato and Aristotle, Aquinas's principal task was to comment on Aristotle's philosophy from the perspective of Augustine's theology. The degree to which Aquinas departs from Augustine has been the subject of great debate. Clearly, Aquinas drew material from the Stoics, as well as Jewish and Muslim theologians and philosophers, who were attempting to interact with Aristotle from within their own religious doctrines.[11] St. Thomas's social ethic seems to reflect both a substantial repudiation as well as an actual synthesis of Augustine's thought.

One of Thomas's fundamental ethical concepts was the notion of the public good under law. Ethics was much more than simply one's inner attitude, as was the case with the Stoics. Aquinas had no radical discontinuity between the city of God and the city of man, as did Augustine. For St. Thomas, well-being and well-doing were both related to law and the common good. Thomas thus marks a return to the strong relationship between ethics and politics that characterized the thinking of Plato and Aristotle. This constitutes a major part of the general synthesis he attempted with Aristotelian philosophy and Augustinian theology. Ethics provided the grounding for fundamental political concepts, and Christian ethics was the basis for both moral law and jurisprudence that applied to everyone, regardless of religious conviction. A great shift occurred between Augustine and Aquinas in their concepts of law. For Aquinas, the purpose of law was to help mold essentially good people; for Augustine, however, law was intended primarily to restrain essentially sinful people. For Aquinas, God's grace was only one of the means for attaining virtue. For Augustine, it was the only way. Aquinas emphasized the Aristotelian idea of developing virtue by training and education.

For Aquinas, the good is based on his concept of natural law, that is, the natural tendencies of a thing. This includes a consideration both of its end and its function. These were considered to be natural, and thus ordained by the creator God. Here he largely adopted categories first introduced by Aristotle, and reworked them in a way consistent with his view of Christian theology. The good promotes what is natural (i.e., ordained by God) and evil interferes with what is natural. To put it another way, the good is that which propels man toward his *telos*, or his God-ordained end, which is happiness.[12] For Aquinas, happiness is knowing God and loving the good, while evil is that which interferes with it. His ideas of what constitutes the good are more clearly understood when set against the backdrop of his concept of law.

Four types of law occur in Aquinas's thought. The first is called *eternal law*. This law refers to God's thoughts about how things could or should be in the world. This is the plan that exists in the mind of God and is the umbrella over all the other types of law. The other types of law reflect the different ways in which God's eternal law is revealed.

The second type of law is called *natural law*, and is the most well-developed and most common form of law for Aquinas. This type of law is based on the natural tendencies of a thing. One's tendencies are tied to one's "equipment" in body and mind that have been given to the person by God. Natural law can refer both to general moral principles, such as justice, fairness, and respect for persons, and to specific moral prescriptions, such as the Roman Catholic prohibition on contraception and other reproductive technologies.

St. Thomas held that the principles of natural law are self-evident precepts from which practical reason deduces moral maxims. Natural law imprints its structure on beings and therefore determines its inclinations to proper acts and ends. Human beings do have choices however, and thus can deviate from natural law. Natural law can be known by reason and is accessible to everyone, regardless of an individual's relationship to God. Thus, both believers and nonbelievers are accountable to natural law.

The Prophetic Books and Wisdom Literature of the Old Testament appear to be consistent with the concept of natural law. God has clearly embedded a natural order in creation (Jer. 31:35–37; 33:19–22). In Proverbs 8:22–31, this is associated with God's wisdom, and in 8:32–36 such wisdom has moral implications for individuals' lives. Further, it is applied to specific cases such as Proverbs 6:6–11 (a moral lesson on diligence learned from observation of the ant), and Proverbs 24:30–34 (same lesson learned by observing human behavior). This is likely the basis for Paul's use of natural law to condemn the pagans in Romans 1–2.[13]

The third type of law is called *human law*. This refers to the law made by men and includes both civil and criminal law. According to St. Thomas, human law is necessary because many things are necessary for social order that do not correlate to nature, and natural law needs to be enforced. With this as the case, it is clear that Thomistic ethics are universal in scope and application. He clearly envisioned natural law being enforced by human law. This fits the Catholic notion of being a universal church, but it also reflects the apex of Catholic influence over all of life, or what is commonly called christendom. There appears to be neither any place for pluralism, nor much distinction between law and morality in Thomas's system. This type of law is also called civil law or positive law.

Finally, the fourth type of law is *divine law*, or special revelation. This is the law that is revealed in Scripture and is also called canon law. This goes beyond natural law and is necessary because some divine law is not evident in nature, such as the place of intentions and motives. Special revelation also includes the context for morality in one's relationship to God and the justification of moral precepts as the commands of God.

St. Thomas made a significant contribution to social ethics that should not be surprising, given the continuity in his thought between ethics and politics. Aquinas saw human beings as essentially social beings. He reasoned that even if the Fall had not occurred, government and the state would still have a place. Thus his social ethic left more room for the state to intervene to improve the lot of society. He saw society through the lens of harmony, not conflict, as had been the case with Augustine. This view of society resembled Plato's view of the city functioning harmoniously. Thomas's view also contributed to the static view of social order in which people had their place essentially dictated by nature, thus severely limiting social mobility but providing a great deal of order. Human society is seen as an organism, in which each part related in harmony. This organic model of society appears regularly in Catholic encyclicals on the church's social mission.

According to St. Thomas, one of the inherent truths in the world is the existance of an innate inclination of human beings to live together in society. Thus, the way in which human beings congregate in social relations reflects the goodness in creation, and is not some sort of "contract" to insure one's survival, as Augustine suggested. Thus social life is based on human nature being in the image of God, not human nature as corrupted by sin and needing society for restraint. Social life together is necessary for the development of a person's potentialities. For Aquinas, institutions exist to encourage the development of good people, reflecting the classical Greek emphasis on developing public virtue. But for Augustine, institutions exist to restrain essentially bad people. Obviously, a substantial conflict of visions in social ethics exists between Augustine and Aquinas to this day. For example, at the heart of the debate about "big government" is the conflict over the purpose of institutions, a conflict illustrated by the "debate" between Augustine and Aquinas.

For Aquinas, values were both objective and had an ultimately transcendent source in the eternal law of God. Many historians suggest that Aquinas's emphasis on natural law and how it can be discovered by anyone, and his subsequent de-emphasis of revelation (except for matters of faith), opened the door for philosophers such as Thomas Hobbes to develop an ethic grounded in nature apart from a transcendent source. We now turn our attention to the thought of Hobbes.

THOMAS HOBBES

Hobbes marks a major break in the history of ethics in which nature, law, and reason were freed from their transcendent source, namely, the God of the Bible. For Hobbes, law was only functional, and he made no reference to the transcendental or essential qualities of law. In ethics, he marked the beginning of a secular optimism in ethics, which believed that one can derive a plan for well-being from an analysis of human nature. Much of the next century in ethical theory is a response to Hobbes, either essentially an affirmation with a few changes, or a thoroughgoing critique.[14] He is best known for his system of personal ethics, or *egoism*, and his social ethics, with his contract view of civil society. Egoism is the ethical theory in which morality is determined by what is in an individual's self-interest. Consistent with this is his view of society, in which individuals voluntarily give up some freedoms in society to maximize their self-interest in the long run.

Hobbes lived in England for most of his life (1588–1679), absent only during a brief exile in France away from political turmoil in England. He was very interested in and heavily influenced by geometry and mechanistic psychology, and these disciplines played a significant part in the formation of his ethics. His ideas about ethics and politics were considered dramatic in his day, and he was the object of much harsh criticism, since he challenged not only the religious roots of the past, but also the philosophy of Aristotle. He is best known for his shortest work, *Leviathan*, which summarizes a good deal of his ethical and political theory.

The sociological roots of his theory come from the breakup of the medieval worldview, with its static view of the social order. According to the medieval view, everyone had their place in it by nature or by God's plan. Social mobility was very difficult and no real middle class existed. As that view of the world came unraveled, it was not clear what kind of society would emerge. Nor was it clear that order in that society would necessarily prevail. Thus Hobbes was formulating his ethic in a very uncertain sociological context, with the emphasis on individuals outside of the community and few assurances about social order. This affected both his personal and social ethics.

His personal ethics are clearly based on the nature and constitution of a human being, that is, anthropology. His anthropological task is to break man up into his constituent parts and examine the relationships of those parts. Thus, his view of a human being is based on empirical observation. He has an atomistic view of human nature in which, parallel with science, man is viewed as a small, isolated, individual machine. The most basic fact about man is that he consists of motions, both internal and external. External motions are derived from the internal. The internal motions produce two types of endeavor, aversion and appetite, or desire. His definition of the good then emerges out of these two types of endeavor. The object of the appetite is the good, and the object of aversion is evil. However, he is not a hedonist, since pleasure is the feeling associated with the good, not the good itself.

Thus he has an egoistic definition of the good. The good is defined in terms of individual and the individual's self-interest. But it does not mean that the good is relative. It is a relational, not a relative view of the good. It is relational in that the good is defined in relation to a desire. But it does not follow that the good varies or is arbitrary. The reason for this is that Hobbes assumed that aversions and appetites are constant. For example, he assumed that all people desire peace. This is one of his principal laws of nature. According to Hobbes, since people share desires such as the fear of death and the enjoyment of prosperity, universal goods must exist. Accordingly, calling his system relativism is not quite accurate, although it is easy to see how one could make that conclusion. After making observations of human nature that he took to be universal, he then built an ethic that could also be universal. This is clearly the way in which he intended it. Reason functions not to discern the ends, which are already clear from observations of human nature, but to give one the ability to see the best means to satisfy one's desire.

Happiness for Hobbes derives from his notion of desire and the good. Happiness is not the repose of a satisfied mind, as in the classical definition of contemplation. Human beings are always in the process of attaining happiness, but cannot finally attain it. Happiness is in the pursuit, that is, in the progress from one desire being satisfied to another. Hobbes put it this way: "Felicity [happiness] is a continual progress of the desire from one object to another, the attaining of the former being still but the way to the latter."[15] One can never get enough. He called the lust for power a general inclination of all humankind. Thus, there is no greatest good, only the progress of desire and the state of always needing more. Hobbes called this "a perpetual and restless lust for power, that ceaseth only in death."[16]

This leads logically to his social ethic, since this lust for power and for more satisfaction of one's desire can only come in interaction with others, and often, at their expense. Because of this ever-increasing lust for power, we exist in a state of war, what Hobbes called the *state of nature*, or the war of all against all. One of the key questions of Hobbes' critics is how his system of ethical egoism, which defines the good in terms of individual self-interest, tends to result in the state of nature, which he clearly abhors. Many critics have pointed out the inconsistency in the cause-and-effect relationship between an egoistic conception of the good and the resulting state of nature.

Out of his state of nature comes his notion of a *right of nature*. This is the right of self-preservation. This is the fundamental right of every human being, since the desire to live is perhaps the primary desire of a human being. Liberty is related to his right of nature in that liberty is freedom from impediments that would prevent people from using their power to maintain their lives. It is not, however, the same thing as the right of nature.

Hobbes' laws of nature are connected to his right of nature. He defines laws of nature very differently from Aquinas. In fact, to use the term *laws of nature* may even be misleading. Nevertheless, for Hobbes, laws of nature are discovered by reason, not by observation. In other words, reason helps one determine how best to fulfill one's desires. The laws of nature are the dictates of reason concerning an individual's self-preservation, and they determine the best means for insuring one's self-preservation. His laws of nature are premised on the assumption that there is no security in the state of nature. Thus one is to desire peace so that all other desires can be met.

Accordingly, the first law of nature is to seek peace as reason dictates. It is a law of nature in that it is "a general rule of reason." However, when one cannot obtain peace, one is free to seek and use all advantages of war. This he calls the sum of the right of nature, or the right of self-preservation.

The second law of nature is that people must lay down their right to all things as others are willing to do so, and be content with as much liberty as they would allow against themselves. Interestingly, he uses the biblical idea of the Golden Rule to support this.

The third law of nature is that one must keep covenants or promises. This law helped Hobbes define justice and injustice. They refer to the keeping and breaking of covenants. Justice is simply acting in conjunction with covenants that one has made. This reflects what is called a libertarian notion of justice, such as that of Robert Nozick.[17] Hobbes admitted, however, that reason alone is insufficient to compel covenant-keeping, especially since the breaking of covenants may be in one's self-interest. Therefore, covenants are enforced by the sovereign, and to have justice and injustice one must have a commonwealth, or community, into which people have voluntarily entered in order to achieve the self-preservation necessary to satisfy all other desires.

Other laws of nature exist that are all related to furthering one's self-preservation. These laws establish justice, gratitude, modesty, equity, and mercy as the principal virtues. Hobbes called these laws of nature "immutable and eternal" and considered them binding. He maintained that they were necessary to avoid the inevitable decay of society that would result if humankind remained in the state of nature. The fact that the laws are grounded in the desires and inclinations of human beings make them easy to observe.

Thus, he is what is called a realistic social ethicist, clearly following the Augustinian social vision. He viewed society as a voluntary association, not a divine order in which all have their place. Society is the place where free and equal individuals clash to maximize self-interest. The goal of government is to provide minimal order to safeguard one's pursuit of self-interest. He inaugurated the idea of government by consent, but an absolute ruler, which he called Leviathan, was needed to protect man from others. According to Hobbes, self-interest made it difficult for people to keep their covenants; therefore, a totalitarian ruler was needed to enforce the laws of nature. The political philosophy of Western liberal democracy borrowed from Hobbes' diagnosis of human nature, but not his cure. The cure he offered was unnecessary, since the Judeo-Christian ethic embraced by the West possessed an internal check for self-interest.

DAVID HUME

Hume is the first in a line of what are called *moral sense theorists*. The moral sense that an individual possesses makes an action right or wrong. This is very different from the Christian idea of the conscience recognizing right and wrong. Conscience would be a thermometer that measures right and wrong, whereas in Hume's system, one's moral sense is a thermostat that actually determines right and wrong. Virtue, or goodness, is defined as "whatever mental action or quality gives to a spectator the pleasing sentiment of approbation and vice the contrary."[18] Moral distinctions are thus independent of reason, and, for Hume, reason is only the slave of the passions.

Hume was born and raised in Scotland (1711–1776) and was not an academic philosopher by profession. He was turned down for positions at the Universities of Glasgow and Edinburgh, and spent much of life in various diplomatic roles. He was a historian as well as a philosopher and wrote a history of Great Britain in addition to his numerous philosophical works. Among his treatises in philosophy, he attempted a complete philosophical system, entitled *A Treatise of Human Nature*, the lukewarm reception of which left him deeply disappointed and more motivated to make his further philosophical work more accepted. He wrote about metaphysics, epistemology, anthropology, philosophy of religion, political philosophy, and ethics. He was a very popular person in literary circles during his lifetime, although he received much criticism for his philosophical works.

Hume's ethics come out of his overall worldview, which is known as empiricism; that is, the only matters of fact are those discernible by the senses. Thus, moral facts and moral sense as perceptible objects do not exist. The rules of morality are not derived by reason. In fact, reason is inert when it comes to determining the morality of an action. He compared vice and virtue with sounds, colors, heat, and cold. They are not qualities in objects but perceptions in the mind. These moral perceptions are all that is necessary to regulate moral behavior. He stated, "Nothing can be more real, or concern us more, than our own sentiments of pleasure and uneasiness; and if these be favorable to virtue and unfavorable to vice, no more can be requisite to the regulation of our conduct and behavior."[19]

Morals have to do with sense, not reason. Reason can only determine means to accomplishing ends. Thus, reason and the passions can never be at battle. Reason only serves the passions, and they are not subject to reason. Reason is also powerless to incite action necessary to actually do the good.

The content of the moral sense is a critical notion for Hume. It identifies virtue, which Hume called "personal merit," by its usefulness or immediate agreeableness, either to the individual or to others. These qualities give one the pleasing sentiment of approbation. This seems to reduce morality to a matter of taste. Hume did hold to legitimate moral distinctions, constituted by approbation or usefulness. One question raised by his criteria for virtue is the way in which usefulness and agreeableness relate to each other. Hume did not synthesize the concepts of usefulness and agreeability in any coherent way, which most commentators on Hume cite as a serious flaw in his system. Also, he had to borrow the notion of utility to find a way to maintain social order. This inevitably involves the use of reason in the determination of morality, which he rejected. For Hume, morality is not fact, but feeling or sentiment. John Stuart Mill and Jeremy Bentham later developed Hume's concept of usefulness and discarded his concept of agreeability in their utilitarian theories.

Hume's theory worked something like this: our nature is designed to feel approbation for certain actions; trait "X" is the object of approbation as useful or immediately agreeable; therefore, trait "X" ought to be exercised. According to Hume, one's moral sentiments have a hortatory function, exhorting one to action as well as pronouncing a judgment on an action. Reducing morality to matters of opinion or feeling (or even taste) is at the heart of Hume's project. The reason his theory is important is that it is widely followed today. Morality is becoming increasingly subjective and is losing its propositional nature as people in our culture insist that judgments of right and wrong are merely individual subjective feelings or opinion, as evidenced by the contemporary creed, "If it feels good, do it!"

IMMANUEL KANT

Widely regarded as one of the greatest philosophical minds and contributors to ethics, Kant lived during the height of the Enlightenment (1724–1804). He was raised in Prussia and educated at the University of Königsberg, where he later spent most of his teaching career. He wrote voluminously about metaphysics, logic, epistemology, philosophy of religion, and ethics, and enjoyed an outstanding reputation throughout Europe during his lifetime. He lived an uneventful life outside of his teaching and writing. He never married and spent his life fulfilling responsibilities of professor and scholar.

Kant devised a principle-based ethic, based not on a religious system, but on reason alone. He represents the epitome of Enlightenment ethics in that he attempted to construct an adequately grounded ethical system based on the use of reason alone. His system was not dependent on divine revelation, either special or natural. Also, it was not based on any particular view of human nature, since nature could be interpreted in many different ways. Insisting that a valid moral system must be independent of empirical observation, his ethics were in part a response to the ethics of Hume, his contemporary.

Underlying his moral system are three critical assumptions about morality. First, to have a valid moral system, one must have power to constrain people without being deterministic. In other words, reason must have the power to motivate action, but it must also leave one genuinely free to not do one's duty. In contrast to Hume, reason governs the passions, not vice versa.

Second, what is a valid duty in circumstance "X" is the same for all rational beings. This is his principle of fairness and is foundational to his central concept known as the *categorical imperative*. He does acknowledge relevant differences among people, but the point is that moral obligations do not vary based on the circumstances. Here Kant appears to be anticipating the utilitarians such as Bentham and Mill for whom morality depended on the consequences of an action, which depended largely on one's circumstances.

Third, people cannot change their moral obligations or duties merely by changing their desires. Moral imperatives based on desire are what he called hypothetical imperatives. A true moral imperative is what he called categorical, since it is not based on some desire.

Kant's system revolved around the notion of the good will. This is his first proposition on the nature of morality. The good will is seen as being the key to being worthy of happiness. In this notion, he reversed the emphasis of the classical Greek philosophers, that virtue would essentially bring one well-being. For Kant, happiness followed if one was morally worthy of possessing it. The good will is capable of acting from motives other than the desire to be well off. It recognizes that one's duty is inherently good apart from any consequences that it produced. What makes the good will good is that is operates independent of consequences. He cited two cases in which one can have a bad will that produces good results, and a good will that produces bad results. Kant reasoned that since one cannot control all the consequences, moral worth cannot depend on things that are beyond the control of the individual making the moral decision. The good will is the will which acts for the sake of duty. Thus, the idea of duty is set up in accordance with the above three assumptions. One's duty can be contrary to one's inclination, but does not have to be. For Kant, being moral is more than acting according to one's inclination.

Actions are determined either by desire or inclination, or by what Kant calls a *maxim*. A maxim is the plan of action where an individual in circumstance "X" does act "A" to bring about result "R." But the result is not what gives the act worth, because one does not control all the results of one's actions. Thus the question is raised, What is it about the maxim that makes the will good?

The good will is the only unconditional good. The good will is one which acts from duty. The value of an act done from duty is not in its consequences. Hence, it must be from its maxim. But what distinguishes the good maxim from the bad? The good maxim must be able to motivate every rational being in the specified circumstance. Thus, it must have something that is the "same for all." This is the form of the law, or its ability to be universalized. In other words, all beings can act on the maxim without making it impossible for any to act on it. Thus, what Kant called the categorical imperative is not based on circumstances.

Within his concept of the good will is the idea of the contradiction of the will. This assumes that if everyone did it, no one would ultimately be able to do it. In his test for universalization he asked, Would it be fair, or could we live with it if everyone did this? The categorical imperative is often applied in a bit different way, by asking, Could we live with a state of affairs if everyone did *not* do things that Kant suggested are to be universal maxims? For example, if everyone violated the duty to tell the truth, could we live with the kind of society that would inevitably result from this?

To put it another way, he might ask, Are you ready for your action to be regarded as the equivalent of a law of nature? Thus, we're constrained to do something because we respect the law that can be universalized and thus we feel a sense of duty as a result. Duty and inclination are not necessarily opposed, but a moral act is one done out of duty, not simply because one wants to do it. Moral maxims, or plans of action, must be categorical, that is, they must be binding and independent of one's desires. This categorical imperative actually has four different formulations, which are listed below:

1. Act only according to that maxim by which you can at the same time will that it should become a universal law.
2. Act as though the maxim of your action were by your will to become a universal law of nature.
3. Act so that you treat humanity, whether in your own person or in that of another, always as an end and never as a means only. From this formulation the fundamental principle of respect for persons is derived. (This is one of the most significant legacies of the ethics of Kant.)
4. Do no action according to any maxim which would be inconsistent with its being a universal and thus ..., act only so that the will through its maxims could regard itself at the same time as universally law-giving. This is what he calls his principle of autonomy. Since we derive the principles from our own rational nature, we are autonomous and self-determined, and thus by our actions, we "legislate" morality. Moral con-

straint is thus possible without individuals losing their genuine free-dom of moral choice.

To summarize, no will is morally good because it does what it wants to do. A motive other than the passions must exist. It is the feeling of respect for law. Free from determination, the rational will acts on the basis of respect for law. But since not all are purely rational beings, human beings *ought* to act under the con-straint of the categorical imperative. The moral purpose of reason is to illumi-nate us to our "ought," independent of sensation. The highest good for Kant is both happiness and being worthy of it. That is achieved by adherence to duty.

CONCLUSION

Numerous other thinkers could have been included in this overview. Some of them will be addressed in the next chapter, "Ethical Systems and Ways of Moral Reasoning." For example, the system known as utilitarianism will be addressed in some detail. Accordingly, Jeremy Bentham and John Stuart Mill, the seminal thinkers who developed utilitarianism, will be discussed in the context of exam-ining the entire system. The ethical theorists mentioned in this brief chapter con-stitute the primary contributors to ethical theory and have left a significant legacy to moral theory. In fact, various aspects of their theories survive in popu-lar culture today, despite the difficulties raised by scholarly critics. Taking this chapter together with the one that follows, the student should be well-equipped to identify and critique the various types of moral reasoning employed in many of the current debates on various issues.

FOR FURTHER READING

Sidgwick, Henry. *Outlines in the History of Ethics*. Indianapolis: Hackett Publishing Co., 1988.

MacIntyre, Alasdair. *A Short History of Ethics*. New York: Collier Books, 1966.

Melden, A. I. *Ethical Theories: A Book of Readings*. New York: Macmillan, 1967.

NOTES

[1]For example, Martin Luther had few complimentary things to say about Aristotle, calling him "that buffoon who misled the Church."

[2]This is not to say that parts of the Constitution were not heavily influenced by Judeo-Christian moral principles. But there is great debate over whether the right to privacy is a right supported by Scripture, particularly as it is used in the debate over abortion.

[3]For a good example of the similarities within various pre-philosophical law codes, see C. S. Lewis, *The Abolition of Man* (New York: Macmillan, 1947), 97–121.

[4]The best known of these attempts was by the medieval Catholic theologian Thomas Aquinas, who lived and wrote in the thirteenth century. Roughly contemporary with him were the Islamic theologians Averroës and Avicenna, and the Jewish theologian Moses

Maimonides, all of whom attempted to wed Aristotelian philosophy and their theology. The Reformers, however, had little patience with this synthesis.

[5]Perhaps the best known example of this is the landmark work by Alasdair MacIntyre, *After Virtue* (Notre Dame, Ind.: University of Notre Dame Press, 1984), and his subsequent work, *Whose Justice? Which Rationality?* (Notre Dame, Ind.: University of Notre Dame Press, 1988).

[6]This concept of a craft or skill is at the heart of the Hebrew concept of wisdom. In the Old Testament, wisdom is compared to a skill, such as woodworking or embroidery, which is done well. The wise person is the one who is skilled at living life and maintaining right relationships with God and the community.

[7]It may be that the New Testament teaching on justification was written to correct the Platonic idea of justice. The Greek term *dikaiosune*—translated "righteousness," from which we receive the idea of justification—is in the same word family as "justice." Plato held that justice could be achieved by training and education, whereas the Pauline doctrine is that justice is a free gift from God that cannot be earned or achieved by individual effort (Rom. 3:21–26).

[8]Interestingly, the word Aristotle uses for "happiness" in classical Greek is the same word that Jesus uses to describe life in the kingdom of God. It is translated "blessed" and used repeatedly in the Beatitudes (Matt. 5:1–12).

[9]Epicurus to Menoeceus, cited in A. I. Melden, *Ethical Theories* (New York: Prentice Hall, 1967), 145-46.

[10]St. Augustine, *The City of God*, cited in Melden, *Ethical Theories*, 169.

[11]The principal Muslim philosophers include Avicenna and Averroës, from Spain, and the primary Jewish theologian engaged in this type of synthesis is Moses Maimonides. St. Thomas tried to balance the place of reason and revelation in ethics, although some might suggest that he effectively jettisoned revelation, given his emphasis on reason and natural law. The result of the Islamic debate was quite different from the Thomistic synthesis, since revelation essentially vanquished reason as the principal determinant of ethics. Islam emphasized dependent reason and denied that objective moral values existed apart from revelation. Jews under Maimonides essentially maintained a similar balance between reason and revelation that Aquinas emphasized.

[12]In seeing happiness as the *telos* of a human being, Aquinas is heavily influenced here by Aristotle. He has adapted Aristotle's notion of happiness to Augustine's concept of the highest good, namely, knowing God and enjoying fellowship with him.

[13]For a more detailed discussion of natural law as a moral system, see chapter 2.

[14]The main lines of response to Hobbes are twofold: the rationalists such as Cudworth, Clarke, Price, and the empiricists such as Locke, Shaftesbury, Hutcheson, Butler, Hume, Bentham, and Mill. The rationalists are also called the Cambridge Platonists or the British moralists, who were critical of Hobbes' arbitrary and variable nature of morality. The empiricists were characterized by their emphasis on the observable regularities and connections within the human self. Butler is perhaps the chief representative of this school.

[15]Thomas Hobbes, *Leviathan*, cited in Melden, *Ethical Theories*, 221.

[16]Ibid.

[17]For the classic statement of this philosophy, see Robert Nozick, *Anarchy, State and Utopia* (New York: Basic Books, 1974).

[18]David Hume, *An Enquiry Concerning the Principles of Morals*, cited in Melden, *Ethical Theories*, 309.

[19]David Hume, *A Treatise of Human Nature* (New York: Oxford University Press, 1978), 456.

4

ETHICAL SYSTEMS AND WAYS OF MORAL REASONING

As people in our contemporary culture wrestle with ethical decisions, they employ a wide variety of methods of moral reasoning. One obvious place to observe this is in the debate over various social issues. In fact, one of the primary reasons why many of these debates remain unresolved is that the participants are applying different methods of moral reasoning.

Take, for example, the debate over euthanasia. Imagine that you are listening to a community panel discussion on the morality of physician-assisted suicide. The participants are (1) an eighty-year-old man with terminal cancer and approximately six months to live; (2) the head of the local chapter of the Hemlock Society, an organization that advocates assisted suicide; (3) a physician who specializes as an oncologist, that is, a cancer specialist; (4) a Catholic priest who is an outspoken opponent of euthanasia; (5) an atheistic philosophy professor from the local college; (6) an attorney; and (7) a Protestant minister. Each one will use a different type of moral reasoning as they present their respective positions. Each panel member will offer a brief opening statement to define and defend their position.

Participant #1: The 80-year-old Man with Terminal Cancer (Ethical Egoist)

"All this moral discussion of euthanasia really bothers me. You see, for me it all boils down to the fact that I am the patient and what I want should be the thing that counts. It's my interests that really matter here, not whether euthanasia violates the Hippocratic Oath or the Fifth Commandment (Thou shalt not kill), or what consequences allowing euthanasia produces for the general society. I am the patient, and the one most directly affected, and that's why it should be my decision. Whatever is in my best interest in terms of euthanasia should be OK."

Participant #2: The Head of the Local Chapter of the Hemlock Society (Deontologist)

"I am in substantial agreement with our first participant, though for a different reason. I, too, support active euthanasia, or physician-assisted suicide, but from a slightly different perspective. One of the fundamental principles, or rights, that Western societies have affirmed for centuries is the right of individual autonomy and self-determination, that is, the right of people to make private choices concerning their lives without interference from the state. Surely matters of life and death for people are so private that they ought to have the freedom to do as they choose without undue interference from the authorities, as long as no one else is harmed. This is a fundamental right that is based on the principle of respect for persons and individual bodily integrity. I appeal to this fundamental moral principle in order to affirm my support for euthanasia."

Participant #3: The Physician Who Specializes as an Oncologist (Utilitarian)

"In most cases, I, too, support active euthanasia, but for still different reasons than we have heard so far. You see, I hold that it is not necessarily principles that determine right and wrong, but the consequences produced by the actions in question. If a particular course of action or decision produces the best set of consequences, then it seems to me that it should be allowed. To put it another way, the action that produces the greatest balance of benefits over harms is the one that is the most moral. So in the case of euthanasia, I think that the first two participants have framed the question incorrectly. What is important to determine is whether or not active euthanasia would produce the greatest good for the greatest number of people. I can see that allowing physician-assisted suicide could produce a lot of good for the people involved. It would relieve the patient of needless suffering, stop the family's anxiety about their loved one's condition, end a needless drain of the family's financial resources, and allow everyone involved to get on with their lives. Now, there may be situations in which euthanasia may produce, on balance, more negative than positive consequences. In those cases, it should not be allowed. We should be cautious in setting hard-and-fast rules that don't fully consider the consequences."

Participant #4: The Catholic Priest (Deontologist)

"I am opposed to all active euthanasia because of a principle that is foundational to our civilization. Even for those without any religious inclination, the principle that 'Thou shalt not kill' is still one of the core values on which most civilized people agree. Now I also happen to believe that this principle comes from God, but a person does not have to believe in God to accept the importance of this moral rule. I hold that active euthanasia is killing an innocent person, and that is something our society should not allow, regardless of the person's desires. Underlying the moral rule that 'Thou shalt not kill' is the more important principle of respect for the dignity of a person. Now again, I believe we should respect people because they are made in God's image, but you don't have to believe in God to accept such a basic moral principle. People have an innate tendency toward self-preservation, and that is one of the basic reasons it is immoral to take innocent life. You see, like my opponent at the Hemlock Society, I, too, hold a high place for principles, but I differ on how they are applied. For me, the principle of respect for persons does not mean that we should necessarily let them do whatever they want to do. What it does mean is that we should never take innocent life, because life is sacred, and when it shall end is not our prerogative."

Participant #5: The Atheistic Philosophy Professor (Emotivist)

"I hate to throw a monkey wrench into this whole discussion, but in my view, all of the participants so far are trying to do the impossible. So far each person has attempted to make some kind of determination of what is right or wrong in the case of active euthanasia. I don't think this is possible. They are really using the language of right and wrong to mask their own personal preferences. What I mean is that anytime a person says that something is right or wrong, all they are saying, and can say, is that they either like or dislike the action or position under consideration. It is obvious that the elderly gentleman and the representative of the Hemlock Society are really saying that they personally approve of euthanasia. It is equally obvious that the priest is really saying that he personally disapproves of euthanasia. We should be honest and admit that we're only talking about our preferences, and that we're simply using moral language to give greater persuasive power to our argument."

Participant #6: The Local Attorney (Relativist)

"I wouldn't go quite as far as my professor friend, but I do think he's moving in the right direction. I'm not prepared to say that there is no such thing as genuine right and wrong, but I do think that there is no universal, absolute standard of right and wrong. What is moral depends on the situation, and on what the cultural consensus of right and wrong is at that time. In the case of euthanasia, if the culture has reached a consensus that it should be allowed, then I see no reason why it should not be allowed. Conversely, if the culture is opposed to the practice, I see no good reason why euthanasia should be forced on them. I know that in the Netherlands, for example, the majority believes that euthanasia is right, and that should be respected. We could say that it is right for them. But in the state of Utah, where there are so many religious Mormons, or in the Bible Belt, where there are so many conservative Christians, the culture will undoubtedly be against euthanasia, and that should also be respected."

Participant #7: The Protestant Minister (Virtue Theorist)

"I'd like to put a slightly different slant on the issue of euthanasia. You see, I believe that there's more to morality than simply making decisions when a person is faced with a moral quandary. There is more to the moral life than simply doing the right thing and making the correct decision. We cannot neglect the place of an individual's character, or virtue, when considering ethical questions. In my view, the important questions still have not been asked. For example, what does a person's desire for active euthanasia tell us about that individual's character? What does support for euthanasia, or opposition to it, say about our society? Does it say that we as a society lack compassion for the suffering terminally ill, as proponents of euthanasia suggest? Or does it say that we have lost some of our reverence for life and our commitment to care for the dying, as opponents of euthanasia would suggest? These are very important questions that cannot be ignored in any discussion about the morality of euthanasia."

Each person on this panel has argued his position using a distinctive method of moral reasoning from a specific ethical system (each participants' method is noted within parentheses above). They represent each of the main positions adopted by people when applying moral reasoning to the moral issues currently debated in society. As you witness the news media's coverage of various debates over current ethical issues, observe the various methods utilized by those engaged in the debates. If you are careful, you will likely detect the regular use of most of these systems discussed in this chapter. For the remainder of this chapter, we will analyze each of the ethical systems used by the panel participants, highlighting the positive elements of each system as well as offering a critique of each.[1]

ETHICAL EGOISM

Ethical egoism is the theory that the morality of an act is determined by one's self-interest. Actions that advance self-interest are moral, and those that do not are not moral. A common misunderstanding is that an ethical egoist is someone who is egotistical. The ethical egoist simply uses self-interest to make moral decisions, which does not necessarily mean that the person is narcissistic.

In addition to Participant #1, who made his moral decision about euthanasia based strictly on his self-interest, many other contemporary examples illustrate the practice of ethical egoism. For example, medical doctors frequently make decisions based upon their potential exposure to medical malpractice suits. In many cases, nothing is inherently wrong with the desire to avoid lawsuits. Our point here, however, is simply to illustrate the use of ethical egoism in making moral decisions. For the physician who is an ethical egoist, the right thing to do is what will protect him from being sued, or what is in his self-interest.

Another example of ethical egoism is what we commonly call "whistle blowing." This occurs when an employee's superiors ask the employee to do something that the employee believes is immoral; like falsifying data, offering bribes, or deceiving customers or regulators. The employee may refuse to fulfill the request, and instead may "blow the whistle" on the company, revealing the immoral, and at times, illegal, practice that they have been asked to do. In most cases, however, whistle blowers lose their jobs and are blacklisted from the industry, leaving them unable to support themselves and their families. In short, whistle blowing often has devastating results for the employee. When deliberating about blowing the whistle, many employees become ethical egoists, using their own self-interest as the determining factor for what they should do in the situation.

Ethical egoism is also used in the Bible as a way of motivating people to be obedient to God. For example, the covenant blessings and curses set forth in Deuteronomy 27–30 promise Israel agricultural prosperity and military peace as consequences of obedience, and threaten the opposite should the nation turn to idolatry and disobey God. What is in Israel's national self-interest is clearly a motivation for doing the right things. Other examples of this use of self-interest include becoming a Christian and receiving eternal life as a result, which is clearly in a person's self-interest. Doing altruistic acts because of the good feelings we receive is egoistic. Some have even suggested that the Bible is entirely egoistic, and simply changes the categories of what constitutes a person's self-interest. However, that is probably too strong a statement. While the Bible never condemns self-interest, it does require that it be balanced with concern for others (Phil. 2:4). It is one thing to occasionally appeal to self-interest as the Bible does, but quite another to claim that egoism is a sufficient ethical system, as do thoroughgoing ethical egoists. We will examine this latter claim in the following paragraphs.

In ethical egoism, one's only moral duty is to one's own self-interest. This is not to say that a person should avoid actions that help others, since a person's interests and the interests of others can coincide. It may be that helping others may be a means to the end of a person's own self-interest. It is also not to say that one's short-term interests are primary. One may forego an immediate advantage to insure long-term interests. Thomas Hobbes, the original egoist, suggested that to prevent the pursuit of self-interest from destroying society, people should voluntarily give up some of their freedom to pursue their interests so that each one's long-term interests might be protected.[2]

Its Principles

The principal arguments offered in support of ethical egoism are as follows:[3]

1. *Looking out for others is a self-defeating pursuit.* Looking out for others is self-defeating for three reasons. First, the egoist claims that we know only our own needs, and we have much less ability to understand or meet the needs of others. Second, being concerned with the needs of others invades their privacy. Third, people find it demeaning to accept the help of others. Interestingly, the logic of this argument is actually very *unegoistic*. The argument runs like this: (a) we ought to do whatever will promote the best interests of others; (b) this will happen best if we all pursue our own interests exclusively; (c) therefore, each of us should adopt the policy of pursuing our interests exclusively. The end result is that we act like egoists, but reason like altruists. Following this argument to its logical end, we would have to conclude that we are not egoists at all, but altruists with a strange view of what makes for the general welfare.

2. *Ethical egoism is the only moral system that respects the integrity of the individual human life.* This is the argument of the most well-known spokesperson for egoism, the libertarian novelist-philosopher Ayn Rand.[4] Her argument is as follows: (a) Since a person has only one life to live, this life is of supreme importance; (b) the ethic of altruism regards the life of the individual as something that one must be ready to sacrifice for the good of others; (c) thus, altruistic ethics does not take seriously the value of the individual human; (d) egoism, which allows each person to view his own life as having ultimate value, does take the individual human seriously; (e) therefore, ethical egoism ought to be accepted.[5] The problem with this argument is that it portrays the two alternatives of self-interest and altruism as polar extremes and mutually exclusive. In her view, altruism demands that one's interests have no value, when in reality one's self-interest can be balanced with a concern for others. When the argument is presented in this way, it is easy to see how egoism can have appeal, since the alternative is so unattractive. Very few people would choose a life in which they could never look out for their own interests.

3. *Egoism is the hidden unity underlying our widely accepted moral duties.* The egoist accepts that people can genuinely look out for others, yet tries to explain it as an outworking of self-interest. For example, doing harm to others is to be avoided because others will be more inclined not to harm us. Truth-telling is in our interest, since people will trust us and be truthful with us. Likewise, keeping promises or entering into mutually beneficial arrangements, or contracts, is in our interest. One could reply that this is only a general rule, since one might

gain from harming another, or lying, or breaking promises or contracts. When this is so, the obligation not to harm others cannot be drawn from egoism. Also, one could argue that altruism is to one's advantage. But it does not follow that this self-interest is the only, or even the most fundamental, reason for doing something altruistic. It only proves that it is also to my advantage to do something altruistic. To derive a duty from self-interest, one would have to prove that self-interest is the only motive for being altruistic.

Its Problems

Not only can one rebut the main arguments for ethical egoism, but one can point out other problems that it has. First, egoism has no means to settle conflicts of interest between individuals and groups without appealing to some other system. What happens when my self-interest conflicts with yours? All the egoist can do to resolve the conflict is to reassert his basic premise of self-interest. To think that interests never conflict is naive. Yet this assumption seems to be necessary if ethical egoism is to be a viable system.

Second, ethical egoism ultimately collapses into anarchy. For example, Hobbes' system required an absolute monarch (who he called *Leviathan*, the title of his work that explains this concept) to keep egoism from disintegrating into anarchy. Yet there were no guarantees that the monarch would not also pursue his own self-interest, too. It takes great faith to believe that some kind of "invisible hand" mysteriously works all things out.[6] Again, for the system to work, it requires resources outside of itself. To make egoism work, one must assume some sort of natural law to control egoism, which would discredit the underlying premise known as psychological egoism (that people are incapable of acting except in their own self-interest). The Bible teaches that depravity drives people toward self-interest, whereas common grace and the creation of people as bearers of God's image balance that force even for the unbeliever. For the believer, the resources also include the indwelling Holy Spirit to balance depravity.

Third, egoism is an arbitrary ethical system.[7] It divides people into two groups and says that the interests of one group count more than the interests of the other. For example, both anti-Semitism and racism illustrate this. Advocates of those ideologies insist that the interests of their group count more than the interests of Jews or any other race different than their own, simply because of the difference in race. In general, treating groups differently is justifiable if there are relevant differences between the groups. An anti-Semite or racist cannot point consistently to any criteria that justify anti-Semitism or racism. Egoism advocates that we divide the world into two groups—me and the rest of the world—and that we regard the interests of the first group as more important than the second, but putting myself into such a privileged category simply cannot be justified.

Fourth, ethical egoism is built on the false premise of psychological egoism, that is, the notion that individuals are only capable of acting in their self-interest, and that genuine altruism does not exist. This premise is false for two primary reasons. First, sometimes we simply act spontaneously, without any concern for self-interest. For example, people who perform feats of heroism generally do them by instinct, without any thoughts of possible recognition. Second, in our closest human relationships, namely, friendship, marriage, and parenthood, we often sacrifice our well-being and interests for those we love. The egoist will insist that on the surface your actions only look like altruism. But if you look at the deeper, unconscious motives, you'll find that your motives are entirely egoistic. At this point, however, egoism becomes an untestable theory. This reveals the deepest flaw of egoism, since the egoist has announced his determination to interpret people's behavior in a way that corresponds to his theory, no matter what they do. Thus, nothing that anyone could do could count as evidence against the theory. However, the argument could just as easily be turned around by saying that at the deepest level, one's motives are altruistic, not egoistic. Further, this argument confuses a motive and a benefit. Just because someone receives a benefit from an altruistic act, it does not follow that it is the motive for doing the act. We would actually hope that people receive good feelings from doing altruistic things even though that may not be the entire motive.

Fifth, ethical egoism as a sufficient system ignores the fact that the Scriptures call believers and unbelievers to a balance of self-interest and altruism. We are called to care for the needs of others because they are comparable to our own and because a significant part of being a disciple of Christ is following his altruistic example. Believers are called to be servants, and that invariably involves periodically putting others' needs ahead of our own. It does not, however, obligate believers to neglect their legitimate self-interest. The Bible does not call believers to the kind of extreme altruism that ethical egoists claim it does. One should remember that at times even Jesus separated from the crowds to seek solitude with his heavenly Father. Thus, the Bible seems to suggest that self-interest has a legitimate place, but it needs to be balanced by a compassionate concern for the interests of others.

UTILITARIANISM

Utilitarianism is what is known as a teleological system (taken from the Greek word *telos*, which means "end," "goal"), in which the morality of an act is determined by the end result. In fact, sometimes utilitarianism and teleological ethics are used interchangeably. Utilitarianism commonly argues that the moral choice is the one that produces the greatest good for the greatest number of people, or the moral choice is the course of action that produces more good consequences than harmful ones. Thus, this type of moral reasoning is also called consequentialism, because of its overriding emphasis on the consequences of an action.

Utilitarianism has its roots in the philosophies of Jeremy Bentham (1748–1832) and John Stuart Mill (1806–1873). Bentham held to a hedonistic utilitarianism, which maintains that the most moral acts are those that maximize pleasure and minimize pain. Mill developed his approach away from hedonism and toward a more general concept of maximizing the general happiness, or the greatest good for the greatest number. When it was proposed, utilitarianism was a radical theory, since it divorced morality from divine revelation and from any view of nature. According to utilitarianism, moral behavior no longer required faithfulness to divine ordinances and rigid moral rules.

Utilitarian modes of moral reasoning are widely applied to many of the currently debated moral issues. Most of the public policy in the United States and Western Europe is still decided on overwhelmingly utilitarian grounds. As was evident from Participant #3 in the euthanasia debate, a good deal of the discussion about active euthanasia is conducted on utilitarian grounds, where principles take a backseat to consequences. If, on balance, euthanasia provides more beneficial consequences for more people, then a utilitarian would consider it to be the most moral choice. Another example of utilitarianism is when a company considers closing plants or laying off workers to maintain their competitive position in the marketplace. While acknowledging that this will produce harm for some, the company justifies such measures by asserting that it is safeguarding the jobs of the rest of the employees. Keeping the company in business, management argues, will produce greater benefits than harms.

Its Appeal

The appeal of utilitarianism rests on a number of factors. First, it is a relatively simple theory to apply. All one must do is weigh the anticipated good consequences of an action against its anticipated harmful ones and see if the bottom line produces a greater balance of benefits over harms. If it produces greater benefits, then it is the most moral course of action. Second, it avoids the rigidity of deontology, that is, it keeps morality from being reduced to abstract principles that must be strictly followed, regardless of the consequences produced by them. Without question, deontological, principle-based systems can be legalistic and can sacrifice people at the expense of holding to one's principles. Third, it doesn't require special appeal to divine revelation for morality; rather, it appeals to nonmoral criteria for determining the good. This makes it a logical choice in an increasingly secular world, in which people are growing more skeptical of religiously based morality. Many people in society view the divorce of morality from religion as a good thing, and see utilitarianism as a substitute for divisive moral systems based on revelation. Also, the presumed neutrality of utilitarianism has special appeal to a world that still prides itself on being value free and objective. Fourth, most people know intuitively that the consequences of one's actions must be taken seriously. No matter how tenaciously one holds to principles, one must take the consequences of one's actions into account to have a fully functioning moral system. Utilitarianism enables one to do just that, since the consequences of an action determine its morality.

Utilitarianism may be divided into two primary schools, known as *act utilitarianism* and *rule utilitarianism*. Act utilitarianism uses the consequences of any given course of action to determine its morality. In doing so, the act utilitarian treats each moral decision separately, and weighs the consequences of each isolated act. Rather than depending on a separate calculation of consequences each time one needs to make a moral decision, rule utilitarians have formulated moral rules to guide them in decision making. The rule utilitarian formulates rules based on the tendency of certain actions to produce a predictable set of consequences. For example, rape would be an immoral act, not because of a principle that prohibits it, but because rape, every time it occurs, produces more harmful consequences than beneficial ones. The rule utilitarian could say the same about many other actions, such as truth-telling, promise-keeping, murder, fraud, and deceit. Thus, a rule utilitarian appears very similar to a deontologist, yet they have entirely different foundations for their rules.

Although utilitarianism has appeal, especially in a secular society, it also has shortcomings. The most common charge against utilitarianism is that it cannot protect the rights of minorities, and sometimes it can even justify obvious injustices when the greater good is served. For example, in the antebellum South, slavery was clearly justifiable from a utilitarian point of view. It provided cheap labor that made the South very prosperous and clearly benefited more people than it harmed. But no one today would justify slavery on any grounds, let alone utilitarian ones. The good consequences that it produced appear not only irrelevant, but callous toward the suffering endured by so many slaves. The reason that slavery was immoral has little to do with the balance of consequences. Rather it has to do with a universal principle that directs us to safeguard the basic rights and dignity of people, ultimately because they are made in the image of God.

Also, utilitarianism can justify obvious injustices, such as contriving evidence against an innocent person to prevent widespread social unrest that would result in loss of life and substantial property damage. On strictly utilitarian grounds, framing someone is not only justifiable, but morally obligatory, to prevent significant harmful consequences. But most people have a deep, intuitive sense that framing someone is wrong, regardless of the consequences.

A utilitarian may reply that the cases cited beg to be questioned, since they assume the priority of the principles of justice and fairness. Here it is crucial to demonstrate to the utilitarian how difficult it would be to live with the implications of their theory. For example, how would utilitarians justify slavery?

The utilitarian may also take the position of a rule utilitarian, instead of an act utilitarian. This prevents individual actions from being judged by the principle of utility. Rather, the rule utilitarian would approach the situation differently. The rule utilitarian would not reason as an act utilitarian, but would step back from the situation and ask, What rules of conduct tend to promote the greatest good for the greatest number?

Given two societies, one which had a rule against bearing false witness and another that did not, from the perspective of utility, the first one would clearly be the better one. By appealing to the rule against bearing false witness, the person would conclude that he should not frame the innocent person to quell the riots. Thus, the utilitarian has shifted the focus from the justification of individual actions to the justification of general rules (on the principle of utility) to avoid the charge of injustice. Whether the utilitarian has avoided the charge of injustice is not clear, however, since it could be argued that a society that uses false witness in specific circumstances to prevent widespread social unrest might be a good society. It is not clear that the retreat to rule utilitarianism can help ease the tension created by act utilitarian situations.

Its Problems

Even if the utilitarian can escape the charge of justifying obvious injustices, this system has other problems. First, not only are the consequences of actions difficult to predict and measure, but the notions of benefit and harm are not value neutral. What may be a benefit or a harm to one person may not be to another. It is not entirely accurate to say that the utilitarian uses nonmoral criteria to evaluate the morality of an action. In many cases, one must appeal to principles to give substance to the idea of a benefit or to arbitrate competing claims about a benefit.

Second, utilitarianism lacks criteria to direct the distribution of benefits in a group. It tends to be an aggregate theory in that what really counts is the overall amount of benefit, that is, the greatest good for the greatest number. The distribution of benefits is just as important, if not more so, as the overall amount of benefit accorded to the aggregate group.

Third, utilitarianism offers no place for the idea of individual merit.[8] For example, an employer promotes a responsible employee rather than an irresponsible one not because it serves the general utility, but because the responsible employee has earned it. Without being guilty of discrimination, we recognize merit as a reason for treating people in different ways, regardless of the consequences for treating people that way.

In spite of these problems with utilitarianism, it is important to take the consequences of actions and decisions seriously, since there may be times when an appeal to principles will not resolve a dilemma. Also, consequences may force us to realize that sometimes there are exceptions to our deontological principles.

EMOTIVISM

The debate over moral issues such as euthanasia, abortion, and homosexuality illustrates the overlap between moral judgments and personal preferences. For example, many people who say that homosexuality is wrong actually mean that they find it distasteful or disgusting. This is another way of describing ethical subjectivism (see the following section on "Relativism"). The subjectivist holds that morality depends on how an individual feels about an action. When someone makes the statement that "X is wrong," the subjectivist will conclude that the person simply disapproves of X, since morality to the subjectivist is in the eye of the beholder. Many of the same criticisms of ethical relativism also apply to ethical subjectivism.

Emotivism goes beyond subjectivism and is a theory about metaethics, that is, the language of morality. The emotivist holds that moral language simply expresses a person's emotions about a subject. Thus, nothing that anyone says in moral language can be true or false. The emotivist considers ethical statements to be attitudes masquerading as facts. Emotivism as a moral theory has its roots in the moral philosophy of David Hume, who held that morality is a matter of sentiment rather than fact.

There is an essential difference between the subjectivist and the emotivist. For the subjectivist, moral judgments are reports or statements of fact about the attitude of the person who says them. For the emotivist, moral judgments are not facts at all, but emotional expressions about an action or person. The subjectivist will say, "Homosexuality is wrong!" This means, "I disapprove of homosexuality." For the emotivist, the same statement means, "Homosexuality, yeech!!! Boo!!" Emotivism is thus a more sophisticated theory than subjectivism. Both share the idea that moral judgments are not normative statements, and that objective moral facts are nonexistent.

Philosophical Developments in Emotivism

Two philosophical developments contributed to the rise of emotivism. The first was a reaction to a moral theory called *intuitionism*, in which morality was directly intuited by the person making the moral decision. Since intuitionism seemed arbitrary to many philosophers, and, therefore, untenable as a moral theory, emotivists went a step further than intuitionists. They claimed that the language of morality expressed one's emotions about the situation or person under consideration, but that nothing was said about what was right or wrong.

A second philosophical development that contributed to emotivism was the rise of *logical positivism*. Logical positivists claimed that only two types of statements are possible: (1) analytical statements, such as definitions; and (2) factual statements that are empirically verifiable. In other words, the only things that can be considered as facts are definitions and statements that can be either proven or disproven empirically. According to the logical positivists, moral judgments are more than definitions and are not empirically verifiable; therefore, they cannot be factual statements. All they can be are statements that simply express and arouse emotion.

Thus, for the emotivist, moral language has three purposes.[9] First, it expresses emotions or feelings. This is the primary use of moral language. Second, it is imperative, that is, it is used to lend authority to a command to someone to do something. Third, it is persuasive, that is, it is used to influence another's actions, primarily by bending another's will to fit one's own. Emotivism does give us something positive, a reminder that moral language is emotionally charged and can be used improperly to manipulate people under the guise of getting them to do the right thing. Unfortunately, because moral language is so emotionally charged, people often dismiss it today as too divisive or incapable of verification.

Its Problems

Emotivism as a moral theory can be criticized in three primary ways.[10] First, the verification theory of meaning, which is the foundation of logical positivism, has problems. Specifically, it fails its own test of meaning. Emotivism maintains that the only statements capable of having meaning are those that are empirically verifiable, but this underlying principle is itself not empirically verifiable. There is no good reason to limit meaningful statements to those that are verified empirically.

Second, emotivism is actually a theory of the use of moral language, not of its meaning.[11] The emotivist has jumped from a theory of use to a theory of meaning without any justification for that leap.

Third, emotivism cannot account for the place of reason in ethics. Emotivism sets up a false dichotomy, as the following demonstrates:

(a) Either there are moral facts, like there are scientific facts, or
(b) Values are nothing more than expressions of our subjective feelings.

But there is another possibility, namely, moral truths are truths of reason, or a moral judgment is true if it is supported by better reasons than the alternatives. As Christians we would also say that moral truths are also truths of revelation, and that there is a strong connection between the facts of creation and the facts of morality. Good reasons usually resolve moral disagreements, but for the emotivist, giving good reasons and manipulation would essentially be the same thing. There is no good reason to assume that moral language is not also factual language, or that moral judgments are just expressions of emotion or preference rather than cognitive statements. It should not be surprising that ethical statements are not empirically verifiable, since right and wrong are not empirically observable qualities. But neither are they simply emotive expressions.

RELATIVISM

Ethical relativism became popular as a result of the findings of cultural anthropologists, who observed that different cultures have widely varying moral codes and concepts of right and wrong. Its key advocates include anthropologists, such as William Graham Sumner, Ruth Benedict, and Melville Herskovits, and philosopher John Ladd.[12]

As these scholars studied different cultures, they discovered the lack of a uniform concept of right and wrong. For example, some cultures practice polygamy, while others practice monogamy. Some cultures consider it a moral obligation to give one of their children to an infertile couple. Some cultures, such as certain Eskimo groups, practice euthanasia and infanticide in ways that seem ghastly and immoral to many other cultures. Among the Auca Indians of South America, treachery was considered the highest virtue. In fact, after sharing the gospel with the Aucas, the missionaries were shocked to learn that the Aucas saw Judas as the hero of the gospel, not Jesus. In colonial India, the Indians burned widows following the death of their husbands, which was a widely practiced custom considered to be morally legitimate. What the natives of Polynesia considered as taboo astonished Captain Cook's sailors. Despite the fact that the women had much freedom in the area of sexual relations, the natives considered it taboo to eat a meal with someone of the opposite sex. These illustrations offer merely a sample of the various ways in which people conceived and practiced morality.

In response to these observations, scholars drew new conclusions about the nature of morality. In view of such moral diversity, they suggested that it was impossible to believe in universal moral values. Such moral diversity called into question ethical systems that posited absolute, unchanging moral principles that could be universally applied. The more "enlightened" way of viewing morality was to allow for morality to be relative to the culture. Rather than being universal, morality was seen as relative to the cultural consensus.

Types of Relativism or Its Different Forms

Some anthropologists, however, merely pointed out the differences between the moral codes of various cultures. They held to what is called *cultural relativism*, which simply means that different cultures in the world have widely differing standards of right and wrong. But many other anthropologists espoused a stronger form of relativism, called *ethical relativism*. This form of relativism holds that all values are culturally created, and, therefore, are not objective, universal moral principles applicable to all cultures and time periods. In other words, the culture determines the values. Whereas the history of ethics has shown how sociological conditions have strongly influenced the emphases of different thinkers,[13] the ethical relativist says that morality is actually dependent on the cultural context in which one finds oneself. Consequently, there are no objective, universal moral principles that are binding for all cultures and time periods.

Another form of relativism practiced today is *ethical subjectivism*, which says that morality is determined by the individual. Expressed in its popular form, ethical subjectivism says, "What's right for me is right, and what's right for you is right." This view of morality is often applied to sexual morality where one's moral code for sexual behavior is considered a private matter and where one can subjectively and individually determine what is right. Inevitably, relativism reduces to subjectivism.

A second form of relativism prevalent in the popular culture is called *conventionalism*, which maintains that cultural acceptance determines the validity of principles. While morality may need cultural acceptance to function properly, it is quite another thing to insist that cultural acceptance *determines* the validity of principles. In practice, little difference exists between ethical relativism and conventionalism. In both instances, the culture determines the morality, and the standards of that culture are considered normative for that culture, without being universal.

A third form of relativism smuggled into the popular culture is called *situation ethics*. Popularized by Joseph Fletcher in the 1960s and 1970s, situation ethics holds that all morality is relative to the situation in which one finds oneself, and one's moral obligation is to do the loving thing in that situation. Technically speaking, situation ethics is not relativism, since the law of love actually functions as an absolute. (As biblical support for his position, Fletcher repeatedly cites Rom. 13:8, "Owe nothing to one another, except to love one another.")

To bolster their position, situationists cite the classic case of the woman in the Nazi concentration camp who asked a guard to impregnate her so that she could be released to her family. Unless she were ill or pregnant, she knew that she would remain in prison. So she decided to become pregnant to be reunited with her family. Situationists will argue that her illicit affair was justifiable, since love for her family motivated her act. In determining the morality of her action, the situationist views the act of adultery as irrelevant.

Ethical relativism, the view that morality is determined by the cultural context in which one finds oneself, is the predominant form of relativism today. It is widely applied in the popular culture in two principal areas, namely, international business and a recent phenomenon called multiculturalism.

One of the most significant challenges to doing business comes from ethical relativism. Imagine yourself as a business executive responsible for expanding your firm into international markets. As a result of different ethical standards of doing business, you will be faced with the temptation to offer bribes to high government officials to secure access to the market for your product. Although bribes are considered immoral and illegal in much of the West, your clients in this new market will expect them as a normal part of doing business. What will you do? Will you adhere to what you consider to be a universal standard that does not permit bribery? Or will you adopt the philosophy, "When in Rome, do as the Romans do," and justify offering bribes because that is acceptable in that culture?

Imagine now that you are a project manager for a large construction company that is expanding its business into the Third World, where safety and environmental standards are significantly lower than in the United States. By adopting lower safety standards, your company can save a great deal of money, but it presents safety hazards for some of the people living in the community. Do you build according to higher safety standards, or do you simply follow the inferior codes of the foreign country and increase your company's profits? All kinds of things once considered immoral can now be justified if one becomes a relativist and uses culturally acceptable standards.

So as not to be pointing an accusing finger at other countries and cultures, imagine a situation that frequently occurs here in our own country, the United States. In an attempt to avoid paying higher income taxes, business people will claim deductions for expenses that they did not have. Dishonest activities such as padding expense accounts and falsifying other data are often done simply because it is considered a permissible action in the context of the corporate world. The fact that "everyone else does it" is taken as permission to perpetuate such blatant corruption.

A second principal area where ethical relativism is applied is in multiculturalism, which is a movement that seeks to foster greater appreciation of and tolerance for cultures different than one's own. This takes the form of things like cultural exhibits and education to avoid language and other behavior that offends particular cultural groups. Relativism has been perhaps inadvertently associated with multiculturalism, since to take any culture seriously, one must come to grips with its values. Failure to take a culture's values into account may actually result in trivializing it. Once you begin to promote tolerance and understanding of a culture's distinct values, you must take the next logical step, which is to accept their values as equally valid as yours. In the name of appreciating cultural diversity, one accepts the values of a culture as normative within that culture. Then it becomes more difficult to make value judgments about a culture for fear of creating offense and not appearing tolerant. In many circles, if you're not a relativist, you are accused of being ethnocentric and even a cultural imperialist.

An extreme example of this occurred when an Arab-American family moved to California from the Middle East. When the adult daughter expressed her desire to choose her own husband, the girl's father insisted that her marriage be arranged according to traditional Middle Eastern custom, in which parents arrange the marriages of their children. When the girl refused and announced her engagement to a man of her own choosing, her father took disciplinary action considered appropriate to his Middle Eastern background—he killed her. Accordingly, he was charged with murder. His defense attorney argued that since his behavior was normative in his Middle Eastern culture, the morality of his action should be determined by his cultural context. In other words, the attorney appealed to ethical relativism to justify an otherwise heinous act.[14]

Its Appeal

Despite its philosophical shortcomings, ethical relativism does have appeal, particularly to the popular culture. The first appeal of relativism is based on the important idea that morality does not develop in a sociological vacuum. Some of our values are formed either in reaction to or affirmation of the social conditions of the time. Unfortunately, these values can be mistaken for absolute standards, when in reality they are little more than cultural biases dressed up in moral language. Slavery during the Civil War era aptly illustrates this. Although it was clearly immoral for human beings to own and mistreat other human beings, many Southerners attempted to justify slavery, sometimes on biblical grounds. Created to supply cheap labor in the agricultural South, slavery was deemed moral, and the right to own slaves was regarded as an absolute right. In reality, slavery was merely a cultural creation that was regarded as an absolute moral right.

A second appeal of relativism comes from the way it is presented. Frequently relativism is presented as though it and its opposite, called absolutism, were the only two valid alternatives. The absolutist rigidly holds to absolute moral principles and does not allow for any exceptions, regardless of the circumstances. This is clearly not an attractive or realistic position to hold, and if relativism is presented as the only alternative to this kind of absolutism, it is not difficult to see why people would prefer relativism. It is better to see morality on a continuum, with absolutism at one extreme and relativism at the other. One can hold to objective moral principles and not be an absolutist, that is, one can be what is called a prima facie absolutist, or an absolutist "on the surface." While recognizing the importance of unchanging, objective, moral principles, the prima facie absolutist allows for periodic exceptions to general principles. On selected issues, most people who hold to the importance of principles would admit exceptions. For example, many people would agree that in the rare cases when a pregnancy presents imminent danger to a woman's life, it is justifiable to end the pregnancy. Similarly, if someone breaks into my house with a loaded gun and asks where my wife is, I am not obligated to tell him the truth. Thus, the relativist's appeal rests on a false dichotomy.

A third appeal of relativism comes from the emphasis in the 1990s on multiculturalism, that is, sensitivity to different cultures. This trend emphasizes tolerance for the distinctives of other cultures, including values, which moves one strongly in the direction of being a relativist. Yet most people realize that limits must be drawn somewhere, and that some standards must transcend culture if society is to arbitrate between competing cultural values.

A fourth appeal of relativism comes from the modern emphasis on scientific objectivity. When applied to morality, this takes the form of value neutrality, presumed by the culture to be a good thing. Yet scholars are increasingly recognizing that value neutrality is actually a myth, and even if it were possible, it may not even be desirable. In the popular culture, a person who holds to absolute values that transcend culture is perceived, at best, as somewhat unenlightened, and, at worst, as a narrow, rigid fundamentalist. Given this alternative to relativism, it is not surprising that relativism has appeal.

Its Weaknesses

In spite of its appeal and widespread use in the popular culture, relativism has significant philosophical shortcomings. First, in terms of the observations of the cultural anthropologists who developed relativism, the degree of moral diversity is overstated and the high degree of moral consensus is understated. A good deal more moral consensus exists among cultures than was first believed. Anthropologist Clyde Kluckhohn has noted the following:

> Every culture has a concept of murder, distinguishing this from execution, killing in war and other justifiable homicides. The notions of incest and other regulations upon sexual behavior, the prohibitions on untruth under defined circumstances, of restitution and reciprocity, of mutual obligations between parents and children—these and many other moral concepts are altogether universal.[15]

A second weakness of relativism is related to the first. Many of the observations of moral diversity were differences in moral practices. But diversity in practice does not necessarily equal diversity in underlying values or principles. Much less moral diversity exists than many anthropologists think they have observed. A person who holds to the reality of objective moral values can easily account for varieties in practices from the perspective of the underlying principles.

A third weakness of relativism is that ethical relativism cannot be drawn from the observations of the cultural relativist. In other words, the strong form of relativism, in which values are dependent on the cultural context in which one finds oneself, cannot be drawn from the weaker form, or from the phenomena of moral diversity. Ethical relativism as a system does not follow from the empirical data of moral diversity among cultures. Simply because different cultures have different moral standards, even if the degree of moral diversity were not overstated, it does not follow that there is no such thing as absolute values that transcend culture.

A fourth weakness of relativism is that it provides no way to arbitrate among competing cultural value claims. This is important as many countries recognize the high degree of cultural diversity in their populations, and thus, the clash of cultures that is inevitable. For example, in the Los Angeles riots of the early 1990s, a serious conflict occurred between the Korean and African-American cultures that lived in South Central Los Angeles. Although many African-Americans condemned the rioters, some African-Americans felt that their status as an oppressed people, symbolized by the acquittals of the police officers accused of beating African-American motorist Rodney King, justified their expression of outrage in the riots. On the other hand, the Koreans felt victimized by looters who had destroyed what many of them had worked their entire adult lives to build, and they felt justified in using force to defend themselves and their property. The relativist can offer very little to resolve this conflict since the relativist can neither condemn either group nor umpire their competing claims.

The fifth and most serious charge against relativism is an extension of the fourth weakness. The relativist cannot morally evaluate any clearly oppressive culture or, more specifically, any obvious tyrant. Cultures that relegate women to the status of second-class citizens cannot be evaluated by the relativist since morality is dependent on the cultural context. Similarly, the relativist cannot pass judgment on someone like Hitler, who oppressed a minority with the permission, if not approval, of the majority, since no moral absolute that transcends culture exists to which the relativist can appeal as a basis for that judgment.

A sixth weakness of relativism is that it allows no room for moral reformers or prophets. Since the reformer stands against the cultural consensus that is supposed to determine the valid moral values for the relativist, the relativist cannot offer the praise due most moral reformers. The relativist can only explain the moral reformer as an example of the clash of cultures. Yet moral reformers often stand alone, apart from any support from the culture, until the movement gathers momentum.

A final objection to relativism is the charge that its central premise, namely that moral absolutes do not exist, is a self-defeating statement, since the premise itself is an absolute. However, the relativist could respond that the premise is only a formal absolute, not a material one, that is, it is a statement that describes the procedure of relativism, not a moral principle that is absolute. While that distinction is correct, the relativist still has a moral absolute that makes the system self-defeating, namely, the absolute of tolerance and respect for the values of other cultures. The relativist could hardly tolerate any culture that had intolerance as one of its central virtues.

VIRTUE THEORY

All of the normative theories examined thus far are action-oriented ethical systems. The exception to this is emotivism, which is a theory about moral language, rather than a theory that attempts to provide moral direction. Most ethical theories in modern times have focused on doing the right action, or making the right decision when confronted by a moral dilemma. Many of the major debates in ethics have revolved around the basis for determining what is the right action, whether consequences or principles provide that basis and whether the right action is universal or relative.

Virtue theory, which is also called aretaic ethics (from the Greek term *arete*, "virtue"), holds that morality is more than simply doing the right thing. The foundational moral claims made by the virtue theorist concern the moral agent (the person doing the action), not the act that the agent performs. Dating back to Plato and Aristotle, the tradition of virtue theory is a long one, including the Epicureans, the Stoics, the New Testament Gospels, and Thomas Aquinas. With the collapse of the medieval worldview during the Renaissance and Enlightenment periods, one of the unfortunate casualties was Thomas's emphasis on Aristotelian virtue theory.

Some virtue theorists hold that virtue theory can stand alone as an adequate system of ethics. Others hold that virtues and moral rules or principles are interdependent, but exactly how they fit together is a point of debate. In the face of both natural law and divine commands, it is difficult to see how the Christian could not embrace some sort of deontological ethics. But it is equally difficult to see how the Christian could ignore virtue theory in favor of act-based ethics, given the emphasis in the New Testament on developing the character of Christ, which would seem to precede action. It may be that virtues are logically prior to principles in that the virtues emerge out of God's character, and that moral rules and principles are those that are consistent with the outworking of God's virtue.

Some of the main differences between virtue ethics and act-oriented ethics include an emphasis on being rather than doing, an emphasis on who a person should become more than what a person should do, the importance of following people with exemplary behavior instead of following moral rules, an emphasis on a person's motive in place of action, and a stress on developing character more than simply obeying rules. Virtue theory is an ethic of character, not duty. These emphases are certainly consistent with the biblical emphasis on sanctification and becoming more like Christ in character. One could also argue that act-oriented systems do not adequately produce moral people, not to mention spiritually mature people. It would seem that some component of virtue theory is needed to supplement act-oriented systems. Given the biblical emphasis, it would appear that act-oriented ethics alone give a person an overly narrow view of the moral life.

In Favor of Virture Theory Versus Act-oriented Ethics

Advocates of virtue theory have pointed out some of the shortcomings of act-oriented ethics.[16] First, they reduce ethics to solving moral dilemmas and difficult cases that most people encounter infrequently. This is a reductionistic view of morality in which ethics has been moved to the extremes of life. The real substance of the moral life, the day-to-day decisions that people must make, is ignored.

Second, the virtue theorist points out that moral duties involve attitudes as well as actions. It is ludicrous to say that two people who perform the same right action, but with different attitudes are both equally worthy of praise. Act-oriented ethics focus on the act and tend to minimize the dispositions and character of the moral agent. Thus, act-oriented ethics is a truncated view of the moral life, particularly for the Christian, who is commanded to develop virtuous character. One of the primary moral rules emphasized in Scripture is to cultivate virtue (Gal. 5:22–33).

Third, act-based systems provide little motivation for doing the right thing.[17] This is especially true of the apex of action-based morality, the system of Kant, who held that the good will was the will that performed its moral duty for the sake of duty. According to most virtue theorists, action-oriented ethics are largely negative prohibitions that involve hair-splitting distinctions that do not usually move people to action.

Fourth, action-based systems can become legalistic and encourage people to hide behind a facade of morality. They may actually mitigate against cultivating long-term adherence to moral principles.

Fifth, and finally, act-based ethics overemphasize individual autonomy, or the ability of people to arrive at their moral duties by reason or revelation alone.[18] Since virtues are usually developed in some sort of a relationship or community, virtue theory gives proper emphasis to the communal context of ethics.

Virture Theory on Its Own

Some virtue theorists hold that considerations of virtue are sufficient in and of themselves, and thus all act-oriented systems of ethics are unnecessary. Typically, a virtue theorist develops a theory in three stages. First, one must develop some conception of the ideal person, or the purpose of a person. Without this first stage, virtues that the theorist determines to be essential would appear ungrounded, suspended in philosophical midair. For the Christian, this first stage is defined by the purpose of a human being, which is to glorify God by becoming more like Christ. Second, the theory involves developing a list of virtues necessary for achieving the person's proper purpose as outlined in the first stage. Third, people need to be shown how they can develop these virtues, either by divine grace, training, discipline, emulation, education, or a combination of these. For the virtue theorist, the moral virtues must be lived and cannot be taught in isolation from real life.

According to Aristotle,[19] virtues are those habits that enable one to live well in the community. They are tied to the end of a human being, which is to use reason in pursuit of the good life. He defined virtues in terms of the golden mean, that is, between the two extremes of excess and deficiency. Virtues are developed by exposure to virtuous people, namely, watching and imitating them. This parallels the emphasis in Christian ethics on imitating Christ and developing his character, although a Christian's ultimate purpose differs from that described by Aristotle.

Problems with Virture Theory on Its Own

Nevertheless, any virtue theory that attempts to stand alone, without a partnership with moral rules or principles, will have problems. The classic criticism of virtue theory is that it fails to give guidance for resolving moral dilemmas. Whether this criticism is entirely fair is debatable, since it does seem possible to use considerations of virtue to make difficult moral decisions. It does not offer the clear directions provided by a rule-based system, but that is not to say that it gives no direction.

A virtue theory that stands alone, however, does have one primary problem. Since virtue theory relies on the emulation of ideal individuals in order to develop virtue, and since we have no way of observing or evaluating a person's character apart from that individual's actions, some emphasis on one's actions is essential in order to recognize a virtuous person. Virtue ethics seems to presuppose that you will simply know that a person is virtuous when you meet one, a debatable assumption at best. Two other related problems include the inability of virtue theory to make sense out of cases in which good people do harmful actions, and the inability of virtue theory to provide any way for society to notice when good persons have gone bad, since the theory emphasizes the person's character as opposed to actions. A final criticism of virtue theory is that virtue ethicists are overly optimistic about the power of virtue to stem social evils. Since notions about what constitutes virtue are so diverse, society must depend on rules that are based on principles to maintain social order.

Virtue Theory in Relation to Principles

Many other virtue theorists hold that virtues and principles must somehow coexist. They hold that virtues without principles are blind, but principles without virtues are impotent to motivate people to action.[20] The debate is whether virtues derive from principles (called the *correspondence view*) or complement principles as equals (called the *complementary view*).[21] According to the correspondence view, moral rules obligate people to perform certain actions, regardless of whether they possess the requisite virtues. Thus, the virtues must be secondary and the principles primary. Virtues are dispositions to obey the rules or perform certain actions. Each virtue corresponds to a moral principle that governs the action that exhibits that virtue. The virtues do not have intrinsic value, only instrumental value. Their role is to motivate one to perform right actions and eliminate wrong actions. Principles help one evaluate the act, and virtues help one evaluate the moral actor. Both are important because those with the particular virtues are more likely to perform the right actions.

According to the complementary view, however, people have a moral obligation to be a certain kind of person, and whether it results in action is irrelevant in many cases. Some rules require action, but some require virtue. Virtues are more than simply dispositions to act in certain ways, since they include attributes that do not necessarily involve action. To be sure, the only way we can tell if a person has those virtues is when they issue in action. As a Christian, the moral virtues cannot be said to be derivative or not have intrinsic value. Right consists in doing the right thing with the right motive and attitude. It is insufficient to do the right thing for the right reason if the underlying attitude is absent. Virtues are a constitutive element of the good life and especially of being like Christ. Thus, a complementary view of virtues and principles would appear to be more consistent with Scripture. Perhaps virtues are even logically prior to principles, insofar as God's character expresses itself in virtues, and moral rules and principles then are those that are consistent with the outworking of God's virtues.

CONCLUSION

Most of these systems are still widely embraced in the contemporary culture. As you encounter the debate of different moral issues in public, observe which methods of moral reasoning are employed by those in the debate. The shortcomings of these systems illustrate the need for a method of moral reasoning that is based either on general revelation, natural law, or special revelation. The Bible does employ different types of moral reasoning, but nowhere does it suggest that any of the systems mentioned in this chapter are all-sufficient. Blending divine command, natural law, and virtue, the biblical emphasis seems to be strongly deontological with periodic appeal to egoism and utilitarianism.

FOR FURTHER READING

Frankena, William. *Ethics*. New York: Prentice-Hall, 1973.

Holmes, Arthur. *Ethics: Approaching Moral Decisions*. Downers Grove, Ill.: InterVarsity Press, 1984.

Pojman, Louis P. *Ethics: Discovering Right and Wrong*. Belmont, Calif.: Wadsworth, 1990.

Rachels, James. *The Elements of Moral Philosophy*. Philadelphia: Temple University Press, 1986.

NOTES

[1]The reader may notice that deontological systems, or ethical systems based on principles, are not outlined in this chapter. This is because there are three main types of deontological system: Kant's categorical imperative, which is discussed in chapter 3, nat-

ural law and the divine command theory, both discussed in chapter 2. This chapter contains the major non-deontological systems. For the sake of rounding out the hypothetical debate on euthanasia, two representatives of deontological ethics have been included, though their positions will not be analyzed.

[2]For further discussion of Hobbes' system of ethical egoism, see chapter 3.

[3]James Rachels, *The Elements of Moral Philosophy* (Philadelphia: Temple University Press, 1986), 67–73.

[4]See her classic exposition of ethical egoism in *The Virtue of Selfishness* (New York: Signet, 1961).

[5]Louis Pojman, *Ethics: Discovering Right and Wrong* (Belmont, Calif.: Wadsworth, 1990), 48.

[6]In his defense of capitalism of an economic system, Adam Smith employed ethical egoism to some degree in his justification of it. He argued that there was an "invisible hand" that coordinated each person's pursuit of self-interest and made it work for the common good. It should be recognized that Smith held to an *enlightened* self-interest, presumably self-interest regulated by Christian morality as the key to making capitalism work. See his classic work, *The Wealth of Nations*, for further discussion of this.

[7]Rachels, *The Elements of Moral Philosophy*, 76–78.

[8]Ibid., 102–3.

[9]Pojman, *Ethics: Discovering Right and Wrong*, 145–46.

[10]Ibid., 147.

[11]This is the point made by Alasdair MacIntyre in chapter 1 of his *After Virtue*. His critique of modern ethics is that emotivism is philosophically bankrupt and essentially all that remains after the Enlightenment efforts to create morality by reason alone had failed. See MacIntyre, *After Virtue* (Notre Dame, Ind.: University of Notre Dame Press, 1984).

[12]Their main works in this area are as follows: William Graham Sumner, *Folkways* (New York: Ginn, 1906); Ruth Benedict, *Patterns of Culture* (New York: New American Library, 1934); Melville Herskovits, *Cultural Relativism* (New York: Random House, 1972); John Ladd, ed., *Ethical Relativism* (Belmont, Calif.: Wadsworth, 1973).

[13]For a survey of the history of ethics, see chapter 3. Each thinker is analyzed in terms of his sociological context and the contribution to his emphases.

[14]Neal Gabler, "Moral Relativism: You Don't Get It," *Los Angeles Times,* 14 June 1992, M1–2.

[15]Clyde Kluckhohn, "Ethical Relativity: Sic et Non," *Journal of Philosophy* (1955): LII. See also E. O. Wilson, *On Human Nature* (New York: Bantam Books, 1979).

[16]Some of the main proponents of virtue theory are Alasdair MacIntyre (*After Virtue*), Edmund Pincoffs (*Quandaries and Virtues*, University of Kansas Press, 1986), Richard Taylor (*Ethics, Faith and Reason*, New York: Prentice-Hall, 1985), Philippa Foot (*Virtues and Vices*, Blackwell, 1978), James Wallace (*Virtues and Vices*, Ithaca, New York: Cornell University Press, 1978). Two very helpful collections of essays on virtue theory are Robert Kruschwitz and Robert Roberts, eds., *The Virtues*, (Belmont, Calif.: Wadsworth, 1987), and P. A. French, T. E. Uehling, and H. K. Wettstein, eds., *Ethical Theory: Character and Virtue,* Midwest Studies in Philosophy, vol. 13 (Notre Dame, Ind.: University of Notre Dame Press, 1988).

[17]Pojman, *Ethics: Discovering Right and Wrong*, 116.
[18]Ibid., 119.
[19]This briefly summarizes his system, which is developed further in chapter 3.
[20]Pojman, *Ethics: Discovering Right and Wrong*, 126.
[21]Ibid., 124–30.

5

MAKING ETHICAL DECISIONS

CASE #1: MEDICAL ETHICS[1]

A twenty-year-old Hispanic male was brought to a hospital emergency room, having suffered abdominal injuries due to gunshot wounds received in gang violence. He had no medical insurance, and his stay in the hospital was somewhat shorter than expected due to his good recovery. The attending physicians felt that he could complete his recovery at home just as easily as in the hospital, so he was released after only a few days in the hospital.

During his stay in the hospital, the patient admitted to his primary physician that he was HIV positive, having contracted the virus that causes AIDS. This was confirmed by a blood test administered while he was hospitalized.

When he was discharged from the hospital, the physician recommended that a professional nurse visit him regularly at home in order to change the bandages on his still substantial wounds and to insure that an infection did not develop. Since the patient had no health insurance, he was dependent on Medicaid, a government program that pays for necessary medical care for those who cannot afford it. Medicaid refused to pay for home nursing care, however, since someone was already in the home who was capable of providing the necessary care. That person was the patient's twenty-two-year-old sister, who was willing to take care of her brother until he was fully recovered. Their mother had died years ago and the sister was accustomed to providing care for her younger siblings.

The patient had no objection to his sister providing this care, but he insisted that no one disclose to her that he had tested HIV positive. Although he had always had a good relationship with his sister, she did not know that he was an active homosexual. Even greater was his fear that his father would learn of his sexual orientation and lifestyle. Hispanics generally look upon homosexuality with extreme disfavor.

Since a physician is bound by a code of ethics that places a high priority on keeping confidentiality, the young Hispanic man's physician cannot divulge information about his medical condition. Some would argue that the responsibility of confidentiality is even greater with HIV and AIDS, since disclosure of someone's homosexuality normally carries devastating personal consequences for the individual who is forced "out of the closet." On the other hand, the patient's sister will be putting herself at risk by providing nursing care for him. Doesn't she have a right to know the risks to which she is subjecting herself, especially since she willingly volunteered to take care of her brother?

If you were the physician, what would you do? Would you breach the norm of confidentiality to protect the patient's sister, or would you keep confidentiality to protect the patient from harm that might come to him from his family members, especially his father?

Perhaps a better question in this situation is, How would you decide what to do? The process of making a moral decision can be as important as the decision itself, and many ethical decisions that people face are so complex that it is easy to exhaust oneself talking around the problem without actually making any progress toward resolving it. Where do I start? is the question asked by many people facing moral dilemmas. People who are faced with these decisions often need direction that will enable them to move constructively toward resolution.

A MODEL FOR MAKING MORAL DECISIONS

To address adequately the ethical dilemmas that people regularly encounter, we will present a procedure for making moral decisions. We offer it not as a formula that will automatically generate the "right" answer to an ethical problem, but rather as a model designed to make sure that the right questions are asked in the process of ethical deliberation.

Given the ethnic and religious diversity of our society, the model used for making ethical decisions should be able to accommodate a variety of different moral and ethical perspectives. The model presented here is not tied to any one particular perspective, but can be used comfortably with a variety of cultural, ethnic, and religious backgrounds. Although this model is consistent with the Scriptures and allows Christians to use biblical principles, it is not a distinctively Christian model.

As we mentioned earlier, what makes many moral dilemmas so difficult is that the Scriptures do not always address an issue clearly, if they speak to it at all. More general biblical principles may be brought to bear on the issue at hand. In these instances, however, there is often disagreement about which biblical principles are applicable to the specific issue under discussion. In the preceding scenario, for example, the physician could invoke the biblical principle of compassion to protect his patient from harm that might befall him if his homosexuality were disclosed. At the same time, however, he could invoke the same principle of compassion to protect the sister from the risks of exposure to AIDS. Appeal to principles alone will not necessarily resolve this case. Thus, insisting that all ethical dilemmas be resolved simply by appeal to biblical principles seems to oversimplify the case. Certainly, appealing to the Scriptures can conclusively resolve many moral questions, but there are other cases in which that does not happen. That is not to say that the Scriptures are not sufficient for the believer's spiritual life, but that the special revelation is often supplemented by the general revelation of God outside of the Scriptures. This model makes room for both general and special revelation, and gives each a place in helping to resolve the difficult moral dilemmas facing people today.

Following is a list of the elements of a model for making moral decisions:[2]

1. Gather the Facts

Frequently ethical dilemmas can be resolved simply by clarifying the facts of the case in question. In situations that prove to be more difficult, gathering the facts is the essential first step that must be taken prior to any ethical analysis and reflection. In analyzing a case, we need to know all of the available facts. Later, we may need to acquire additional information pertaining to the case. Thus, to make an intelligent ethical decision, one needs to ask two primary questions: What do we know? and What do we need to know?

2. Determine the Ethical Issues

Ethical issues are stated in terms of legitimate competing interests or goods. These competing interests are what actually create an ethical dilemma. The issues should be presented in an X versus Y format in order to reflect the competing interests in a particular ethical dilemma. For example, the interests of the HIV-positive Hispanic man conflict with those of his sister. In this case, the conflict is his interest in confidentiality versus her interest in being protected from contracting the AIDS virus.

3. What Principles Have a Bearing on the Case?

In any ethical dilemma, certain moral values or principles are central to the competing positions. It is critical to identify these principles, and in some cases, to determine whether some principles are to be weighted more heavily than others. Clearly, biblical principles should be weighted more heavily. Also, principles that speak to the case may come from other sources, such as the Constitution or natural law, which would supplement the applicable biblical principles.

4. List the Alternatives

Part of the creative thinking involved in resolving an ethical dilemma involves developing alternative courses of action. Although you will probably rule out some alternatives without much thought, in general, the more alternatives that are listed, the better the chance that your list will include some very good ones. In addition, you may come up with some very creative alternatives that you had not considered earlier.

5. Compare the Alternatives with the Principles

At this point, the task is one of eliminating alternatives according to the moral principles that have a bearing on the case. In many instances, the case will be resolved at this point, since the principles will eliminate all alternatives except one. In fact, the purpose of this comparison is to see if there is a clear decision that can be made without further deliberation. If a clear decision is not forthcoming, then the next part in the model must be considered. At the least, some of the alternatives may be eliminated by this step of comparison.

6. Consider the Consequences

If the principles do not yield a clear decision, then a consideration of the consequences of the remaining available alternatives is in order. Both positive and negative consequences are to be considered. They should be informally weighted, since some positive consequences are more beneficial than others, and some negative consequences are more detrimental than others.

7. Make a Decision

Deliberation cannot continue indefinitely. At some point, you must make a decision. Realize, too, that ethical dilemmas often have no easy and painless solutions. Frequently, the decision that is made is one that involves the least number of problems or negative consequences, not one that is devoid of them.

APPLYING THE MODEL

Using the preceding model, let's return to the case of the young, HIV-positive, Hispanic man. Here we will illustrate how to apply the model and clarify the meaning of each of the elements in the model. Two additional cases will be presented and analyzed in the framework of this model to insure that it can be used profitably.

CASE #1: MEDICAL ETHICS (AS PRESENTED EARLIER)

1. Gather the Facts

The relevant facts in this case are as follows:

- The patient is a homosexually active, young man, infected with HIV.
- He suffered fairly severe abdominal wounds but is recovering well.
- Homosexuality is looked down upon in Hispanic communities.
- The patient has insisted that his physician maintain confidentiality about his HIV status.
- The patient is afraid of rejection by his father if his homosexuality is discovered, an understandable fear given the stigma that homosexuality has in the Hispanic community.
- He was wounded by gunfire in gang violence. Although not certain, it is a reasonable assumption that he is a gang member. As a result, he likely fears rejection and perhaps retribution from his fellow gang members, especially if they discover that he is HIV positive.
- He is uninsured and cannot afford professional home nursing care.
- Medicaid refuses to pay for professional home nursing care.
- The patient's sister is willing and able to provide the necessary nursing care for her brother. She is accustomed to providing care for her brothers and sisters.
- The patient has specifically requested that his sister not be told of his HIV status. She does not know that he is an active homosexual.
- The patient's sister would be changing fairly sizable wound dressings for her brother. Her chances of coming into contact with his HIV-infected blood are high, but the probability of her becoming infected with the virus is difficult to predict.

2. Determine the Ethical Issues

The competing interests in this case are those of the sister who will provide the care and the patient who will receive it. Both have interests in being protected from harm. The patient fears being harmed in a psychosocial way if his homosexuality and HIV status are discovered. Thus, he has put the physician in a difficult situation by demanding his right to confidentiality. This could be stated as a conflict between confidentiality for the patient and the right of his sister to know the serious condition of her brother and the health risks that he presents to her. The conflict could be summarized as the need for confidentiality versus the duty to warn someone of potential health risks.

3. What Principles Have a Bearing on the Case?

This case revolves around a conflict of duties that the physician has toward his patient and toward the patient's sister. He is called to exercise compassion toward both, but what compassion (or the duty to "do no harm") demands depends on which individual in the case is in view. Thus, two principles are paramount. First, patients have a right to have their medical information kept confidential, particularly if the information could be used to harm them if it were disclosed. Second, the physician has the duty to warn interested parties other than the patient if they are at risk of imminent and substantial harm.

One of the difficult aspects of any ethical decision is knowing what weight to give the principles that are relevant to the case. Here, the principle of confidentiality is considered virtually sacred in the medical profession. Most physicians will argue that confidentiality is necessary if patients are to trust their physicians and continue coming for treatment. But confidentiality is often considered subordinate to the duty to warn someone who will likely be harmed if certain information is not disclosed. For example, if a psychologist believes that his patient will either kill or severely beat his wife, the psychologist has a moral and sometimes legal obligation to inform the wife of the imminent danger. In such cases, the duty to warn someone of imminent and severe harm is usually considered a more heavily weighted principle than confidentiality.

The key question here in weighting the principles of confidentiality and the duty to warn is the degree of risk that the patient's sister is taking by providing nursing care for her brother. If the risk is not substantial, then that could weight confidentiality more heavily. But if the risk is significant, then the duty to warn is the more heavily weighted principle. This is particularly so, given the fact that the sister has volunteered to perform a very self-sacrificing service for her brother. Some would argue that her altruism is an additional factor that weights the duty to warn more heavily. Others would suggest that his contracting HIV is an example of "reaping what one sows," and that minimizes consideration of the patient's desire for confidentiality. An additional factor that should be figured into the deliberation is that the risk to the patient, though it may have a higher probability of happening, is not as severe as the risk to the sister. After all, in the worst case scenario, the father would disown his son and the gang would expel him, although the gang might do something even more severe than expulsion. He would recover from all of that. But if his sister contracted HIV, she would not recover. Although the probability of the worst case scenario is higher for the patient, the results of the worst case are clearly higher for the sister.

4. List the Alternatives

Various alternatives exist that would involve compromise on either the patient's or his sister's part. Two alternatives, however, do not involve compromise, but reflect a weighting of the principles. The first alternative is to tell the sister that her brother is HIV positive. This alternative results from assigning a higher priority to the duty to warn. The second alternative is to refuse to tell her that information, upholding the patient's request for confidentiality. This alternative gives more weight to the confidentiality principle.

Yet there are also other alternatives. For example, the physician could warn the patient's sister in general terms about taking appropriate precautions in caring for her brother's wounds. Specifically, she must wear gloves and even a mask at all times when handling the bandages. Should she get any blood on her clothes or body, she is to wash immediately with a disinfectant soap. In other words, she is to take universal precautions that any medical professional routinely takes in caring for patients.

Another alternative is to request that the patient inform his sister of his condition. He could then request that she not tell any other family member or any or his friends. If he refused, then the next step might be to tell him that you will.

5. Compare the Alternatives with the Principles

In many cases, the principles resolve the case. Depending on how one assesses the relative weight of the principles, that may happen in this case. In fact, it may be that the alternative of encouraging universal precautions for the sister, but not telling her why, comes close to satisfying all the relevant principles. Certainly, questions about the adequacy of those precautions will arise. Will she follow them strictly, or treat them casually? Assume for the moment, however, that appeal to principles will not resolve the dilemma.

6. Consider the Consequences

Here the task is to take the viable alternatives and attempt to predict both the positive and negative consequences of each. In addition, one should try to estimate how beneficial are the positive consequences and how severe are the negative ones, since some consequences will be clearly more substantial than others.

In many cases, when two opposing alternatives are presented, the consequences of one are the mirror image of the other. Such is the case here with the alternatives of telling the sister, or not telling her about her brother's status.

If the sister is informed regarding her brother's HIV status, several consequences would likely follow:

- The sister would be properly warned about the risks of taking care of her brother, minimizing the risk of her contracting HIV, and saving her from the risk of developing a fatal illness.
- The brother's HIV status would be out in the open, leaving family and gang friends to hypothesize about his sexual orientation. If they draw the right

conclusion, which is likely, he will possibly suffer psychosocial harm from his family, and probably more significant harm from the gang members.

- Trust between the physician and the patient will suffer, and he may refuse to see that physician or any other one again until a dire medical emergency. This would be unfortunate, since he will require ongoing medical care due to his HIV status.

If the sister is not informed regarding her brother's medical condition, either because the physician refuses to disclose the information or the brother refuses to tell her, then we would expect the following consequences:

- The sister would not know about the risk she is taking, being exposed to a contractable infection for which there is no cure. The degree of risk that she is taking is debatable. Some would argue that if the degree of risk is any more than minimal, then warning her would be justifiable, since the virus produces a fatal disease.
- The patient's HIV status would be a secret, as would be his homosexuality. But it is unlikely that either his HIV status or his homosexuality would be kept a secret forever, since as HIV develops into full-blown AIDS, both will likely be revealed in the future.
- Trust between the physician and patient would be maintained.

If the sister is merely told to take general precautions, the following are likely consequences:

- She may exercise appropriate caution, but she may not. She may treat the precautions casually and unknowingly put herself at risk. If the physician tells her about the precautions in very strong terms to insure her compliance with them, she may become suspicious and start questioning the doctor. In fact, the doctor may be hoping that she will start questioning her brother and ultimately be informed by him.
- In general, the patient's HIV status and homosexual orientation would be kept secret, and confidentiality would be honored, but the question of how long it would remain a secret is unknown, and it is likely that it will become known eventually.
- Trust between the physician and patient would be maintained. However, if the sister feels compelled to ask her brother some pressing questions about the necessity of the precautions, he may conclude that the physician has prompted his sister to ask these questions, leaving him feeling betrayed.

7. Make a Decision

What would you decide in this case? Which principles are the most weighty? Would you include others? Which alternatives are the most viable? Would you suggest others? Which consequences seem to be the most severe? Do you think others will occur?

At some point, however, you need to realize that you must stop deliberating and make a decision, as uncomfortable as that may be.

CASE #2: BUSINESS ETHICS

You are the manager of a toxic waste dump located outside of Sacramento, California. The parent company is located in downtown Los Angeles. Some years ago, a cement "pond" was built to store toxic waste from the firm's operations throughout northern California. Supposedly, the pond was built in impermeable soil. After the toxic waste was combined with other chemicals, it was rendered considerably less toxic and was considered to be safe in the pond. This operation has worked well for a number of years.

A few months ago, you noticed a change in the taste of the drinking water in your office and home. As a result, you ordered some tests to be run and to your dismay the tests revealed some leakage that was moving toward the water table. The engineers who conducted the tests could not determine with certainty if the waste was leaking into the water table, since the soil outside the pond acts as a partial filtering agent.

Being a responsible manager and concerned about the community, you report this to your boss in L.A. He consults with the top management of the company and their response is the same as his. Since the facility passed the state inspection only a few months earlier, they choose to ignore the problem, citing prohibitive costs involved for cleanup and compliance with state standards.

You maintain that the state's standards clearly are not adequate, but the company is adamant. They will do nothing about the problem unless they are found to be in violation of state standards. You protest that decision, and they warn you not to do anything more. You are told to keep to managing the facility and leave these other decisions to them.

Your dilemma is compounded by the fact that "whistle-blowers" almost always lose their jobs and are frequently blackballed from the industry. Since you have a wife and three school-age children, you cannot afford to lose your job.

As the manager of the facility, what would you do in this situation? How would you justify your actions? What options do you have as the manager?

1. Gather the Facts

The relevant facts are as follows:

- Although you are in a management position, you do not have final authority on how the facility is run. You have lodged complaints with upper management. Their response has been that they will not do anything about the site until the state orders them to do so. Upper management still holds you in high regard, but they are getting tired of your raising the issue of this leak with them.

- You believe toxic materials are leaking into the groundwater of your community, endangering the water supply. This belief comes from your experience as an engineer and a noticeable difference in the taste of the community's drinking water. You have started buying bottled water for your family and are discreetly encouraging your friends to do likewise.
- Tests to determine whether the waste has reached the water table are inconclusive so far. The facility has met all tests and guidelines issued by the state. It is in compliance with state environmental regulations.
- You have a secure job with the company that supports you, your wife, and your three school-age children. You are aware that people who blow the whistle on their employer are often fired from their job and are frequently blackballed from the industry.

2. Determine the Ethical Issues

Companies have a right to make a fair profit, and that profit provides jobs and a good living for those in the community. Yet companies also have a responsibility to avoid endangering the community in which they operate. Thus, one ethical issue in this case would be the conflict between profit and the public good, namely, environmental protection.

A second ethical issue concerns the manager himself. He has a responsibility to his family to support them and not do anything that would endanger that support. Yet as the manager of the facility, he has an obligation to operate it safely and make sure that it does not harm the community water supply. This is a conflict between his responsibility to his family and his responsibility to the community. In other words, he has a conflict in his duty to tell the truth (protecting the community) and his duty to take care of his family (protecting his job).

3. What Principles Have a Bearing on the Case?

As is often the case, the ethical issues here are chiefly a conflict of principles. The manager is confronted with the principles of taking care of his family and telling the truth to protect the community from harm. The company has an interest in maximizing its profit, which will be jeopardized if it has to expend money for cleanup costs. But the company also has an obligation to pursue profit in a morally responsible way. Perhaps another principle might be employee loyalty, which would not want to expose the company to unnecessary risk and negative publicity.

As was true in Case #1, the weighting of the principles depends on the degree of risk that is known at this time. If the chances of the waste leaking into the water table are great, then more consideration should be given to the principle of truth-telling, which would curtail harm to the community. If the manager simply suspects a leak but cannot verify it, then the principle of loyalty to one's family and company will carry more weight. At this point, the manager does not have data that clearly indicates that waste is leaking into the community's water table. If he waits until he has more conclusive data, it may be too late and too expensive to clean up the damage. The fact that the facility has passed all state inspections to date is significant, too, but ethics frequently involves responsibilities that go beyond mere legal compliance.

4. List the Alternatives

The manager has two main alternatives with several options. First, he could go public with the information about a leak at the facility. Second, in an effort to keep the discussion within the company, he could run his own tests to determine if any waste has leaked into the community's water table. If he proves that leaks have occurred, he could take the new information to upper management and again request that they fix the problem. This latter alternative would be both prudent and moral, and would satisfy all the principles that have a bearing on this case.

In reality, however, ethical dilemmas are not usually resolved quite so easily. Let's assume that the manager procedes with additional testing that indicates leakage, and management still tells him to keep quiet until the state forces the company to take action. Then his options for disclosing the information about the leak would encourage "whistle-blowing," a term that describes the efforts of an informer to reveal the covert and usually illegal activities of another. If he chooses to blow the whistle, the manager can select one of several options.

The first of these options would be to "blow the whistle" directly to the state environmental regulators and request that they immediately schedule an inspection of the facility. He could do this anonymously, but it is unlikely that his involvement would remain a secret for long, given his past record of complaints to upper management about the problem. Thus, whether it is done anonymously or directly, the result would likely be the same.

A second option would be to reveal his concerns to the press. This would assure him of wide coverage, and perhaps public outcry would be sufficient to persuade the company to fix the problem. However, if he uses this option, he runs the risk of losing his job and being blackballed from the industry.

A third option is to keep the information to himself, except for a few discreet suggestions to friends and acquaintances in the community to avoid drinking the community's water. By suggesting this to anyone beyond his close friends, he takes the risk that the story will be dispersed to the entire community. Perhaps he wants this to happen, so that the burden of "blowing the whistle" will be on someone else and will not be traced back to him, thus preserving his job.

A fourth alternative is to clean up the waste and fix the leak himself, using his facility budget for the cleanup and repair. This way he could safeguard his job and insure the safety of the community's water supply. If this did not involve a substantial amount of money, this would be a feasible, if not the best, alternative. For a problem of large magnitude, however, he could probably not afford the costs associated with resolving the problem. Even if it were within his budget, a substantial expenditure of money would likely be noticed by upper management, and he would risk their censure. But this approach presents less of a risk than blowing the whistle on the company. For the sake of this discussion, let's assume that the amount of money needed to fix the problem is more than the manager has to spend.

5. Compare the Alternatives with the Principles

The only way to get a clear decision at this point is to weight one of the principles more heavily than the others. Knowing the extent of the leak into the water table would help, but given the lack of hard data about this, let's assume that no clear decision is reached at this point.

6. Consider the Consequences

The only other alternatives for the manager are either to find another means for disclosing the information or just keep it to himself until the next state test of the facility. As in the previous case, the positive consequences of one option are the reverse of the negative consequences of the other. Thus, the weight which those making the decisions assign to the various consequences is important in determining the direction that the consequences will take.

If the manager discloses the information, the likely consequences of his action would include the following:

- The company will either be tested immediately by the state or it will receive much negative publicity. But remember, the facility is in Sacramento and the company's headquarters is more than 400 miles away in Los Angeles. If the pond is tested and found to be substandard, the company will have the responsibility to fix it. However, the facility may still pass the state tests.
- The manager will likely lose his job for defying direct orders from upper management. He may be blacklisted from the industry and have to seek employment in another field. His family may have to move, and he may suffer significant financial distress. Keep in mind, however, that the Christian can depend on God's sovereignty in situations like this and trust him to provide for one's family when standing up for principles like the good of the community.

If the manager does not disclose the information, the likely consequences will be the following:

- The leak will continue unabated, perhaps heading toward the community's water table.
- The manager will have to live with the fact that he had the opportunity to save the community from possible harm and did not.
- His job will remain secure, as will his income and his family's material needs.
- Should the facility be investigated at a later point, he may be blamed for harm to the community and may be held liable. However, in his defense, he could appeal to his correspondence that he sent to the home office to alert them to the problem, thereby possibly absolving himself of culpability. At the very least, he will be held responsible by his friends and peers in the community if the problem worsens.

7. Make a Decision

The decision in this case is difficult. What would you do? Is there sufficient evidence to justify going "out on a limb" and making the information public, either to the press or to the state? Does the biblical principle of self-sacrifice for the good of the community require disclosing the information? Does the community also include one's family, giving the manager a responsibility to them, too? What role does the sovereignty of God have in the decision? Would the decision be different if the manager was not a Christian?

CASE #3: PARENTAL RIGHTS AND THE PATIENT'S BEST INTEREST

An eight-year-old Korean child was brought to the Medical Center on December 31 by his parents. His symptoms included a high fever, canker sores around his mouth, swollen lymph glands, and an inability to move his head. He was given antibiotics but did not respond. After analysis of the lab results, he was diagnosed with Kawasaki's disease. Although the origin of the disease is unknown, it causes a number of symptoms, which include rashes, high fever, and skin lesions. The major problem produced by the disease is the prospect of heart disease and aneurysms. This disease is known to affect the heart seriously in 30% of the cases. The treatment for this disease includes aspirin and gamma globulin, a blood by-product that greatly reduces the possibility of heart problems.

On the evening of January 5 doctors started gamma globulin treatment. Upon realizing that this treatment included blood by-products, the mother presented a written document to the doctor stating that she was a Jehovah's Witness and that she wanted no blood by-products for her son.[3] Accordingly, she had the intravenous treatment discontinued. The father also wanted the treatment to be stopped because of his belief in Oriental herbal medicine. He had lost confidence in traditional medicine since it had not been effective to date.

On January 6 the physician contacted the ethics committee members. His wish was to continue treating the minor while allowing for the usage of Eastern herbal medicines. The parents, however, wanted to remove the child from the hospital against medical advice. The physician believed that the possibility of cardiac complications was too great to allow this to happen. The physician wanted to have a meeting with the parents and the Director of Chaplaincy Services (also a member of the Ethics Committee) to explore possible treatments, but the father refused to speak to the physician. Then the Director of Discharge Planning was contacted. She called the Child Protective Services and investigated the possibility of a police hold.

In consultation with the Chair of the Ethics Committee and the hospital's ethicist, the Director of Chaplaincy Services and Director of Pediatrics decided to withhold treatment until a court order could be obtained. They decided to meet first with the parents to clarify the issues.

For the purpose of discussion here, assume that the meeting with the parents resolved nothing. Following the doctrine of the Jehovah's Witnesses, the mother insisted that her son receive no blood by-products in the treatment. The boy's father, however, wanted to continue to use herbal medicine to treat his son.

As a member of the Ethics Committee, you are the representative who will now meet with the family and attempt to resolve this ethical dilemma between parental rights and the child's best interests. Walk through the seven-step model and make a decision on how you will resolve the case.

1. Gather the Facts

The relevant facts are as follows:

- Patient, a minor child, was admitted to the hospital on December 31. He is diagnosed with Kawasaki's disease.
- Traditional treatment adversely affects the heart in 30 percent of the cases. (Questions: How serious is the effect on the heart? Life threatening? Is a 30 percent probability high for a child of his age?)
- Treatment with gamma globulin, which contains blood by-products, was started on January 5 to minimize the negative effect on the patient's heart. (Question: What took place between December 31 and January 5 when the gamma globulin was started?)
- Mother objected to blood products being introduced into her son's body. She produced a written document, testifying that she is a Jehovah's Witness and that membership in that community forbids the use of blood or blood products in medical treatment.
- Korean father advocates the use of herbal medicine, being skeptical of traditional Western medicine. His relationship with the attending physician has deteriorated beyond repair.

- Both parents wanted treatment to stop for their respective reasons. Later they wanted to remove the child from the Medical Center against medical advice.
- On January 6, Child Protective Services was contacted and the prospect of a police hold on the patient was pursued. The process to obtain a court order to continue treatment against the parents' wishes was also begun on January 6.
- Physician was willing to allow the father to use his herbal medicines, but unwilling to discontinue traditional treatment.
- On January 6 treatment was stopped in an effort to maintain communication and rapport with the parents. The Ethics Committee decided that they could reintroduce the gamma globulin without harm to the patient. This was only a temporary step and the prospect of using a court order to force treatment was entertained. A meeting with the parents was arranged to seek a resolution apart from the court.
- Patient responded very well to the initial treatment of choice prior to its being temporarily discontinued.

2. Determine the Ethical Issues

Here the issues revolve around the rights of the parents to do what they think is best for their child versus a course of medical treatment that is in the child's best interests. Thus, the autonomy of the parents and the child's medical well-being are juxtaposed.

3. What Principles Have a Bearing on the Case?

Parental autonomy—the freedom to make medical decisions for the children under their care.

Beneficence toward the patient—the responsibility to pursue the best interest of the patient ("do no harm" principle). This principle is highlighted by the fact that the patient is a minor child, unable to make his own medical decisions.

Right of the physician to administer treatment in a way he considers the most effective for the patient.

4. List the Alternatives

Continue treatment against the parents' wishes. This would be contingent on a court order and perhaps a police hold on the patient.

Accept the parents' wishes by allowing herbal treatment in conjunction with most of the other means of treatment. No blood or blood by-products would be included, forcing the parents to assume the risk of their child developing heart problems.

Reach a compromise with the parents by allowing the herbal treatment in conjunction with the gamma globulin treatment. This option would require an appeal to the local authorities of the Jehovah's Witnesses to allow an exception in this case.

5. Compare the Alternatives with the Principles

A great deal depends on the degree of risk to the child if he does not receive the gamma globulin treatment. If the risk of cardiac complications is severe and life-threatening, then the weight given to beneficence toward the child should be increased. If the risk is something that the physician and treatment team can accept, however uncomfortable that may be, then the autonomy of the parents should be weighted more heavily. There appears to be no reason why the father's herbal medicine could not be used in conjunction with the normal course of treatment. However, if the two methods conflict, or if the herbal treatment some-how interferes with the normal treatment, then beneficence toward the child should be weighted more heavily.

It is not clear that a decision has been reached at this point.

6. Consider the Consequences

Each of the three alternatives presented above remains a viable option at this point. Comparing the principles does not yield a clear decision; neither does it elim-inate any of the alternatives. Let's consider the consequences of each alternative.

If the first alternative is chosen (i.e., continue treatment against the par-ents' wishes with a court order), the following consequences could be expected:

- Further alienation of the parents from the medical center and its staff.
- The parents will remove their child from the hospital. The parents have already threatened to do so, and they probably will if they know that a court has ordered treatment. This will force the medical center to use a police hold on the patient to keep the parents from removing the boy from the hospital. If this happens, all trust between the medical center and the parents will disintegrate.
- The boy will get the necessary medical care, insuring that his best inter-ests are protected.
- According to the parents' religious beliefs, the child could be condemned for eternity for accepting blood products into his system.
- The parents may sue the medical center for usurping their parental rights and authority.

If the second alternative is taken (i.e., accept the parents' wishes to allow herbal treatment but forbid blood products), here are the likely consequences:

- Trust between the medical center and the parents will be restored, perhaps opening the door for further discussions about the boy's treatment.
- The risk of a lawsuit or the parents' removal of the child from the hospital will diminish.
- Possible cardiac complications arising from not receiving the blood products will jeopardize the boy's health.
- According to the parents' beliefs, the boy's spiritual state will remain secure.
- To be required to follow a course of medical treatment that is not the best for the boy may have an adverse effect on morale in the medical center.

If the third alternative is selected (i.e., allow herbal treatment in conjunction with the treatment that includes blood products), the likely consequences are as follows:

- For the most part, the boy's health will be protected, assuming that the father's herbal treatments do not interfere with the normal course of treatment.
- This will honor the father's wishes, but not the mother's, which will likely alienate her from the hospital and perhaps the parents from each other.
- If an appeal to Jehovah's Witnesses officials succeeds and they grant an exception, the mother will likely be satisfied and the boy's health will be protected. If the appeal fails, the mother will still have a problem with this alternative, since it affects her son's spiritual condition. Regarding the doctrinal issue, you could attempt to explain to the parents that their biblical proof text has been misinterpreted. You could properly interpret the text and try to persuade them that their view rests on a faulty interpretation of Scripture.

7. Make a Decision

If you were the physician, what would you decide? This case aptly illustrates the way in which ethics must deal with different cultures and worldviews. You cannot assume that everyone shares a Christian worldview, and, to a point, you must respect the beliefs of others. How do you balance the rights of the parents with what you believe are the best interests of the child? Would you seek a court order to force treatment against the parents' wishes? Or do you continue discussion with the parents and try to persuade them to continue the medical treatment? To what extent do you compromise the best interests of the child to avoid further alienating the parents? When dealing with people whose culture and worldview differ from yours, you must frequently face difficult choices.[4]

CONCLUSION

It is hoped that this model offers a helpful way of insuring that all of the relevant questions are asked when attempting to resolve an ethical dilemma. It is not, however, a formula or a computer program that will automatically enable a person to easily resolve ethical dilemmas. But when faced with what appears to be a confusing maze of facts and feelings, this model will provide you with some guidance in the decision-making process.

NOTES

[1] Taken from the *Hastings Center Report* 22 (January/February 1992).

[2] I have adapted this model from the seven-step model of Dr. William W. May from his course, "Normative Analysis of Issues," taught at the School of Religion, University of Southern California.

[3] Jehovah's Witnesses are well known for their refusal of blood transfusions and blood products such as gamma globulin. This doctrine is taken from their interpretation of Acts 15:29, which states, "You are to abstain ... from blood." In context, this passage does not refer to human blood as used in transfusions, but to eating meat that still had blood in it. In Acts 15 the issue was whether Gentile believers who had received Christ had to obey the Mosaic law, a claim made by their Jewish brothers. The issue was resolved by the Jerusalem Council, which ruled that Gentiles were not subject to the Mosaic law. However, to avoid offending their Jewish brothers in Christ, the Gentile believers were instructed to abstain from certain things, including eating meat with the blood still in it.

[4] Here is how the case was resolved. After a lengthy conversation with the parents, the hospital reached the understanding that the herbal medicines would be used in conjunction with the standard course of treatment. The father wished to have his beliefs regarding the use of herbal medicine heard and honored. The mother received permission from the Jehovah's Witnesses to make her own decision regarding the use of blood by-products. She expressed concern over the physical side effects of the treatment, but she and her husband ultimately agreed to continue the treatment. In addition, the father asked that the attending physician be changed to another doctor with whom he had better rapport. He also asked that the new doctor examine the contents of the herbal medication that the father would be administering to his son to enhance the doctor's understanding of Eastern medications. The Directors agreed to pass along this request, but made no guarantees that the physician would fulfill the request. At the conclusion of the meeting, the parents thanked the Directors for their time and willingness to hear their perspective. The Child Protection Worker was advised that the situation was resolved and that her presence was no longer needed. It was thought best that she not address the parents, since this likely would have caused greater anxiety.

6

ABORTION

On January 20, 1973, the United States Supreme Court decided the landmark *Roe v. Wade* case that legalized abortion. As a result, the battle over abortion erupted into full-scale warfare. For pro-choice advocates, the decision amounted to the emancipation of women from having to carry unwanted pregnancies to term. For pro-life supporters, on the other hand, the decision was tantamount to an assault on the most vulnerable segment of society, the unborn. For over two decades, the abortion debate has intensified and it shows no signs of being resolved. It is still the debate which defines the current cultural conflict in America, and will likely remain so in the foreseeable future.

On January 20, 1993, the political landscape surrounding the abortion debate changed dramatically. While thousands of pro-life supporters marched outside the White House during their annual protest of the *Roe v. Wade* decision, newly inaugurated President Clinton, with one stroke of the pen, reversed more than a decade of executive support for the unborn. He signed executive orders that did three specific things. First, he lifted the "gag rule" that had prohibited workers in federally funded health clinics from mentioning abortion as an alternative to dealing with an unwanted pregnancy. Second, he lifted the federal prohibition against performing abortions on military bases and in military hospitals. Third, he ended the moratorium on federal funding for research that utilizes fetal tissue procured from induced abortions. He further vowed to do whatever he could to have Congress overturn the Hyde Amendment, which prohibits the use of federal funds to pay for abortions, an amendment that affects primarily poor women. In 1993, however, Congress defeated an attempt to overturn the amendment, and currently it is still in force.

The literature on the subject of abortion is vast, from both pro-life and pro-choice perspectives, and on both popular and scholarly levels. It would likely take a lifetime to become familiar with all of it. Many philosophers, lawyers, theologians, and ethicists have devoted much of their professional lives to pursuing the abortion issue. This chapter is structured in such a way as to help you get at the heart of the problem by looking at four aspects of the abortion issue.

The first aspect of the abortion issue concerns the legal background that has developed since the *Roe v. Wade* decision in 1973. Four more key Supreme Court cases will be presented, with special emphasis on the two most recent cases, which restrict abortion rights while affirming the basic direction of *Roe v. Wade*. The second aspect is the biblical background, where we will outline the relevant passages of Scripture. The third aspect is an analysis of pro-choice arguments for abortion rights. The fourth and final aspect of the problem deals with the issue of personhood and asks the question, At what point in the process of gestation does the unborn become a person?

THE LEGAL BACKGROUND OF ABORTION

Although numerous legal battles have been carried out in the courts over different aspects of the abortion issue, the cases that have reached the Supreme Court are the most influential in setting the terms of the debate and the general direction of its outcome. Five specific cases in the past two decades have been particularly important, both in establishing the right of a woman to obtain an abortion, and in limiting that right. Beginning with the *Roe v. Wade* decision that initially legalized abortion and continuing through to the recent *Planned Parenthood v. Casey* decision that affirmed but limited the right to abortion, the abortion debate has continued to focus on the courts, rather than on the U. S. Congress or state legislatures.

Roe v. Wade (1973)[1]

In this landmark case, Norma McCorvey* (Jane Roe) claimed she had been raped and that Texas law was forcing her to continue her pregnancy, even though she had been impregnated against her will. Although she later admitted that she had not been raped but had become pregnant due to birth control failure, the Court ruled that Texas' laws prohibiting abortion except to save the mother's life were unconstitutional. Such laws were claimed to violate the due process clause of the Fourteenth Amendment of the Constitution, which protects a person's right to privacy. The idea of privacy was extended to a woman's womb, allowing her the right to end her pregnancy.

The Court ruled that although a woman does have a constitutional right to an abortion, the state also has an interest in protecting the woman's health and the potential life of the fetus. The Court saw this as growing and becoming compelling as the pregnancy progresses. They therefore divided pregnancy into three

---

*In August 1995, McCorvey changed her views about abortion, quit her job at a Dallas women's clinic, and joined a church pastored by a leader of Operation Rescue.

trimesters and held that the state has different interests during each of the trimesters. The justices affirmed a woman's unquestioned right to abortion on demand during the first trimester of pregnancy. After the first trimester, however, the state may regulate abortion in ways that are reasonably related to the health of the mother. For example, this would be done by requiring that abortions be done in licensed medical facilities by licensed medical personnel. Thus, after the first trimester, abortion is available, but not entirely on demand. After viability (i.e., the point at which the fetus can live on its own outside its mother's womb), due to the state's interest in the potential life of the fetus, the state may regulate and prohibit abortion, except in cases necessary to preserve the life or health of the mother. Although the decision did not technically legalize abortion on demand, *Roe v. Wade* along with its companion case, *Doe v. Bolton*, would eventually make abortion on demand legal throughout pregnancy.

Doe v. Bolton (1973)[2]

In a companion case decided on the same day as *Roe v. Wade*, the Court struck down a Georgia law that limited abortions to accredited hospitals, required the approval of the hospital abortion committee and confirmation by two other physicians, and limited access to abortion in Georgia to state residents. Again citing the woman's right to privacy, and for the first time, the physician's right to conduct medical practice, the Court declared the statute unconstitutional. Any attempts to limit the woman's right to obtain an abortion must be consistent with what the Court called "a compelling state interest," of which there was none in this case.

An exception in the Georgia law allowed for abortion in the case that a continued pregnancy would either endanger the pregnant woman's life or threaten her health. The decision about a threat to the woman's life or health was made according to the "best clinical judgment" of the physician. The right of the physician to exercise judgment in this way constituted a significant broadening of the *Roe v. Wade* decision, and made abortion on demand available throughout a woman's pregnancy. The *Roe v. Wade* decision allowed states to prohibit abortion after viability, except when continuing the pregnancy threatened the life or health of the mother. The decision in *Doe v. Bolton* expanded what was meant by the life and health of the mother.

The Court interpreted the health of the mother to include much more than simply her physical health. It also included her psychological and emotional health. Thus, if she would be significantly harmed emotionally by continuing the pregnancy, then the physician could authorize an abortion. The Court put it this way:

> That statute [the Georgia law in question] has been construed to bear upon the psychological as well as physical well-being.... We agree that the medical judgment [of the woman's physician] may be exercised in light of all factors—physical, emotional, psychological, familial and the woman's age—

relevant to the well-being of the patient. All these factors may relate to health [of the pregnant woman].[3]

Thus, if the physician sees the pregnancy as a threat to the woman's health in virtually any way, the Court ruled that he can authorize an abortion at any stage of the pregnancy. If continuing the pregnancy would affect the emotional health of her family (the familial factors cited by the Court), an abortion could also be justified. The way in which the Court expanded the idea of the woman's health and how the fetus can threaten it opened the door to abortion for virtually any reason. This decision, along with the *Roe* decision, established a constitutional right to abortion on demand.

Planned Parenthood v. Danforth (1977)[4]

This case struck down limits on the freedom to obtain an abortion according to the standards set down in *Roe v. Wade*. At issue was a Missouri law that required that a woman's husband also consent to the abortion, and that the parents of a minor child consent to her abortion. The Court ruled that a woman's right to abortion cannot be limited by the requirement that a spouse or parent of a minor child must grant prior consent. The Court ruled that the decision to abort must be left to the pregnant woman and the best medical judgment of her attending physician, and that blanket provisions of consent were overreaching and, therefore, unconstitutional. For many opponents of abortion it was inconceivable that a pregnant teenager could obtain an abortion without either her parents' consent or even their knowledge. Accordingly, this decision created substantial controversy.

Webster v. Reproductive Health Services (1989)[5]

This case marked one of the first significant limits to the right to abortion. The Court reversed decisions by the District Court and the Court of Appeals and upheld a Missouri law that prohibited the use of public funds or medical facilities for "nontherapeutic" abortions (i.e., abortions not necessary to safeguard the life of the mother). The Court held that the right to abortion established in *Roe v. Wade* does not obligate the state to pay for abortions for those women who cannot afford them. The denial of public funds to secure an abortion does not violate *Roe v. Wade*, since it places no governmental obstacle in the path of a woman seeking an abortion. It simply leaves her the same choices as if the government had decided not to operate any public hospitals at all. In addition, the use of public funds for childbirth, which is constitutional, and not for abortion does not violate *Roe v. Wade*, since states are allowed to make value judgments in their allocation of public funds.

Whereas the Hyde Amendment addressed the use of federal funds for abortions, *Webster v. Reproductive Health Services* concerned the right of states to prohibit the use of its tax dollars to pay for abortions. Proponents of abortion argued that the right to obtain an abortion is an empty right if a woman cannot afford it and if the state refuses to help her pay for it. The Court ruled that the responsibility of government, at any level, to pay for abortions does not follow from the woman's right to obtain an abortion free from state interference. The Court rightly distinguished between a negative and a positive right. Negative rights are the rights to be left alone, to be free from governmental interference (in this case, in procuring an abortion). In other words, the state cannot place deliberate obstacles in the way of a woman who desires an abortion. A positive right is a right that also obligates someone to provide it for you (in this case, the state who provides the funds to pay for the abortion). As outlined in *Roe v. Wade*, the right to an abortion is a negative right, a right to be left alone and free from interference in pursuing an abortion. That negative right does not obligate the state to provide a way for a woman to obtain the abortion.

Planned Parenthood v. Casey (1992)[6]

The most recent challenge to *Roe v. Wade* concerned a Pennsylvania law and was considered by abortion opponents to be the best opportunity for the Court to actually overturn *Roe v. Wade*. At issue in the case were the provisions of the law that required a 24-hour waiting period before the abortion (during which time a woman must be given information about the procedure and risks of abortion and about the probable gestational age of the fetus), parental consent for a minor seeking an abortion (although the law provided a way to bypass that requirement by getting a judge's consent, called the judicial bypass), and notification of the woman's husband of her decision to obtain an abortion. A woman could be exempt from all of these requirements in cases of "medical emergency."

Sensing that this case was a challenge to the basic tenets of *Roe v. Wade*, the Court went to great lengths to reaffirm the basic direction of that decision and to continue to safeguard a woman's right to choose an abortion, much to the disappointment of pro-life advocates. The Court reasoned that abortion rights are consistent with the notion of the right to privacy that emerges out of the idea of liberty in the Constitution. They further reasoned that abortion rights are consistent with the ideas of personal autonomy (the right to make one's major life decisions for oneself) and bodily integrity (the right to have one's body left alone), parallel to the right to refuse medical treatment. These arguments constitute a significant part of the pro-choice position that will be examined more closely in the next section.

However, the Court did uphold some of the provisions of the Pennsylvania law, much to the dismay of pro-choice advocates. First, the Court upheld the 24-hour waiting period in which the woman would be provided information about the risks of abortion (both to the woman and the fetus), and the probable age of the fetus. Even if the information presented (which had to be presented fairly and in a way that was not misleading) resulted in the woman choosing childbirth over pregnancy, it did not constitute an undue burden to a woman seeking an abortion. Second, the Court also upheld the parental consent with judicial bypass provision of the law as reasonable. Third, the Court declared the spousal notification provision of the law invalid because of the risk that it could pose to a woman and because it would be a significant obstacle for some women in obtaining an abortion.

Thus, both pro-life and pro-choice advocates were disappointed with the ruling. Pro-life supporters felt as if the best chance to overturn *Roe v. Wade* had been lost and vowed to continue the fight in state legislatures across the country. Pro-choice supporters were disappointed at the restrictions that the Court upheld, believing them to be undue burdens on women seeking abortions. The legality of abortion appears to be safe for the time being, however, with *Roe v. Wade* having survived the challenges to its constitutionality. With the Clinton administration committed to pressing ahead with the Freedom of Choice Act, which would cement the basic right to abortion affirmed by the Courts into federal law, it would appear that the chances of significantly restricting abortion through the Courts are not very great. That makes the place of moral debate and persuasion even more important, and underscores the significance of the biblical data and the moral arguments used in the debate.

THE BIBLICAL BACKGROUND OF ABORTION

Although the Bible never specifically states that "the fetus is a person" and "Thou shalt not have an abortion," it is misleading to insist that the Bible nowhere prohibits abortion. The general tenor of Scripture is resoundingly pro-life. Although some texts on the surface appear to support a pro-choice position, such support is not borne out by further examination of the texts in their context.

The Bible clearly prohibits the taking of innocent life in the Fifth Commandment: "You shall not murder" (Ex. 20:13). The biblical case against abortion, therefore, is made by equating the unborn child in the womb with a child or adult out of the womb. It is not sufficient to show, as some pro-life advocates attempt to do, that God is deeply involved in fashioning the unborn in the womb, and thus deeply cares about the unborn. Given his role as Creator of all the universe, the same thing could be said of the animals. God is involved in the creation of animals and cares deeply for them as well. But from that alone, it does not follow that animals have the same rights as people, since God also gave people dominion over the animal kingdom.[7] The pro-life advocate must show that God attributes the same characteristics to the unborn in the womb as to a person out of the womb. In other words, God must use person-language in referring to the unborn. The argument would run as follows:

1. God attributes the same characteristics to the unborn as to an adult.
2. Therefore, God considers the unborn to be a person.

3. Abortion is killing an innocent person.
4. Killing innocent persons violates the Fifth Commandment (Ex. 20:13).

The passages cited below are not an exhaustive list of texts that could refer to abortion, but they represent the clearest passages that attribute aspects of personhood to the unborn.

In the account of the first birth, when Eve gave birth to her son Cain, person language is used to describe Cain. In Genesis 4:1, the text states that, "Adam lay with his wife Eve, and she became pregnant and gave birth to Cain. She said, 'With the help of the LORD I have brought forth a man.'" Here Cain's life is viewed as a continuity, and his history extends back to his conception. Eve speaks of Cain with no sense of discontinuity between his conception, birth, and postnatal life. The person who was conceived was considered the same person who was born. Had Eve not given birth to Cain, she still would likely have said that she conceived Cain, the person.

This continuity between conception and birth is clearer in Job 3:3, which states, "May the day of my birth perish, and the night it was said, 'A boy is born!'" This poetic passage employs what is called *synonymous parallelism*, in which the second line of poetry restates the first one, essentially saying the same thing in different language. This type of parallelism suggests that the child who was "born" and the child who was "conceived" are considered the same person. In fact, the terms *born* and *conceived* are used interchangeably in the passage, suggesting that a person is in view at both conception and birth. What was present at birth was considered equivalent to what was present at conception. This is strengthened by the use of the term *boy* in the second half of the verse, which speaks of conception. The woman did not conceive a thing or a piece of tissue, but a "boy," a person. The Hebrew term for "boy," *geber*, is also used in other parts of the Old Testament to refer to a man (Ex. 10:11; Deut. 22:5; Judg. 5:30). Thus, in the same sense that an adult man is a person, the individual conceived in Job 3:3 is a person.

Other passages describe God knowing the unborn in the same way he knows a child or an adult. For example, in Jeremiah 1:5, God states, "Before I formed you in the womb I knew you, before you were born I set you apart; I appointed you as a prophet to the nations." Here it seems clear that God had a relationship with and an intimate knowledge of Jeremiah in the same way he did when Jeremiah was an adult and engaged in his prophetic ministry. In the womb he was called to be a prophet, something that was commonly done with other prophets when they were adults. A similar text occurs in Isaiah 49:1, which states, "Before I was born the LORD called me [literally, "from the womb the LORD called me"]; from my birth he has made mention of my name." Here the person in question was both called and named prior to birth, indicative of a personal interest that parallels the interest God takes in adults. Since the person in view in Isaiah 49:1

is the Suffering Servant, Jesus Christ, this passage may be a reference to preexistence. Another indication that the unborn are objects of God's knowledge may be found in Psalm 139:13–16, which clearly shows that God is intimately involved in forming the unborn child and cultivating an intimate knowledge of that child.

Some people may object to the use of these texts, suggesting that all of these refer only to God's foreknowledge of a person prior to birth. However in passages such as Genesis 4:1 and Job 3:3, the person who eventually grows into an adult is the person who is in view in the womb. A second objection that can be raised is that texts such as Psalm 139:13–16 speak only of the *development* of a person in the womb, not of the fact that what is in the womb is indeed a person. However, these texts suggest that in the womb from conception is a person with potential for development, not merely some being who will develop into a person at some point in the gestational process.

Two other passages attribute characteristics of personhood to the unborn. Psalm 51:5 says, "Surely I was sinful at birth, sinful from the time my mother conceived me." Here David is confessing not only his sins of adultery with Bathsheba and premeditated murder of her husband, Uriah the Hittite (see 2 Sam. 11–12), but also his innate inclination to sin. This is a characteristic shared by all people and David's claim is that he possessed it from the point of conception. Thus, the inclination to sin is attributed both to adult persons and the unborn. Using synonymous parallelism similar to that in Job 3:3, David appears to treat birth and conception as practically interchangeable terms. Finally, the Greek term for "baby," *bréphos*, is applied to a child still in the womb in Luke 1:41–44 as well as to the newborn baby Jesus in Luke 2:16.

The general tenor of Scripture appears to support the idea that the unborn is considered a person by God, being described with many of the same characteristics that apply to children and adults. However, a handful of passages seem to indicate that the unborn is less than a full person, and that the Bible does not consider the unborn to be the equivalent of an adult in terms of its essential personhood. The primary text that calls this into question is Exodus 21:22–25, which records a specific law designed to arbitrate a very specific case. The passage states,

> If men who are fighting hit a pregnant woman and she gives birth prematurely but there is no serious injury, the offender must be fined whatever the woman's husband demands and the court allows. But if there is serious injury [i.e., to the woman], you are to take life for life, eye for eye, tooth for tooth, hand for hand, burn for burn, wound for wound, bruise for bruise.

Pro-choice advocates contend that since the penalty for causing the death of the fetus is only a fine, whereas the penalty for causing the death of the mother is death, the fetus must not be deserving of the same level of protection as an adult person. It must have a different status, something less than that full personhood that merits a life-for-life penalty if taken. However, there is significant debate over the translation "gives birth prematurely." For the pro-choice advocate, the interpretation has no scholarly consensus. The most likely translation is "she gives birth prematurely" (so NIV), implying that the birth is successful, creating serious discomfort to the pregnant woman, but not killing her or her child. The normal Hebrew word for miscarriage is the term *shakal*, which is not used here. Rather the term *yasa* is used. It is normally used in connection with the live birth of one's child. The fact that the normal term for miscarriage is not used here and a term that has connotations to live birth is used suggests that the passage means a woman who gives birth prematurely.[8] This would make more sense of the different penalties accruing to the guilty party. Perhaps the phrase "if there is serious injury" in verse 23 would apply to either the woman or to the child, so that if the woman actually did have a miscarriage, then the punishment would be life for life. Even if the correct translation were "she had a miscarriage," it would not necessarily follow that the unborn has less of a claim to personhood, since penalty and personhood are not necessarily related.[9]

THE ARGUMENTS FOR THE PRO-CHOICE POSITION

The pro-life position has in effect only one argument, based on the notion that the unborn is a person, that must be answered. Throughout the past two decades, however, pro-choice proponents have put forth a number of arguments to support a woman's right to choose abortion. In the next section, we will examine the pro-life claim that the unborn has personhood from the point of conception. Here we will examine the various pro-choice arguments that have been articulated both in popular and scholarly forums.[10] Most of the arguments for abortion rights commit the logical fallacy known as "begging the question," or assuming the conclusion one wishes to reach without offering any evidence for its validity. For example, in order for their various arguments to work, pro-choice advocates assume that the fetus is not a full person. The pro-life advocate will rightly point out the question-begging fallacy in order to focus the debate on the central issue—the personhood of the unborn.

1. A woman has the right to do with her own body whatever she chooses.

This is by far the most frequently presented argument in favor of abortion rights. It is the fundamental principle of the pro-choice movement—the woman's right to choose. This is foundational to the woman's constitutional right to privacy and was appealed to by the Court in the *Casey* decision when they referred to the preservation of a woman's bodily integrity and to her personal autonomy to choose abortion. Many people who personally oppose abortion and would never have one themselves nevertheless support a woman's right to choose abortion on the basis that it is her body and, therefore, her choice.

In response, we would note that a person's right over his or her own body is not absolute. In most states, prostitution is illegal, and nowhere is it legal to pour illegal drugs into one's body. In addition, the fetus is technically not part of the woman's body. It is a genetically distinct entity with its own genetic code, and early on in the pregnancy it has its own heart and circulatory system. In many cases, it also has a separate gender identity that is present from the moment of conception. It would be difficult to account for the presence of a differently gendered "part" of the woman if the fetus is a part of the woman's body. This argument confuses the fetus being attached to the woman carrying it and being a part of the woman carrying it. It does not follow that just because the fetus is attached to its mother by an umbilical cord that the fetus is a part of her in a way that denies its own separate identity. To put it differently, this argument confuses the fetus living inside the woman with being a part of her. Again, these are not the same and being a part of her does not follow necessarily from the fact that the fetus lives inside of her.

This argument further begs the question of the nature of the fetus by assuming that it is less than fully human. If pro-choice advocates did not assume this, this argument could not stand. Historically in Western society, when life and freedom (choice) have been in conflict, life always has taken precedence. Only if the fetus is not a person does a woman have a right to make a choice that would result in its death. But if the fetus is a person, then very few freedoms would take precedence over its right to life. The pro-choice advocate may respond that I am also begging the question by assuming that the fetus is indeed a person. That is true, but it is done only in order to show the question-begging nature of this argument. That is, only if one assumes that the fetus is not a person will the argument work. But that is the heart of the debate, and any argument that assumes what is central to the issue cannot be considered valid.

2. If abortion becomes illegal, we'll return to the dangerous days of the back-alley butchers.

This argument takes one back to the days prior to the *Roe v. Wade* decision, when most abortions were illegal and women had to go to less than ideal settings to obtain them, thereby putting their health at significantly greater risk. Unlicensed physicians allegedly performed these abortions in "back alley" clinics with varying degrees of safety. Desperate to be relieved of an unwanted pregnancy, women would thus endanger themselves in the process of obtaining an abortion. No one, the argument goes, would want to go back to those days, and if the pro-life movement has its way, that is exactly where society would be heading.

In response, this argument also begs the question, since one must assume that the fetus is not a person. Otherwise, the person advancing this argument would be arguing that society has the responsibility to make it safe to kill people who have the right to life. Unless the fetus is a person, this argument has little force, for if it is a person, and abortion amounts to killing a person, the issue of making it safe for a person to do so is not only irrelevant, but it is absurd. The only way that the safety of the mother can be a legitimate concern is if the fetus is not a person and if abortion is comparable to any other type of surgery in which a part of the woman's body is removed.

This argument also seems to overstate the potential danger to women receiving illegal, "back alley" abortions. The statistics on the number of women who died procuring illegal abortions are clearly inflated, at times even by the admission of pro-choice advocates.[11] For example, according to numbers available from the Bureau of Vital Statistics, roughly forty women died from such abortions in 1972, the year prior to *Roe v. Wade*. In fact, the number of deaths from abortion-related consequences has decreased consistently since 1942.[12] It is misleading to insist that the majority of illegal abortions were performed by unqualified physicians, since prior to 1973 roughly 90 percent of illegal abortions were performed by licensed physicians in good standing with their state medical boards.[13]

Closely related to this argument is the argument that any substantial prohibition of abortion is unenforceable. To enforce any such law would likely involve intolerable invasions of privacy and would force physicians to break their covenant of confidentiality with their patients. But again, this argument begs the question by assuming that the fetus is not a person, for if it is, then making it safe and legal to abort them does not follow at all. In addition, it can be shown that prior to 1973, restrictive abortion laws were quite enforceable and were effective in limiting abortions. Since 1973 roughly 1.5 million abortions have been performed annually. Prior to 1973 roughly 100,000 abortions were performed annually. This does not mean that enforcement would be free of all difficulties, but it does not follow that abortion should not be limited because of these difficulties.

3. Forcing women, especially poor ones, to continue their pregnancies will create overwhelming financial hardship.

This argument is based on the economic hardship that will likely result from women being without the option of abortion to control the size of their families. Without safe and legal abortion, these women will be condemned to a life of poverty and financial burden, which is also unfair to the children that they bring into the world.

In response, this argument also begs the question by assuming that unborn poor are not persons. This argument can work only by making such an assumption. Otherwise, this argument could be used as a basis for exterminating all those people who are financially burdensome to society. Obviously the reason that society does not do this is that the financially burdensome are persons with the right to life, and their burden to society is irrelevant to their continuing right to life. Only if the fetus is not a person can we say that financial burdensomeness is a criteria for elimination. This argument also confuses finding a solution with eliminating the problem. The solution to unwanted pregnancies is not to eliminate them; by comparison, we could easily solve the problem of poverty by exterminating all the poor. It is better to view adoption as one of the solutions to the problem and recognize that hardship, no matter how severe, cannot justify intentionally killing someone.

4. Society should not force women to bring unwanted children into the world.

Closely related to the economic hardship argument is the argument of the unwanted child. This argument is broader, encompassing pregnancies that are unwanted for more than reasons of financial hardship. Abortion helps society prevent bringing unwanted children into the world, and thus prevents child abuse and child neglect.

In response, this argument also begs the question by assuming that the fetus is not a person, because if it is, then surely abortion is the worst imaginable form of child abuse. In addition, one cannot determine the value of a child based on the degree to which they are desired. If anything, the fact that a child is unwanted is more of a commentary on the parents than the child, and if the fetus is a person, whether it is wanted or not is irrelevant to its right to life. Perhaps the issue of the homeless offers a parallel. They are not wanted in many communities, but the reason they are not eliminated has nothing to do with that. They are persons with the right to life, and one cannot solve a problem by eliminating it. Therefore, this argument hinges on the pro-choice advocate's ability to demonstrate that the fetus is not a person, not on the fact that the pregnancy is unwanted.

Statistics show that since 1973 child abuse has increased substantially, even with the termination of approximately 1.5 million unwanted pregnancies annually. It would appear that the incidence of child abuse is unrelated to liberal abortion laws. If anything, it may be that the callousness toward the fetus engendered by liberal abortion laws has carried over into a greater societal tendency toward child abuse. No evidence shows that being unwanted is necessarily linked with being abused. In fact, some studies have shown that the great majority of abused children were wanted by their parents, and adopted children experience a higher incidence of child abuse than nonadopted children.[14]

5. Society should not force women to bring severely handicapped children into the world.

This is the argument from the deformity of the fetus, which can be detected in utero through the process of amniocentesis. This is becoming more routine in prenatal care, and frequently genetic counselors assume that a woman will have an abortion if tests reveal a deformed fetus. Pro-choice advocates consider it unfair and insensitive to force a woman to carry a pregnancy that she knows will result in a severely deformed child.

In response, abortions in the case of deformity are a relatively small percentage of the overall number of abortions performed annually. These are clearly some of the most difficult cases in the abortion scenario. At best, they only support the right of a person to have an abortion in these difficult cases, but they do not support the right of a woman to choose abortion as a fundamental right. In general, difficult cases do not make the general rule, that is, they do not support the right of a woman to choose abortion on demand.

This argument also begs the question of the personhood of the fetus, since this argument can only be valid if you assume that the fetus is not a person. But if the fetus is a person, then this argument can be used to justify killing all the handicapped. There is no moral difference between the abortion of a handicapped fetus and executing handicapped children. Yet no one accepts the right of parents to kill their handicapped children, precisely because they are persons. Unless the assumption that the fetus is not a person is true, the argument collapses. Thus this argument must rest on whether the fetus is a person, not on the handicapped status of the fetus. In addition, it is presumptuous to say that a handicapped life is not worth living and should be aborted. This may be true in rare and very extreme cases such as anencephaly, where the child is born with only a brain stem and no other part of the brain. But this extreme case cannot be used to justify abortion in cases of more moderate deformities, such as mild Down's syndrome. No evidence supports the notion that unhappiness necessarily accompanies disability.

6. Society should not force women who are pregnant from rape or incest to continue their pregnancies.

This argument is related to the previous one and is one of the most emotionally compelling arguments for a woman's right to choose abortion. Since the woman had sex forced on her against her will, it is argued that she should not be forced to continue a potential pregnancy. This is not a case of carelessness, but rather a lack of consent to sex that made her pregnant. Thus society would be punishing the victim of a violent crime by making her a victim again. At the heart of this argument is the premise that a woman should not be held responsible for sex that is forced upon her, and thus should have the right to end a pregnancy that came about through rape or incest.

In response, the number of pregnancies that result from rape or incest is very small—roughly 1 in 100,000 cases. Yet how the pregnancy was conceived is irrelevant to the central question of the personhood of the fetus. This argument can only work if one assumes that the fetus is not a person, since you cannot justify the homicide of another person just to relieve the mental distress of a trauma such as rape.

Many people argue that the pro-life advocate should not victimize the woman a second time by forcing her to carry the pregnancy against her will. Although they hold that the fetus is just as much a person as if conceived through consensual sex, they maintain that the law should allow an exception to permit abortion in cases of rape and incest. The reason for this is not moral but prudential. They believe that unless a proposed law contains this exception, it will have little chance of being enacted into law by any state legislature. For example, in 1991 the Louisiana legislature passed what would have been the most restrictive abortion law in the United States. Because it did not contain an exception clause for cases of rape and incest, the governor refused to sign the bill. Thus, an opportunity for pro-life supporters to limit abortion was lost due to an unwillingness to compromise and allow this exception. Arguing that it is better to save more unborn children than less, one can make a good case that the exception should have been adopted. Of course, an inherent problem with this is how to enforce such a law, since it might be difficult to verify the claim of a woman seeking an abortion that she had been raped.

7. Restrictive abortion laws discriminate against poor women.

This argument is based on what happened prior to abortion being legalized in 1973. When women of means wanted abortions, they simply traveled to countries where abortion was legal and paid for them. Obviously, poor women did not have such an option. Thus, restrictive abortion laws have the practical effect of discriminating against poor women, who are often the ones who need abortion services the most due to their difficult economic circumstances.

In response, this argument begs the question by assuming that an abortion is somehow a moral good that would be denied to poor women if restrictive abortion laws were enacted. But whether abortion is a moral good is precisely the point being debated. If the fetus is a person, then denying someone an abortion is irrelevant. Society has no obligation to provide equally to all the freedom to kill innocent persons. Thus, this argument can only be valid if it assumes that the fetus is not a person.

All of the above arguments for abortion rights commit the fallacy of question begging. This illustrates how important it is to debate the central issue in the abortion question—the issue of the personhood of the fetus. If the fetus is not a person at the point in the pregnancy at which the abortion is being considered, then most of the arguments for abortion rights are valid. But if the fetus is a person, then none of the arguments for abortion rights hold. If the premise that the fetus is a person is applied consistently, it would lead to morally preposterous implications. We now turn to the critical question of the personhood of the fetus.

THE PERSONHOOD OF THE FETUS

Most philosophers agree that the fetus either has personhood from the point of conception or it acquires it at some point during the process of gestation. A small minority of thinkers hold that not even the newborn baby possesses personhood, thus making infanticide theoretically justifiable in some cases. But most thinkers agree that once the fetus emerges from the womb as a newborn child, it is a person with full human rights. Thus the question under debate is, At what point in the process of gestation does the fetus possess personhood? A wide variety of different points have been suggested. These are called "decisive moments," referring to a "moment" at which the fetus can be said to be a person. In this section we will discuss these different decisive moments.[15]

Often a distinction is made between the fetus being a human being and the fetus being a person. Such a distinction is highly arbitrary, since the essence of the fetus is unchanged throughout the process of gestation. None of the different decisive moments suggest any relevant change in the essence of the fetus. Thus a constant process of growth and development continues from conception to adulthood.

In the abortion debate one commonly hears voices suggest that no one has a way to determine for sure when personhood begins. Taking an agnostic approach to the issue, these people argue that science has provided no clear answer to the question. They maintain that since it is essentially a religious or philosophical issue and cannot be proven conclusively, it should be left to individual choice.

In response to this, the same can be said of the pro-choice view that allows for abortion. By permitting abortion throughout almost the entire nine months of pregnancy, pro-choice advocates are actually making a strong statement that personhood doesn't begin until birth. We will examine birth as a decisive moment below. In addition, if one is admittedly agnostic about when personhood is acquired, then surely it is preferable to err on the side of life. If we are not sure that the fetus is a person, then society should not permit the taking of the life of the fetus through abortion. For example, if I am hunting with a friend who enters the woods and then I hear what sounds like the rustling of a deer at the same spot where my friend entered, I had better not shoot. After all, I cannot be sure whether the rustling sound was made by my friend or the deer. If in doubt, one should not shoot into the trees. Likewise, if in doubt about the personhood of the fetus, one should not risk the life of the fetus, since it may be a person whose life is being ended by abortion. Uncertainty about the status of the fetus justifies caution, not abortion.

The most commonly proposed decisive moment, and the one currently endorsed by the Supreme Court is *viability*, which is the point at which the fetus is able to live on its own outside the womb. At this point of about 24-26 weeks of gestation, the fetus is able to live on its own, a fact that is deemed significant enough to grant it the status of a person. Although it may still depend on medical technology, it no longer depends on its uterine environment.

One problem with viability as a determinant of personhood is that it cannot be measured precisely. It varies from fetus to fetus and medical technology is continually pushing viability back to earlier stages of pregnancy. Thus, viability keeps changing, which raises questions about its reliability as an indicator of personhood. So what does viability actually measure? Viability has more to do with the ability of medical technology to sustain life outside the womb than it has to do with the essence of the fetus. Viability relates more to the fetus' location and dependency than to its essence or its personhood. Thus, no inherent connection exists between the fetus' ability to survive outside the womb and its essence.

Rather viability measures the progress of medical technology in helping the fetus to survive in a different location.

Perhaps the next most commonly proposed decisive moment is *brain development*, or the point at which the brain of the fetus begins to function, which is about 45 days into the pregnancy. The appeal of this decisive moment is the parallel with the definition of death, which is the cessation of all brain activity. Since brain activity is what measures death, or the loss of personhood, it is reasonable to take the beginning of brain activity as the indication of personhood. The problem with the analogy to brain death is that the dead brain is in an irreversible condition, unable to be revived. The brain of the developing fetus is only temporarily nonfunctional. Its electroencephalogram (EEG) is only temporarily flat, whereas the EEG of a dead person's brain is permanently flat. Also, the embryo from the point of conception has all the necessary capacities to develop full brain activity. Until about 45 days gestation, those capacities are not yet realized but are latent in the embryo. Just because a capacity is not exercised is not a necessary comment on the essence of the fetus, since that capacity is only temporarily latent, not irreversibly lost. Thus, a fetus without brain activity for the first four to five weeks of pregnancy is significantly different from the dead person who is without brain activity. Thus, using brain activity as the decisive moment for personhood raises serious questions about its usefulness in determining viability.

A third proposal for a decisive moment is *sentience*, that is, the point at which the fetus is capable of experiencing sensations, particularly pain. The appeal of this point for the determination of personhood is that if the fetus cannot feel pain, then there is less of a problem with abortion, and it disarms many of the pro-life arguments that abortion is cruel to the fetus.

As is the case with the other decisive moments, however, sentience has little inherent connection to the personhood of the fetus. This decisive moment confuses the experience of harm with the reality of harm. It does not follow that the fetus cannot be harmed simply because the fetus cannot feel pain or otherwise experience harm. If I am paralyzed from the waist down and cannot feel pain in my legs, I am still harmed if someone amputates my leg. In addition, to take sentience as the determinant of personhood, one would also have to admit that the person in a persistent vegetative state (i.e., irreversibly comatose), the momentarily unconscious person, and even the sleeping person are not persons. One might object that these people once did function with sentience and that the loss of sentience is only temporary. But once that objection is made, the objector is admitting that something besides sentience determines personhood, and thus sentience as a decisive moment cannot be sustained.

Another idea suggested as a decisive moment is *quickening*, that is, the first time that the mother feels the fetus move inside her womb. Before the advent of sophisticated medical technology such as ultrasound, which can see the fetus from the early stages of pregnancy, quickening was considered the first indication of the presence of life within the mother's womb. Yet quickening as a determinant of personhood cannot be maintained because the essence of the fetus does not depend on someone's awareness of it. This criteria confuses the nature of the fetus with what one can know about the fetus. Philosophically speaking, this decisive moment confuses epistemology (knowledge or awareness of the fetus) with ontology (the nature or essence of the fetus). A similar confusion is involved in the use of *the appearance of humanness* of the fetus as a decisive moment for personhood. The appeal of this is that as the fetus begins to resemble a baby, it makes it at least emotionally more difficult to consider abortion. But the appearance of the fetus has no inherent relationship to its essence. Also, from the point of conception, the fetus has all the capacities necessary to look like a normal human being. Certainly one would not want to determine personhood on such a subjective criteria as the appearance of humanness.

A few hold that *birth* is the decisive moment at which the fetus acquires personhood. But no essential difference exists between the fetus on the day before its birth and the day after its birth. The only difference is location, that is, the baby now lives outside the womb. But as is the case with viability as the determinant of personhood, the essence of personhood involves more than simply location. It does not follow that my nature as a person changes just because I change locations.

Finally, *implantation* has been proposed as a decisive moment for a number of reasons. First, at this point the embryo establishes its presence in the womb by the "signals" or the hormones it produces. Second, 20 to 50 percent of the embryos spontaneously miscarry prior to implantation, which suggests that implantation is critical not only for the development of the embryo but to its essence. It would also suggest that we have the obligation to save all of the embryos, something that very few people consider. Third, twinning, or the production of twins, normally occurs prior to implantation, suggesting that individual human personhood does not begin until after implantation.

Although placing personhood at implantation would not justify very many abortions, the implications of this decisive moment are significant. First, it would make any birth control methods that prevent implantation, such as many birth control pills and the "abortion pill," RU–486, morally acceptable, since an unimplanted embryo is not considered a person. Further, embryos from in vitro fertilization can be discarded or used for experimentation without any moral problem, since those embryos lack personhood.

In response to the proposal of implantation as a decisive moment, it does not follow that personhood is established at implantation just because the embryo establishes its presence by the hormonal signals it produces. The essence of the fetus cannot be dependent on another's awareness of its existence, whether it is physical awareness, as in quickening, or chemical awareness in the production of specific hormones. Second, just because up to 50 percent of conceived embryos spontaneously miscarry, it does not follow that personhood comes at implantation, since the essential nature of the fetus is not dependent on the number of embryos that do or do not survive to implant. Even if the embryo is fully a person, we are not morally obligated to save all of them since we have no moral obligation to interfere in the embryo's natural death. Not interfering to prevent a spontaneous miscarriage is not the same as killing an embryo just as removing life support from a terminally ill patient is not the same as actively killing such a patient. Third, just because twinning occurs prior to implantation, it does not follow that the original embryo was not fully a person before the split. Thus, the proposal of implantation as a decisive moment for personhood generates some very significant questions.

In light of the above discussion, it seems most reasonable to conclude that the fetus has full personhood from the moment of conception. The argument could look something like this:[16]

1. An adult human being is the end result of the continuous growth of the organism from conception (this premise has hardly any debate).
2. From conception to adulthood, this development has no break that is relevant to the essential nature of the fetus (this is the debatable premise, but the above discussion shows that all the proposed breaks are not comments on the nature of the fetus).
3. Therefore, one is a human person from the point of conception onward (no one debates that this conclusion follows from the above two premises).

Also, from conception the fetus has a unique and separate genetic identity, needing only nutrition and shelter to develop into a full newborn baby and later into an adult. From the moment of conception, it possesses all the capacities necessary to develop into a full adult. Thus it is incorrect to say that the fetus is a potential person. Rather, the fetus is a person with the full potential to develop all of its latent capacities. It is a full human being, a person that is in the process of becoming a fully grown adult, with no breaks in the process of its development.

FOR FURTHER READING

Beckwith, Francis J. *Politically Correct Death*. Grand Rapids: Baker, 1992.

Moreland, J. P., and Norman L. Geisler. *The Life and Death Debate*. New York: Praeger, 1990.

Fowler, Paul B. *Abortion: Toward an Evangelical Consensus*. Portland, Ore.: Multnomah Press, 1987.

Rae, Scott B., and John A. Mitchell. "Substance, Property—Things of Human Persons: The Moral Status of Fetuses and Embryos," in Brad Stetson, ed., *The Silent Subject*. Westport, Conn.: Praeger, 1995.

NOTES

[1]410 U.S. 113 (1973).

[2]410 U.S. 179 (1973).

[3]Ibid., 192–93.

[4]428 U.S. 52 (1977).

[5]109 S. Ct. 3040 (1989).

[6]112 S. Ct. 2791 (1992). For other cases in which limits to abortion were struck down, see *Akron v. Akron Center for Reproductive Health, Inc.* (462 U.S. 416 [1983]), *Thornburgh v. American College of Obstetricians and Gynecologists* (476 U.S. 747 [1986]), and *Ohio v. Akron Center for Reproductive Health* (497 U.S. 502 [1990]).

[7]Such dominion involves the freedom to use creation for the benefit of people, but people were also given the responsibility for creation as God's stewards. This responsibility prevents people from exploiting the environment under the guise of dominion over it. See Genesis 1:28–29.

[8]For more on this text, see Umberto Cassuto, *Exodus* (Jerusalem: Magnes Press, 1967), 275, and Gleason Archer, *Encyclopedia of Bible Difficulties* (Grand Rapids: Zondervan, 1982), 246–49.

[9]Bruce K. Waltke, "Reflections From the Old Testament on Abortion," *Journal of the Evangelical Theological Society* 19 (1976): 3.

[10]I am indebted to Dr. Francis J. Beckwith for much of the following discussion. For further development of these arguments and the appropriate counterarguments, see his *Politically Correct Death: Answering the Arguments for Abortion Rights* (Grand Rapids: Baker, 1992).

[11]See, for example, the statements of Dr. Bernard Nathanson, the former cofounder of the National Abortion Rights Action League. He has since changed his position and become a pro-life advocate. See his *Aborting America* (New York: Doubleday, 1978), 193.

[12]John J. Davis, *Abortion and the Christian* (Phillipsburg, N.J.: Presbyterian and Reformed, 1984), 75.

[13]Mary Calderone, "Illegal Abortion as a Public Health Problem," *American Journal of Public Health* 50 (1960): 948–54, cited in Beckwith, *Politically Correct Death*, 240. For further discussion of the statistics on illegal abortion, see the discussion in Beckwith, *Politically Correct Death*, 54–59.

[14]See Beckwith, *Politically Correct Death*, 64–65.

[15]The pro-life case against abortion focuses on the unborn having personhood from the moment of conception, and is widely considered by pro-life supporters as a conclusive argument against abortion. It is often the only argument offered, as opposed to the various pro-choice arguments. If the argument that the unborn has personhood from conception can be sustained, then abortion is killing an innocent person and is prima facie wrong, or wrong in most cases. One possible exception is the rare case in which the presence of the unborn threatens the physical life of the mother. In order to save the mother's life, abortion would be justifiable. Another possible exception for abortion is in cases of rape or incest, yet pro-life supporters have not found accord on this. Some would suggest that the circumstances of an unborn child's conception are irrelevant, and it is wrong to take its life. But others hold that if a woman does not consent to sexual rela-

tions, then she cannot be held responsible for the pregnancy, and thus abortion is justifiable. Still others favor compromise. Maintaining that abortion is always immoral, they believe that a bill that restricts abortion except in cases of rape and incest has a better chance of becoming law.

[16]The argument is stated like this in Richard Werner, "Abortion: The Moral Status of the Unborn," *Social Theory and Practice* 4 (Spring 1975): 202.

7

REPRODUCTIVE TECHNOLOGIES

On March 27, 1986, Mary Beth Whitehead gave birth to a little girl whom she named Sara. On that same day, Elizabeth and Daniel Stern named the same baby Melissa. Both were convinced that the child (called Baby M in the press) belonged to them and were prepared to take drastic measures to insure that they took custody of the baby they believed was their child. The Sterns had hired White-head to bear their child. To this day she is the most well-publicized person who ever performed the role of a surrogate mother. The contest over Baby M was carried on in court for almost two years, and it illustrates the potential problems and complexities connected to many of the new reproductive technologies.

Medicine has made some remarkable accomplishments in the field of reproductive technology. The term *reproductive technology* refers to various medical procedures that are designed to alleviate infertility, or the inability of a couple to produce a child of their own. They include artificial insemination, in vitro fertilization (which produces "test-tube" babies), and surrogate mother-hood. Until recently, adoption had been the only viable way for an infertile couple to have a child. Yet with adoption, the child was not genetically related to either of the parents. But the above reproductive technologies enable infertile couples to have a child to whom at least one of the parents is genetically related. When successful, these technologies offer the miracle of life to couples who have often spent years trying to have a child and have exhausted all other avenues for conceiving a child of their own. Many of these techniques, however, raise major moral questions and can create thorny legal questions that must be resolved in court. Increasingly, judges are looking for direction in deciding these cases because they lack legal precedents on which to rely, and legislators are looking to ethics to help formulate policies that deal with some of these complex questions before they explode.

New technologies now make all sorts of interesting childbearing arrangements possible. Following is a sample of what is now possible for couples contemplating parenthood in unconventional ways:

1. A man who cannot produce sperm and his wife want to have a child. So she is artificially inseminated with the sperm from an anonymous donor. After this, she conceives successfully and bears a child.

2. A woman who cannot produce eggs and her husband want to have a child. So they hire a woman to be inseminated with the husband's sperm and to bear the child for them.

3. A woman is able to produce eggs, but is unable to carry a child to term. She and her husband "rent" the womb of another woman to gestate the embryo that will be formed by laboratory fertilization of the husband's sperm and his wife's egg.

4. A married couple desires to have a child, but the woman wants to avoid any interruption in her career for pregnancy. So her sister offers to carry the child for her. She accepts and the child is born successfully.

5. A lesbian couple wants to have a child. One of the women provides the egg, and after it is fertilized by donor sperm, the embryo is implanted in the uterus of her partner.

6. A couple desiring to have children cannot produce any of the sperm or eggs necessary for conception. So the woman's sister will donate the egg and the man's brother will donate the sperm. Fertilization will occur in vitro, that is, outside the womb. The embryo will be implanted within the infertile wife, who will carry the child.

7. Two homosexual males want to raise a child. To do so, one man's female friend donates the egg and the other man donates the sperm. Another woman is hired to gestate the child.

These new reproductive technologies raise complicated issues, not only for the law, but also for morality. How should society respond to these technologies that, in many cases, redefine the family and turn traditional notions of reproduction upside down? In addition, what does the Bible teach about these new methods of procreation? Since many of these issues were not directly addressed in Scripture, in what way does the Bible speak to these issues? What basic principles are related to these methods? What does the biblical concept of family and children have to say to these new reproductive technologies?

ARTIFICIAL INSEMINATION

Artificial insemination is a process used to alleviate male infertility. It is a relatively simple procedure in which sperm, either from the woman's husband or from a donor (if the husband is unable to produce sperm), is introduced by a syringe into the woman's uterus directly rather than through sexual intercourse. Usually, a couple will try this infertility treatment method first, because it is simple to accomplish, involves no pain for the woman, and is inexpensive compared to other reproductive technologies. Couples usually try this method when a woman's husband has a low sperm count or when his sperm has poor motility, that is, when the sperm has difficulty in reaching the woman's egg.

When a husband's sperm simply needs help in fertilizing his wife's egg, *artificial insemination by husband* (AIH) is performed. Most people have no moral difficulty with such a procedure, and simply view it as medical technology assisting what could not be accomplished by normal sexual intercourse. The genetic materials that are combined when conception occurs (frequently it takes more than one insemination for conception to occur) belong to the woman and her husband, and they are the ones who plan to raise the child. Most people agree that no morally significant differences exist between AIH and procreation by intercourse. An exception to this is found within the Roman Catholic tradition, which views most reproductive interventions, including contraception, as a violation of natural law. The Catholic view of reproductive technologies will be discussed in more detail below.

In many cases, however, the husband's sperm needs more than just assistance in reaching the egg. Male infertility occurs when the man is unable to produce any sperm. These cases may involve a more controversial procedure called *artificial insemination by donor* (AID). This method utilizes sperm from a donor. The donor is almost always anonymous, so that the father cannot be traced by the child, nor can the father elect to make contact with the child and potentially disrupt a harmonious family. In many cases, the sperm of two or three donors is mixed together, thus making it easier to conceal the identity of the father.

AID raises ethical questions that are not a problem with AIH. Since AIH takes place between husband and wife, the integrity of the family is maintained, as is the continuity between procreation and parenthood. But AID introduces a third party into the reproductive matrix, and someone who donates sperm to be used for AID is now contributing genetic material without the intent to parent the child that will be produced through the use of his genes. The law has attempted to minimize any stigma of illegitimacy on the child born by AID. Anyone who donates sperm cannot be presumed to be the father of the child born to the mother who uses the donated sperm; that is, the father of the child is presumed to be the husband of the woman who gives birth to the child. This has been done to insure that the child is adequately cared for financially and is free from accusations of illegitimacy. Certainly, a child born out of wedlock differs from a child born into a stable family to a woman with an infertile husband who used donated sperm. This greatly differs from what most people think of as an illegitimate child. But the fact remains that procreation and parenthood have been separated, and a third party has been introduced into the family by his contributing genetic material to a child that he will never see.

The Scriptures assume that children are raised by the people who are genetically related to them. The Bible assumes that only a husband and wife are the parents of children, and that a continuity exists between the genetic and social roles of parenthood. Although the Bible does not clearly defend this notion, it assumes it. But Scripture does not dispute the fact that this kind of continuity between procreation and parenthood was considered normative.

Even though techniques like AIH were not the subject of direct biblical teaching, biblical principles can be applied to these different methods of alleviating infertility. Christian tradition surrounding the family has assumed that children will be born into a stable family setting in which sexual relations between monogamous parents result in the child's birth. The principles underlying such an assumption are the integrity of the family and the continuity between procreation and parenthood. It is important to note at this point that adoption does not necessarily represent an invalid option in violation of biblical principle. Rather adoption is widely recognized as an exception to the general rule, or as an emergency solution to the tragic situation of unwanted pregnancy. However, just because a discontinuity between procreation and parenthood is occasionally permitted in cases of adoption, it does not follow that just any such separation of the biological and social roles of parenthood is allowed. Most ethicists acknowledge that emergency solutions such as adoption (although they are fine alternatives) make for poor moral norms. The allowance of an exceptional case does not justify it as the norm.

The Catholic tradition of natural law has also emphasized the continuity between procreation and parenthood, even to the point of denying the moral legitimacy of contraception as something that clearly interrupts that process. This emphasis is also the basis for Catholic opposition to abortion and most reproductive technologies. When everything progresses as God designed it, sexual relations result in conception and childbirth. In the same way that God designed an acorn to grow into an oak tree, he also designed sexual relations to result in the birth of a child. This is the reason sex is reserved for marriage, and is why Catholic tradition makes little room for any reproductive technology that would interfere with the natural process of creation. It also rules out any third party involvement that would replace one of the partners in the married couple. Thus sex within marriage and parenthood have a natural, God-designed continuity.

The most recent Vatican statement on reproductive technology put it this way: "The procreation of a new person, whereby the man and the woman collaborate with the power of the Creator, must be the fruit and the sign of the mutual self-giving of *the spouses,* of their love and fidelity.... in marriage and in its indissoluble unity (is) the only setting worthy of truly responsible procreation."[1] In other words, only in marriage is it morally legitimate to procreate children. A further statement clarifies the unity of sex and procreation, thereby ruling out most technological interventions for infertile couples: "But from a moral point of view procreation is deprived of its proper perfection when it is not desired as the fruit of the conjugal act, that is to say, of the specific act of the spouses union.... the procreation of a human person (is to be) brought about as the fruit of the conjugal act specific to the love between persons."[2] In other words, a unity exists between sexual relations and procreation. Procreation cannot occur apart from marital sexual intercourse, and every conjugal act in marriage must be open to procreation as the natural result of God's creation design.[3]

Catholic tradition does make an important distinction between a technology that *assists* normal intercourse and one that *replaces* it in the process of trying to conceive a child. Anything that assists coitus is considered a part of God's wisdom that may be utilized in reproduction. The important element in such a case is the maintenance of the unity of sex and procreation. What this means more specifically is that conception must occur according to its intended design. The movement of genetic materials may be assisted, but use of technology may not replace normal intercourse. For example, fertilization must always occur inside the body, which means that masturbation may not be used to collect sperm outside the body to be mechanically inserted into the woman.

An example of a reproductive technology that assists intercourse without replacing it is what is called *low tubal ovum transfer* (LTOT). This procedure extracts and relocates the egg to a place where fertilization can occur. This method is used when the woman is infertile due to a blockage in her fallopian tubes. The physician who performs LTOT is able to bypass the blockage and place the egg lower in the fallopian tubes or even in the uterus, where conception can now occur by natural intercourse. The sperm still follows its natural course and fertilization occurs inside the body.

One problem with the Catholic tradition's restrictions on artificial insemination in particular and on reproductive technologies in general is that such restrictions may be inconsistent with the notion of general revelation. The argument is that reproductive technologies may be a part of God's general revelation that is universally available. As a part of creation and the mandate given to people to exercise dominion over the earth (Gen. 1:26), God gave them the ability to discover and apply all kinds of technological innovations. Of course, it does not follow that people have the responsibility to use all of the technology that has been discovered. For example, many people suggest that certain types of genetic engineering, especially what is called *germ line therapy* (a type of genetic "surgery" in which the gene that is corrected is also passed on to succeeding generations), should not be used. For the most part, however, technological innovations that clearly improve the lot of people are considered a part of God's common grace, or his general blessings on creation, as opposed to his blessings that are restricted to those who know Christ personally. Many of the reproductive technologies in question would seem to fit under the heading of general revelation, and whether they should be used depends on whether such a use clearly violates a biblical principle or text.

GAMETE INTRAFALLOPIAN TRANSFER (GIFT)

If artificial insemination fails, an infertile couple will usually try *gamete intrafallopian transfer* (GIFT), a relatively recent development in reproductive technology. In this process, the woman is induced to produce more eggs than she would usually produce in any given cycle. Known as superovulation, this procedure is both expensive (about $5,000) and necessary, since the extraction of the eggs is the most difficult and expensive part of the process. In some cases, the eggs are simply placed back in the fallopian tubes, where fertilization can occur in the body as a result of normal sexual intercourse. However, to increase the chances that fertilization will indeed occur, GIFT often goes one step further. Once the eggs are extracted, the man's sperm, obtained through masturbation, is treated and placed with the eggs in the woman's fallopian tubes. With the sperm and eggs in close proximity of each other, the chance of conception is much higher.

GIFT clearly does more than assist normal intercourse in achieving conception. Since the sperm is acquired through masturbation and rerouted into the fallopian tubes, it is inconsistent with Catholic natural law. But for many Protestants and those from a secular perspective, GIFT presents no inherent moral dilemmas that are different from any other reproductive technologies that utilize genetic material from a husband and wife who plan to raise the child(ren) born to them. No third party is introduced into the procreative picture, and the biological and social roles of parenthood are not separated. While it lacks continuity between sex and procreation, this technology presents no moral tension for those many Protestants and non-Catholics who do not insist on such continuity.

Fertilization is, however, achieved by means that are not entirely natural. GIFT doesn't merely assist intercourse, it actually replaces it. This makes GIFT problematic for those within the Catholic tradition. But for those who reject natural law as a form of moral reasoning, GIFT poses no moral difficulty. The development of the procedure is simply viewed as a part of God's general revelation, enabling people to exercise dominion over the creation more effectively. The problem with the morality of GIFT lies in its association with in vitro fertilization, where the two procedures are used together to insure the best chance of conception in the most cost-effective manner.

IN VITRO FERTILIZATION (IVF)

On July 25, 1978, Louise Brown was born. Her birth was significant because she was the first child ever born through the use of *in vitro fertilization*; that is, she was the first "test-tube" baby ever born. A British gynecologist, Dr. Patrick Steptoe, and a physiologist, Dr. Robert Edwards, successfully fertilized an egg with sperm outside the body, and then implanted the embryo in the mother. Nine months later, Louise Brown was born, and was heralded as a miracle baby around the world. The doctors did not achieve success without a substantial amount of trial and error, however, for they reported that they discarded the majority of the embryos produced in the process, because they were considered incapable of being successfully implanted in the uterus.

In vitro fertilization simply means fertilization "in glass," as in the glass container of a test tube or petri dish used in a laboratory. The procedure first requires the extraction of a number of eggs from the woman. To do this she is usually given a drug that enables her to "superovulate," or produce more eggs in one cycle than she normally does. The eggs are then surgically removed and fertilized outside the body in a laboratory, normally using the sperm of the woman's husband. Since the procedure is very expensive (usually upwards of $10,000), all of the eggs are fertilized in the lab. This is done so that if none of the fertilized embryos are successfully implanted, reimplantation of others can occur without much additional cost or lost time, since extracting more eggs would involve waiting until at least the woman's next cycle. Usually, more than one embryo is implanted in the woman's uterus, because it is uncertain how many embryos will be implanted successfully. If more than one embryo does successfully implant, then the couple may have more children than they originally intended. Twins and even triplets are not uncommon for couples who use IVF.

In most cases, it takes a few weeks to determine if implantation has been accomplished, or if the attempt at conception has resulted in a miscarriage. Should the embryo fail to implant, some of the embryos that were not implanted initially will be used at this point. During the time period in which the couple and their doctor are waiting to see if the embryo is going to develop normally, the remaining embryos are kept frozen in storage. The first child to be born from a stored embryo was born in Australia in 1984.

IVF is often used in conjunction with GIFT. Rather than duplicating the costly procedure of reimplanting both eggs and sperm into the fallopian tubes, especially if the physician is unsure if the husband's sperm can penetrate the egg, the remaining eggs are fertilized in vitro. Should the initial implantation of sperm and eggs fail, the most economical and convenient option is to attempt to implant a fertilized embryo in the woman's uterus.

The amount of fertilized embryos that implant successfully and develop into a child is between 10 and 25 percent with IVF. To keep the procedure as cost effective as possible and to maximize the possibility of a successful implantation, therefore, embryos are frozen in storage to be used later if the first attempt fails. In addition, since there is no guarantee that an embryo will be successfully implanted, more than one is usually implanted at a time. The actual number implanted depends on various factors relating to the condition of the eggs and the health of the woman. It is not unusual to have some, if not all, of the embryos miscarry spontaneously. In some cases, however, more embryos implant successfully than the woman is able to carry without endangering her health.

Both of the above possibilities raise significant legal and moral issues about IVF. What happens if the couple divorces and a "custody" battle ensues over the unused embryos? For example, after a couple in Tennessee who had utilized IVF had finalized their divorce, the woman wanted to use the embryos to have a child. Her ex-husband refused, claiming that he did not want his progeny living without knowing about them. The couple went to court to have their dispute arbitrated, and the court ruled in favor of the ex-husband, holding that one's procreative liberty also gives one the freedom to not procreate, and thus the embryos could not be used without his consent.

An even more complicated case occurred in 1981 when a Los Angeles woman and her wealthy husband flew to Australia for IVF (at that point in time, England and Australia were on the cutting edge of the technology). A number of embryos were frozen and efforts to implant an embryo in the woman were unsuccessful. While the embryos were still in storage in Australia, the couple was killed in a plane crash en route to South America, leaving no heirs to their substantial estate. This created a number of complicated legal questions regarding inheritance rights, both of the embryos, and of any woman who "adopted" the embryos to gestate and raise them. The situation was made more complex by the fact that the embryos were fertilized by sperm not from the husband, but from an anonymous donor. A committee of ethicists recommended the destruction of the embryos, but government officials rejected that idea. The state decided that they should be implanted and then given up for adoption, with no inheritance rights accruing to the child(ren), the birth mother, or the adoptive parents.[4] With the number of unadoptable children exceeding what society can support, one wonders about the wisdom of a decision to create children for the purpose of adoption. But perhaps that is a better option than destroying the embryos.

What to do with unneeded, frozen embryos raises significant questions about the moral status of the embryo. Most people recognize that because of its potential to become a fully developed baby, the embryo cannot be seen as morally neutral and be regarded as merely a piece of tissue. The alternatives include keeping the embryos in storage indefinitely (at a cost of about $150 per year), destroying them, allowing the couple to donate them to another infertile couple, or using them for experimental purposes.

For those who view personhood as beginning at conception, which includes most pro-life advocates, the disposition of these embryos presents knotty moral dilemmas. If the right to life is acquired at conception, then destroying embryos or using them in experiments is problematic. Destroying embryos outside the body would appear to be the moral equivalent of abortion, and science cannot experiment on someone with basic human rights without their consent, particularly since most experimentation on the embryo would result in its destruction. Storing the embryos indefinitely only postpones dealing with this issue. That leaves donation of the embryos as the only viable alternative. Yet this is problematic, too, since it involves a separation of the biological and social roles of parenthood that many Christians believe to be a significant part of the biblical teaching on the family. However, it might be possible to view embryo donation in a way that is analogous to adoption, as a preimplantation adoption in which the couple who contributed the genetic materials to form the embryo consent to give up parental rights to their child after implantation instead of after the child's birth. This would require a significant change in the adoption laws of many states, since they frequently do not recognize any consent to adoption as valid and legal until a period of time after the child's birth.

For those who believe that personhood for the embryo or fetus comes some time after conception, as is the case with most pro-choice advocates, the disposition of embryos does not present such moral problems. In most cases, they would likely authorize the destruction of unused embryos. However, the expense of the procedure, the high failure rate involved, and the perception of overpopulation in the world would generally cause even non-Christians to have hesitation in using IVF.

A second problem arises not from the failures of implantation, but from its successes. Routinely more embryos are implanted than will survive in the uterus. But occasionally a woman is left with more developing embryos than she can carry to term without risk to her health and life or to those of the fetuses. In these cases, the woman, her husband, and her doctor have some very difficult decisions to make.

When multiple implantations do occur, the doctor will usually recommend the *selective termination* of one or more of the developing embryos. This is done at times for sake of convenience, but more often out of a genuine concern for the life of the mother and of the fetuses. Not only does this involve terminating one or more lives, but the doctor must also determine which one(s) to terminate and how to make that decision. If the mother's and fetus's lives are clearly at significant risk in carrying all the fetuses to term, then it would appear justified to terminate one or more of the fetuses in order to save the life of the mother and the fetuses.

This situation would be analogous to cases in which abortion is justifiable because carrying the pregnancy to term would put the mother's life at grave risk. Of course, those who do not hold to such a high view of the sanctity of unborn life would see no problem with the woman terminating the pregnancy. But even for people who do not fit into the pro-life camp, the agony of making such painful decisions must surely be considered prior to utilizing IVF to alleviate infertility.

MICROMANIPULATION

One of the more recent reproductive technologies uses highly technical and precise laser "surgery" on a woman's egg to enable the sperm to penetrate and fertilize it. This is known as *micromanipulation*. Under a very detailed microscope, the technician uses a very fine laser to make a small opening through which the sperm can enter and thereby fertilize the egg. In photographs, the opening looks much like a smile on a person's face, prompting researchers to refer to the opening in the egg as the "happy smile." Initial attempts at micromanipulation have had some success. While the procedure is still quite recent and is still being perfected, it does hold promise for men whose sperm is unable to penetrate the woman's egg. A newer procedure actually enables a physician to inject sperm directly into the egg.

One concern has been raised about the wisdom of a procedure such as this. Since it is the more healthy sperm that finally endure the arduous process of getting to the egg and actually penetrating its surface prior to fertilization, critics of this procedure have asked if making penetration easier for the sperm will lead to inferior sperm being allowed to penetrate, thus resulting in more miscarriages and perhaps more genetic abnormalities in the conceptions that do occur. Although it is still too early to tell whether these concerns are valid, they merit caution in utilizing this technique.

SURROGATE MOTHERHOOD

Undoubtedly, *surrogate motherhood* is the most controversial of the new reproductive technologies. In many cases, the surrogate bears the child for the contracting couple, willingly gives up the child she has borne to the couple, and accepts her role with no difficulty. In those cases, the contracting couple views the surrogate with extreme gratitude for helping them achieve their dream of having a child. The surrogate also feels a great deal of satisfaction, since she has in effect given a "gift of life" to a previously infertile couple. But if, as has happened in some well-publicized cases, the surrogate wants to keep the child she has borne, she may fight the natural father for custody. What began as a harmonious relationship between the couple and the surrogate may end with many doubts about the wisdom of using this type of reproductive arrangement.

Many supporters of reproductive technologies in general are opposed to surrogacy. Most of the states that have passed laws concerning surrogacy have decided either to prohibit it or to strictly regulate it. In general, most states have no such restrictions on other reproductive technologies.

Surrogacy itself is not new, for the Old Testament records two such incidents (Gen. 16:1–6; 30:1–13), and it appears that the use of a surrogate to circumvent female infertility was an accepted practice in the ancient Near East.[5] Today, surrogacy does not usually involve any sophisticated medical technology. Although in vitro fertilization is used in some cases to impregnate the surrogate, conception is usually accomplished by artificial insemination. What makes surrogacy a different concept today is the legal context in which reproduction now occurs. The presence of lawyers, detailed contracts, and even the idea of legal representation for the yet-to-be-born child are the new elements in the previously private area of procreation.

Judicial Cases

The following three cases illustrate the myriad of complexities that can occur in a surrogate parenting arrangement.

The Baby M Case

In the soap-opera drama of the first well-publicized surrogacy case, which became a television movie, William Stern had a special interest in fathering a child to whom he was genetically related. Since most of his relatives had been killed during the Holocaust, he was the only living member of his bloodline. His wife Elizabeth had a mild case of multiple sclerosis, and she believed that pregnancy would be a significant health risk.

The Infertility Center of New York matched the Sterns with Mary Beth Whitehead, a woman of moderate means with two children of her own. She agreed to be impregnated and to surrender custody of the child upon birth for a $10,000 fee and payment of all associated medical expenses. If she miscarried prior to the fifth month, she would receive no fee, but if miscarriage came after the fifth month or if the child was stillborn, she would receive $1,000.

Regretting her decision to give up the child to the Sterns, Whitehead sued for custody after the child was born. The Sterns allowed her to take the child for a week, after which time she fled the area with the child. The child was later recovered forcibly by the police in Florida and returned to the Sterns.

In a decision handed down in March of 1987, a New Jersey Superior Court ruled that the surrogacy contract between the Sterns and Whitehead was valid. Judge Harvey Sorkow ruled that Whitehead was not coerced into signing the contract, and therefore it should be enforced. Using the analogy between a sperm donation and a woman "renting her womb," he ruled that a woman had the right to sell her reproductive capacities. Thus, Whitehead breached a valid contract when she refused to surrender the child and give up custody.

Even though the contract was upheld, a custody hearing was held since the best interest of the child was the primary concern. Due to their refusal to obey the court order and their subsequent flight from the state, Whitehead and her husband took quite a beating in court. The judge ruled that custody should be given to the Sterns, because they would be able to provide a more stable home for the child.

Upon appeal to the New Jersey Supreme Court, that decision was reversed, although the final custody outcome remained the same. In February, 1988, Judge Robert Wilentz, writing for a unanimous Court, ruled that surrogacy contracts violated state laws that prohibit the transfer of money for adoptions. In effect, surrogacy was deemed babyselling, and was prohibited on the principle that human life cannot be bought or sold. The Court cited as evidence the way the fee was paid to Whitehead, who would receive significantly less money from the Sterns if the baby was miscarried or stillborn. Clearly, the Sterns were paying for a child and full parental rights, not just the rental of her womb.

The Court also cited New Jersey laws that protected the fundamental rights of genetic parents to participate in raising their children. Since Mary Beth Whitehead was not an unfit mother and had not abandoned her child, she could not be denied the right of association. In addition, the contract violated laws that stipulated a time period for an adoptive mother to change her mind prior to irrevocably giving up her child. Further, the contract violated established New Jersey public policy on custody that gave the natural parents the right to determine who would raise the child. However, precedent dictated that the decision of who will raise the child cannot be made prior to the child's birth.

The adoption of the child by Elizabeth Stern (facilitated by Judge Sorkow immediately after his lower court decision) was voided and the Whiteheads were to be given visitation rights to be decided by a lower court. They did not receive custody, since the justices held that the child's best interests would be served by custody of the Sterns. Even though Mary Beth announced a pregnancy by another man shortly thereafter and separated from her husband, her visitation rights were not terminated.

Since both William Stern and Mary Beth Whitehead are considered the legal parents, future complications could ensue, as if the ones to this point were not enough. Even though Elizabeth Stern has been the social mother of the child and has established the stronger bond with her, custody would likely revert back to Whitehead if William Stern were to die. Similarly, should the Sterns divorce, Whitehead would have grounds to mount a custody challenge, and would likely win, since the social mother has no legal parental rights. Assuming that Whitehead continued to be a fit mother, there is no compelling reason to deny her custody. In addition there could be issues of child support in the future. Suppose that later on Baby M desires to live with Whitehead. Would Stern then be liable for child support? Under existing law it would appear that he would. Likewise, should Whitehead become financially able, perhaps through book or film royalties, would she become liable for child support? Again, it would seem that she would.

Johnson v. Calvert

In October 1990, another landmark case was decided. In Orange County, California, Mark and Crispina Calvert hired Anna Johnson to be the surrogate mother for their child. This case was different from Baby M in that the surrogate had no genetic relationship to the child. She literally rented her womb for nine months for $10,000, plus all medical expenses. Toward the beginning of the seventh month, Johnson started having second thoughts about giving up the child she was bearing. A month prior to the child's birth, Johnson sued for custody. When the child was born in mid-September, temporary custody was awarded to the Calverts with daily visitation allowed to Johnson. These visits were later reduced to twice weekly until the final custody hearing.

Orange County Superior Court Judge Richard Parslow ruled that the surrogacy contract was valid, and not inherently exploitive. Since Anna Johnson had no genetic stake in the child, she had no parental rights. Thus, the Calverts received exclusive custody of the child and Johnson received no visitation rights. The Judge ruled that the genetic connection took precedence over the fact that Johnson actually gave birth to the child, and that the best interests of the child would be served by custody of the Calverts in any case. Also, testimony was given that undermined Johnson's fitness as a mother. Her roommate testified to the neglect of her current child, and the fact that she was a single mother with minimal financial resources and difficulty holding down a job contributed to the decision to award custody to the Calverts. In addition, the sincerity of her bond to the child was questioned since it was never mentioned until the seventh month of the pregnancy, and then in contradiction to numerous earlier statements to the Calverts that she was carrying their child.

This case bears some resemblance to that of Baby M. For example, in both cases an infertile couple hired a surrogate through an intermediary agency to bear a child for them, with what they considered a valid contract governing the procedure. All medical expenses related to the pregnancy were paid by the contracting couple and the surrogate was to receive a fee of $10,000 for specific performance of the contract. In each case, the surrogate changed her mind and sued to retain parental rights to the child she had borne. In deciding each respective case, the judges were setting new precedents, since neither had any significant legal precedent upon which they could base their decision. In New Jersey, this was the first surrogacy case to receive broad legal and public attention. In California, the precedent set in New Jersey was not that helpful since the relation of the surrogate to the child was different. What made this more difficult is that the law presumes that the birth mother is the legal mother, based on the assumption that genetics and gestation go together. However, the end result of the two cases was the same, in that the contracting couple was given permanent custody of the child, although the way in which the surrogacy contract was viewed was quite different. In each case the court found that the best interests of the child would be served by living with the contracting couple.

These two cases also have some significant differences, however, the principal one being the place of genetic relationship between the surrogate and the child. Whitehead was the genetic mother, having supplied the egg, whereas Johnson was the gestational mother, with no genetic link to the child. Thus the view of the surrogacy contract was different. In New Jersey, the judge ruled that the contract was void because it required Whitehead to give up a fundamental right to parent. But in California, the judge ruled that the contract was valid because with no genetic link between the surrogate and the child, there were no parental rights to be considered. That being so, Johnson had no choice but to give the child to the people the judge considered to be the parents. Genetics made all the difference in the custody award in the Calvert case and in voiding the New Jersey contract. Although the view of the contract was quite different, the child ended up with the contracting couple in both cases; however, Whitehead was granted liberal visitation rights and Johnson was granted none. In addition, the fitness of the surrogate as a mother was considered differently by the courts. Although Whitehead received harsh criticism in the lower court, the New Jersey Supreme Court ruled that she was indeed fit as a mother and that the lower court had been unfairly biased against her. In Orange County, the judge raised significant questions about Johnson's fitness as a mother based on the testimony of her roommate, her status as a single parent, and her employment history. Both the Court of Appeals and the California Supreme Court upheld the lower court's decision.

Moschetta v. Moschetta

A third well-publicized case, also in Orange County, California, has taken a strange twist. In this case, a surrogate sued for custody of a child whom she bore in June, 1990. Elvira Jordan gave birth to Marissa, resulting from Robert Moschetta's sperm and Jordan's egg. In November, Robert separated from his wife Cynthia and took the child. In filing for legal separation, Cynthia, with whom the child had no genetic link, filed for custody, claiming that bonding had taken place with the child and that her role as a social mother should count as significantly as genetics. Jordan also filed a claim for custody, insisting that she did not enter into the surrogate contract to bear a child for a couple that was not going to stay together. So three "parents" were each claiming a right to custody. On January 15, 1991, Judge John Woolley awarded temporary custody to the natural father, visitation rights to his estranged wife, and nothing for the natural surrogate mother. In the spring of 1991, the court ruled that Jordan had legitimate parental rights. In September, Judge Nancy Wieben Stock ruled for joint custody, shared between Jordan and the natural father. Jordan would have custody of the child during the work day, and Moschetta in the evenings and on weekends.

Arguments for Surrogate Motherhood

1. Surrogacy is consistent with the constitutional tradition of procreative liberty.

A long tradition in the Western world gives couples the freedom to make their own decisions about child bearing and child rearing. The family has historically been a place in which the right to privacy has reigned, and for the most part family decisions have been beyond the scrutiny and intervention of the government. Laws have been crafted to insure as much freedom as possible for parents to make choices concerning their children.[6]

A number of Supreme Court cases have set this precedent of family privacy in procreative decision making. For example, in *Meyer v. Nebraska*,[7] the Court ruled that one of the protected constitutional liberties included the freedom for an individual to "marry, establish a home and bring up children."[8] Although at this point the Court could not have anticipated these new reproductive technologies, proponents argue that the freedom to create a family through normal sexual intercourse extends to noncoital means as well.

A second case that opens the door to procreative freedom was *Griswold v. Connecticut*,[9] in which the Court struck down a Connecticut law that forbade the use of contraceptives. The freedom to not procreate a child was broadened by a later decision, *Eisenstadt v. Baird*.[10] In this landmark case, Justice Brennan in the majority opinion stated, "If the right to privacy means anything, it is the right of the individual, married or single, to be free from unwarranted government intrusion into matters so fundamentally affecting a person as the decision whether to bear or beget a child."[11] Although the decision only technically applied to decisions to not bear children, most agree that freedom in decisions to have children are also protected by the right to privacy.

A final decision broadens this freedom even further. In *Carey v. Population Services*,[12] the Court ruled that the state could not unduly burden someone who wanted to purchase contraceptives in the absence of a compelling state interest. In the most sweeping statement on procreative liberty, the Court affirmed the right to marital privacy in decisions involving child bearing. The language of the decision goes far beyond the narrow issue of contraception, and in the view of proponents of surrogacy, strongly implies freedom to involve a third party in procreative efforts. The Courts stated that, "The decision to bear or beget a child is at the very heart of this cluster of Constitutionally protected choices.... decisions whether *to accomplish or to prevent conception* are among the most private and sensitive.... the Constitution protects individual decisions in matters of childbearing from unjustified intrusion by the State."[13]

Thus the right of individuals to make their own decisions about childbearing is well-established in American tradition. Whether these decisions apply to surrogacy is not clear, since the Court has not specifically ruled on a surrogacy case, and since none of these reproductive technologies were in use at the time of these decisions. But it does appear that the full range of procreative decisions is in view in these Court decisions. The debate is over the degree to which Court decisions that apply to individuals using normal coital means of reproduction extends to noncoital means.

In response to this argument, opponents of surrogacy hold that the tradition of procreative liberty only opens the door to *altruistic* surrogacy, in which a woman performs the role of surrogate out of a charitable motive, and only receives reimbursement for reasonable expenses incurred during the pregnancy. This is very different from the way in which surrogacy is normally done. Usually, the surrogate is paid at least $10,000 for her services, and another $10,000–$25,000 is paid to a surrogacy broker for recruiting the surrogate and drawing up the contract that will govern the arrangement. Whether procreative liberty allows for *commercial* surrogacy is another matter, since most states have laws that forbid the exchange of money for the transfer of parental rights to a child.[14]

2. Surrogacy fee is for the rendering of services, not the sale of a child.

Surrogacy proponents are sensitive to the allegation that paying a surrogate a large amount of money for bearing a child for another couple is babyselling. Therefore, the argument is that the fee only pays for the rendering of gestational services, and is not the sale of a child. Proponents insist that it is only fair for a woman to be compensated for her time, risk, and sacrifice that pregnancy entails. People have a right to be compensated appropriately for services rendered. Just as it is legitimate to pay surrogate *childrearers* in a day-care setting, proponents insist that it should be legitimate to pay surrogate *childbearers*.

This argument fails to take into account that the fee is for much more than childbirth services rendered. The service provided in bearing the child is clearly not the intended end product of the arrangement. What really counts in a surrogacy arrangement is not only the successful birth of the child, but also the transfer of parental rights from the surrogate to the infertile wife. She must adopt the child for the "deal to be done." In most surrogacy cases in which the surrogate supplies both the egg and the womb, she is the legal mother of the child.[15] Should she so desire, she may keep the child and share custody with the natural father.

Thus, for any surrogacy arrangement to be completed, she must turn over parental rights to the child. Opponents of surrogacy insist that the fee also pays for this transfer of parental rights, and is thus babyselling.

For example, in the well-known Baby M case, only in the event of the surrogate's delivering a healthy baby to the contracting couple and turning over parental rights, would she be paid the full $10,000. If she miscarried prior to the fifth month of pregnancy, she would receive nothing. If she miscarried after the fifth month or gave birth to a stillborn child, she would receive only $1,000. The contract was clearly oriented to the delivery of the end product, not the gestational process. To be consistent, if the fee paid to the surrogate is only for gestational services rendered, then the surrogate would be paid the same amount whether or not she turned over the child to the contracting couple. If the fee only pays for childbirth services, it is hard to see how a couple could take the surrogate to court to get the child, since the surrogate would have fulfilled her part of the contract once the child was born. In addition, if she miscarried at some point in the pregnancy, her fee should be prorated over the number of months that she performed a gestational service. But this would make surrogacy much too risky for the contracting couple, and it is unlikely that they or the brokers could live consistently with a fee for gestational services scheme.

Proponents of surrogacy will respond that the natural father cannot buy back what is already his; therefore, surrogacy cannot be babyselling. But the child is not entirely his. At best, he can only claim the equivalent of joint tenancy in a piece of property, in which he "buys out" his partner, the surrogate, which is still babyselling.[16]

3. Surrogacy is very different from black-market adoptions.

Some proponents of surrogacy will admit that children are being sold, but that the circumstances are so different from black-market adoptions that it does no harm to exchange parental rights for money. The laws that prevent payment to birth mothers were designed to prevent black-market adoptions, in which birth mothers were exploited financially and in which the well-being of the children was not considered the highest priority. Surrogacy is a completely different situation. Here the natural father is also the adopting father, and surrogacy results from a planned and wanted pregnancy as opposed to an unwanted pregnancy. Thus, the child is not going to a stranger, but to a genetic relative, and the surrogate is not coerced into making a decision she will later regret.

Opponents of surrogacy respond that the differences between black-market adoptions and surrogacy are overstated. For example, screening of the contracting couple is seldom done to insure that they are fit parents and that the best interests of the child are being maintained. In addition, the element of coercion is not entirely absent from a surrogacy arrangement, since it is quite possible that the surrogate could end up being coerced by the contract into giving up a child that she may later want to keep. Further, given the desperation of the contracting couple to have a child, since they usually do not resort to surrogacy until all other means have been exhausted, it leaves them open to exploitation by the surrogacy brokers. Thus, it is inaccurate to suggest that the environment surrounding surrogacy is free from coercion.

Even if the child is treated well and the arrangement comes off without coercion, the problem of babyselling remains. Even if some slaves during the Civil War era were treated well and considered to be family members, the fact remained that they had been bought and sold and had become objects of barter. According to opponents of surrogacy, the circumstances in which such barter takes place is irrelevant.

4. Restriction on the fee means restriction on the practice of surrogacy.

Proponents of commercial surrogacy hold that it is inconsistent to affirm procreative liberty and forbid the fee to the surrogate. If the fee is prohibited, then the number of available surrogates will dramatically decrease and likely curtail the practice. Thus the right to procreate in this way will be an empty right, since the state will have interfered to prevent people from exercising it.

The precedent for this argument is the *Carey v. Population Services* Supreme Court case.[17] In this case the Court struck down a New York law that put burdens on people who wanted to purchase contraceptives, saying that such restrictions infringed on a protected right. This reasoning has been applied to commercial surrogacy by suggesting that a restriction on the fee is tantamount to a restriction on a protected procreative liberty.

One should recognize, however, the significant difference between the issue in Carey and that in surrogacy. In Carey, the sale of *contraceptives* is at stake. In surrogacy, it is the sale of *children*. Although one has a fundamental right to procreate, nowhere does one have a right to sell the "product" of procreation. Any restriction on the sale of children is legitimate, and according to opponents of surrogacy, the argument from the Carey decision does not apply to surrogacy.

Arguments Against Surrogate Motherhood

1. Surrogacy involves the sale of children.

Certainly the most serious objection to commercial surrogacy is that it reduces children to objects of barter by putting a price on them. Most of the arguments in favor of surrogacy are attempts to avoid this problem. Opponents of surrogacy insist that any attempt to deny or minimize the charge of babyselling fails, and thus surrogacy involves the sale of children.

Surrogacy violates the Thirteenth Amendment, which outlawed slavery since it constituted the sale of human beings. It violates commonly and widely held moral principles that safeguard human rights and the dignity of human persons, namely that human beings are made in God's image and are his unique creations. Persons are not fundamentally things that can be purchased and sold for a price. The fact that proponents of surrogacy try so hard to get around the charge of babyselling indicates their acceptance of these moral principles as well.

The debate is not whether human beings should be bought and sold. Rather it is whether commercial surrogacy constitutes such a sale of children. If it does, most would agree that the case against surrogacy is quite strong. As the New Jersey Supreme Court argued in the Baby M case, "There are, in a civilized society, some things that money cannot buy.... There are values ... that society deems more important than granting to wealth whatever it can buy, be it labor, love or life."[18] The sale of children, which usually results from a surrogacy transaction (the only exception being cases of altruistic surrogacy), is inherently problematic, regardless of the other good consequences that the arrangement produces, in the same way that slavery is inherently troubling, because human beings are not objects for sale.

2. Surrogacy involves potential for exploitation of the surrogate.

Most people agree about the potential for commercial surrogacy to be exploitive. The combination of desperate infertile couples, low-income surrogates, and unscrupulous surrogacy brokers raises the prospect that the entire commercial enterprise can be exploitive. Yet statistics on approximately 600 surrogacy arrangements in the 1980s indicate that this potential for exploitation has not yet materialized. Most surrogates are women of average means (the average annual income of a surrogate mother is about $25,000),[19] who are not destitute but are motivated by the money. The fee alone should not be considered exploitation just because it is an inducement to do something that the surrogate would not otherwise do. Money functions as an inducement to do many things that people would not normally do without being exploitive.

This does not mean, however, that the potential for exploitation should not be taken seriously. Should surrogacy become more socially acceptable and states pass laws making it legal, it is not difficult to imagine the various ways in which surrogacy brokers would attempt to hold costs down in order to maximize their profit. One of the most attractive ways in which this could be done would be to recruit surrogate mothers more actively from among the poor in this country, and particularly from the Third World.

Some people have suggested that those with financial need actually make the best candidates for surrogates, since they are the least likely to consider keeping the child.[20] The advantage to using these women is that it dramatically reduces the cost of doing business. John Stehura of the Bionetics Foundation stated that the surrogates from Third World countries would only receive the basic necessities and travel expenses for their services. Revealing a strong bias toward exploitation of the surrogates, he stated, "Often they (the potential surrogates) are looking for a survival situation—something to do to pay for the rent and food. They come from underdeveloped countries where food is a serious issue." But he also suggested that they make good candidates for surrogacy when he stated, "they know how to take care of children.... it's obviously a perfect match."[21] He further speculated that perhaps one-tenth of the normal fee could be paid to these women, and it would not even matter if they had some other health problems, as long as they had an adequate diet and no problems that would affect the developing child.[22] It is not difficult to see the potential for crass exploitation of poor women in desperate circumstances, a potential that is already being seriously considered by brokers in the industry. It is not clear to what degree these statements represent the entire industry, but with the profit motive being a primary factor, it does not take much imagination to see the potential for taking advantage of vulnerable women.

3. Surrogacy involves detachment from the child in utero.

One of the most serious objections to surrogacy applies both to commercial and altruistic surrogacy. In screening women for the most ideal surrogates, one looks for a woman who can easily surrender the child she is carrying. Usually, the less attached the woman is to the child, the easier it is to complete the arrangement. But this is hardly an ideal setting for a pregnancy. Surrogacy sanctions female detachment from the child in the womb, a situation that one would never want in any other pregnancy. Thus surrogacy actually turns a vice, the ability to detach from the child in utero, into a virtue. Should surrogacy be widely practiced, bioethicist Daniel Callahan of the Hastings Center described what one of the results would be:

> We will be forced to cultivate the services of women with the hardly desirable trait of being willing to gestate and then give up their own children, especially if paid enough to do so.... There would still be the need to find women with the capacity to dissociate and distance themselves from their own child. This is not a psychological trait we should want to foster, even in the name of altruism.[23]

4. Surrogacy violates the right of mothers to associate with their children.

Another serious problem with commercial surrogacy might also apply to altruistic surrogacy. In most surrogacy contracts, whether for a fee or not, the surrogate agrees to relinquish any parental rights to the child she is carrying to the couple who contracted her services. In the Baby M case, the police actually had to break into a home to return Baby M to the contracting couple.[24] A surrogacy contract forces a woman to give up the child she has borne to the couple who has paid her to do so. Should she have second thoughts and desire to keep the child, under the contract she would be forced to give up her child.

Of course, this assumes the traditional definition of a mother. A mother has been defined as the woman who gives birth to the child. Society has never had to carefully define motherhood, because medicine has previously not been able to separate the genetic and gestational aspects of motherhood. It is a new phenomenon to have one woman be the genetic contributor, and a different woman be the one who carries the child. Now the debate is whether genetics or gestation should determine motherhood, but in the great majority of surrogacy cases, the surrogate provides both the genetic material and the womb. Thus by any definition, she is the mother of the child. To force her to give up her child under the terms of a surrogacy contract violates her fundamental right to associate with and raise her child.[25] This does not mean that she has exclusive right to the child. That must be shared with the natural father, similar to a custody arrangement in a divorce proceeding. But the right of one parent (the natural father) to associate with his child cannot be enforced at the expense of the right of the other (the surrogate).

As a result of this fundamental right, some states that allow payment of a fee to the surrogate do not allow the contract to be enforced if the surrogate wants to keep the child. Any contract that requires a woman to agree to give up the child she bears prior to birth is not considered a valid contract. This is similar to the way that most states deal with adoptions. Any agreement prior to birth to give up one's child is not binding and can be revoked if the birth mother decides to keep the child. Many states that have passed laws on surrogacy have chosen to use the model of adoption law, rather than contract law that essentially says that "a deal is a deal." The problem with allowing the surrogate to keep the child is that it substantially increases the risk to the contracting couple. They might go through the entire process and end up with shared custody of a child that they initially thought was to be completely theirs. To many people, that doesn't seem fair. But to others, it is just as unfair to take a child away from its mother simply because a contract dictates it.

CONCLUSION

These new reproductive technologies present some of the most difficult ethical dilemmas facing society today. Given the strong desire of most individuals to have a child to carry on their legacy, it is not surprising to see the lengths to which people will go to have a child that has at least some of their genetic material. People's desires to have genetically related children will likely insure a brisk business for practitioners of reproductive medicine, and as a result, society will need ongoing ethical discussion and decision making in this perplexing and confusing area.

FOR FURTHER READING

Congregation for the Doctrine of the Faith. *Instruction on Respect for Human Life in Its Origin and On the Dignity of Procreation.*

Gostin, Larry. *Surrogate Motherhood: Politics and Privacy.* Bloomington, Ind.: Indiana University Press, 1991.

Rae, Scott B. *The Ethics of Commercial Surrogate Motherhood.* Westport, Conn.: Praeger, 1994.

_____ . *Brave New Families?: Biblical Ethics and Reproductive Technologies.* Grand Rapids: Baker, 1996 (forthcoming).

Singer, Peter, and Deane Wells. *Making Babies: The New Science and Ethics of Conception.* New York: Scribner's, 1985.

NOTES

[1] Congregation for the Doctrine of the Faith, "Instruction on Respect for Human Life in Its Origin and on the Dignity of Procreation," *Origins* 16:40 (19 March 1987): 704–5.

[2] Ibid., 706.

[3] For further information on Catholic teaching in this area, see Edward Collins Vacek, S.J., "Catholic Natural Law and Reproductive Ethics," *Journal of Medicine and Philosophy* 17 (1992): 329–46.

[4] Donald DeMarco, *Biotechnology and the Assault on Parenthood* (San Francisco: Ignatius, 1991), 1045.

[5] Both the Code of Hammurabi (1792–1750 B.C.) and the Nuzi tablets (1520 B.C.) authorize surrogacy, and not only for cases of barrenness. Thus surrogacy was not only widely practiced, but it was the subject of detailed legislation to keep the practice within proper limits.

[6] This freedom assumes, of course, that parents are acting in the best interests of their children, and that no harm comes to children in the exercise of freedom on the part of the parents.

[7] 262 U.S. 390 (1923).

[8] Ibid., 399.

[9] 381 U.S. 479 (1965).

[10] 405 U.S. 438 (1972).

[11] Ibid., 453.

[12] 431 U.S. 678 (1977).

[13] Ibid., 685, 687.

[14] This normally applies to adoption. In twenty-five states it is against the law to pay birth mothers a fee beyond expenses to give up her child for adoption. The state rightly wants to protect birth mothers from being exploited and children from being objects of barter.

[15] In cases in which the surrogate does not supply the egg (called gestational surrogacy), there is debate over who is actually the mother, the woman who bears the child (the traditional definition), or the genetic contributor. Good arguments can be made for both genetics and gestation being the determinant of motherhood. For further detail on

this, see Scott B. Rae, *The Ethics of Commercial Surrogate Motherhood* (Westport, Conn.: Praeger, 1994).

[16]This real estate analogy is taken from Alexander M. Capron, "Surrogate Contracts: A Danger Zone," *Los Angeles Times*, 7 April 1987, B5.

[17]431 U.S. 678 (1977).

[18]In the matter of Baby M, 537 A. 2d 1249 (1988).

[19]The statistics on the annual income of surrogates is a bit misleading since it records the income of women who were selected as surrogates. It does not take into account the women who applied to be surrogates but were not chosen. In a 1983 study by psychiatrist Philip Parker, he found that more than forty percent of the applicants to provide surrogacy services were receiving some kind of government financial assistance. See his "Motivation of Surrogate Mothers: Initial Findings," *American Journal of Psychiatry* 140 (1983): 1.

[20]Statement of staff psychologist Howard Adelman of Surrogate Mothering Ltd. in Philadelphia, cited in Gena Corea, *The Mother Machine* (New York: Harper & Row, 1985), 229.

[21]Cited in Corea, 245.

[22]Cited in Corea, 214–15.

[23]Daniel Callahan, "Surrogate Motherhood: A Bad Idea," *New York Times*, 20 January 1987, B21.

[24]This sounds worse than it may be, since Mary Beth Whitehead had left the area with the child because she wanted so badly to keep her. The police were obeying the dictates of a lower court decision that awarded sole custody of the child to the contracting couple. But in any case, they still took the child by force from the woman who bore her. That struck many people as unfortunate, if not barbaric.

[25]In *Stanley v. Illinois*, the Supreme Court stated that, "the rights to conceive and to raise one's children have been deemed essential ... basic civil rights of man ... far more precious than property rights. It is cardinal with us that the custody, care and nurture of the child reside first in the parents." 405 U.S. 650 (1971), at 651.

8

EUTHANASIA

John was terminally ill with incurable stomach cancer that was spreading throughout his abdominal region. His body was wasting away and much of the time, he was racked by pain that could not be adequately alleviated by any pain-killing drugs. As he suffered through his last dying days, he made it clear that he did not desire to live any longer in this terrible condition. He wanted his doctor to "put him out of his misery" by administering a lethal injection of morphine that would quickly and quietly end his suffering. He wanted euthanasia.

Donnie was a strong, athletic, young man in his early twenties when he and his father were standing close to a gas pipeline that exploded, leaving him severely burned over 90 percent of his body and resulting in the loss of his sight and hearing. As he was lying in the field following the explosion, he begged a passerby to shoot him and end the misery that he was experiencing and that he knew he would experience as he underwent painful burn therapy. The passerby refused, and arranged for him to be taken to a burn unit at a metropolitan hospital. The treatment was exactly as Donnie anticipated: slow, depressing, and excruciatingly painful. Repeatedly he asked the doctors to stop the treatments and simply allow him to die. At times, he also asked them to simply end his life in the more humane way, by giving him a lethal injection of drugs. He wanted euthanasia.

Nancy lay in her hospital bed in a permanent vegetative state. She was not in a coma, but all higher brain activity had stopped and only the involuntary functions such as heartbeat, breathing, and digestion, those regulated by the lower brain (brain stem) continued. She had suffered massive head injuries as a result of an automobile accident, and had to be given life-sustaining food and liquids through a tube that had been surgically inserted into her stomach. Only in her late twenties, she was likely to live in this condition for years, perhaps decades, before the rest of her body aged naturally. The cost of maintaining her under these circumstances was high, and since her medical condition was irreversible, her family wanted to withdraw the feeding tubes that were keeping her alive. Confident that they were accurately representing her wishes, they wanted euthanasia for her.

The common element in each of these cases is the desire of the patient to enlist the assistance of medicine to facilitate their own death. The idea of medical killing is at odds with a long tradition of medical practice. But the long-standing taboo against euthanasia has come under increasing scrutiny since the mid-1970s. In recent years, well-publicized organizations such as The Hemlock Society and The Society for the Right to Die have increased their efforts to legitimize euthanasia. In 1991 Derek Humphry, The Hemlock Society's founder, published a best-selling book that was the boldest statement to date in support of euthanasia and assisted suicide. Titled *Final Exit: The Practicalities of Self-Deliverance and Assisted Suicide for the Dying*, it is a "how-to" book, describing the way in which one can be released from the torments of a terminal illness, with or without professional medical assistance. Right to die initiatives are appearing on ballots more frequently. The best known of these has been The Humane and Dignified Death Initiative in California, which nearly gathered enough signatures to get on the 1988 ballot (influential state legislators confidently predict its eventual passage). In the state of Washington, Initiative 119 did receive enough signatures to appear on the 1991 ballot, but was narrowly defeated. Colorado and Florida are considering similar initiatives. Oregon passed such an initiative in 1994, though it is currently tied up in court.

In the late 1980s and early 1990s, Michigan pathologist Dr. Jack Kevorkian made the headlines with his "suicide machine," a simple device that allowed a terminally ill patient to release a lethal dosage of drugs into his body, thereby ending his life. Once the patient was connected to the machine, releasing the drug was a simple matter left in the hands of the patient, not the physician. Kevorkian was indicted on two occasions for second-degree murder. Although the charges were eventually dropped, he has been prohibited by state law from assisting people with euthanasia.

A similar prohibition exists in many countries in Europe, but in the Netherlands, for example, the law is rarely enforced, making euthanasia legal for all practical purposes. The degree to which it is practiced is difficult to accurately determine. The Dutch Ministry of Justice maintains that only approximately 200 deaths per year result from euthanasia, but pro-euthanasia groups insist that close to 20,000 people die by euthanasia annually, accounting for more than 15 percent of the Dutch mortality rate. Clearly, very few euthanasia cases ever come to a prosecutor; the few that do, seldom make it to court.[1]

Two strong traditions in Western societies, the sanctity of life and the "inevitable" progress of medicine, have created a legacy of aggressive medical treatment that has only recently been reexamined. The increasing ability of medicine to prolong life in circumstances of increasingly poor quality of life has contributed to a growing fear among the elderly to face-end-of-life medical decisions. These fears include: ending up powerless to make these decisions for themselves, being held "hostage" to life-sustaining medical treatment that they do not want, and living out their last days with an extremely poor quality of life. Thus there are growing pressures to legalize active euthanasia and allow consenting physicians to assist a dying patient in ending his or her life.

However, it is not clear that this trend reflects the views of the general public or the medical professional community. The morality of euthanasia is still widely debated, and a long tradition that goes back to the Sixth Commandment ("You shall not murder") and the Hippocratic Oath prohibits doctors from assisting in suicide. In addition, some people fear that the practice of euthanasia will expand beyond acceptable moral limits, and include those who are not terminally ill. As a result, most scholars, and even some advocates of euthanasia, urge great caution in determining new parameters for end-of-life medical decisions.

DEFINITION OF KEY TERMS

Euthanasia is derived from classical Greek and literally means "good death." It refers to the process by which a person eases into death without unnecessary pain and suffering. Death is considered a natural and normal part of life, and after a certain point it is not something to be resisted any longer. Euthanasia is often associated with terms such as "death with dignity," highlighting the indignity of the dying process surrounded by unwanted medical technology.

However, some hold that a "good death" is actually a contradiction in terms. Death is said to be the ultimate indignity, coming as a result of sin and the Fall. The Protestant ethicist Paul Ramsey has suggested that death is something wholly alien to people, imposed upon them as a consequence of sin. He thus rejects any concept of death that is considered natural and a part of the normal cycle of life. Since in Christ a person is destined for eternal life, Ramsey argues that death is an indignity, inconsistent with one's eternal destiny in Christ.[2]

Active and Passive Euthanasia

The distinction between *active euthanasia* and *passive euthanasia* is critical. Active euthanasia, commonly called "mercy killing," refers to the direct and intentional efforts of a physician or other medical professional to aid a dying patient in suicide. Normally, a physician accomplishes it by administering a lethal injection of drugs into the patient. Passive euthanasia refers to withdrawing (terminating treatment that has already been initiated, such as a respirator) or withholding (not initiating treatment that one considers futile, such as cardiopulmonary resuscitation for a near-death, terminally ill cancer patient) medical treatment from a dying patient and allowing the patient to die. Unlike active euthanasia, passive euthanasia is not a means for intentionally causing death; rather the disease or condition affecting the patient is simply allowed to take its natural course. Thus the disease rather than the doctor is responsible for the patient's death. The principal difference between the two is that in active euthanasia the patient is killed, whereas in passive euthanasia, the patient is allowed to die. Increasingly, the term euthanasia is used to refer to active euthanasia, since passive euthanasia is becoming more accepted, thus restricting the debate to legalizing physician-assisted suicide.

Ordinary and Extraordinary Means of Treatment

In end-of-life medical decisions, distinctions are often made between *ordinary* and *extraordinary means* of treatment. The term *ordinary means* refers to the course of treatment for a disease that offers a reasonable hope of benefit to the patient, without being excessively burdensome. Antibiotics for curing an infection is an example of this type of treatment. *Extraordinary means* are those that do not offer such hope and place undue burdens on the patient. For example, placing a patient on a respirator is normally considered extraordinary means. Ordinary means are considered morally obligatory and extraordinary means are morally optional.

In the past, these terms have functioned as somewhat rigid guidelines governing treatment decisions, but today there is more flexibility in their application. The terms should be defined relative to the state of medical technology, since many ordinary treatments today were considered extraordinary fifty years ago. In addition, they should be defined relative to the circumstances surrounding a patient. Some treatments may be ordinary in some cases and extraordinary in others, depending upon the patient's condition and prognosis. Many bioethicists prefer the terms *obligatory* and *optional* to "ordinary" and "extraordinary" to take into account the way in which differences in the circumstances play an important role in determining which treatments are morally required and which ones are not.

Living Will

In some cases, people will decide before the end of their lives what kinds of treatments they desire, and more importantly, what kinds they do not want. This kind of advance directive is called a *living will*. Often drawn up by an attorney, it contains varying degrees of specificity concerning the kinds of treatments a person facing end-of-life decisions desires. Some wills are quite general, stating that the person does not want to be maintained on mechanical life-support systems if there is no reasonable hope of recovery, or if one's quality of life dramatically diminishes. Other wills are more detailed, designating the kinds of treatments one desires and refuses. For example, one can request to not be given food and water by medical means or be placed on a respirator under certain conditions. One common request made in a living will is a "do not resuscitate" order, abbreviated by its initials, DNR. This is also called a "no code" order. For example, if a terminally ill patient suffers a heart attack, DNR would indicate that the patient is not to be resuscitated, or that no emergency code is to be announced at the hospital.

The advantage of a living will is that it allows a person to make end-of-life medical decisions prior to the occurrence of a medical crisis. In a crisis, a person must make decisions about treatment options without having the necessary time to think them through carefully. The living will allows time to get the necessary counsel from qualified people so that decisions can be considered carefully and made without pressure.

Living wills are becoming more common, and most states make them available at low or no cost. The 1991 Patient Self-Determination Act now requires that whenever a person is admitted to the hospital, they are to be given information on a living will for their future medical decisions. This is being done so that people can make many of the end-of-life treatment decisions while they are still competent to make them.

In medical ethics *competence* refers to the capacity of the patient to understand the treatment options and give informed consent to the option that is chosen. Patients normally become *incompetent* to make treatment decisions when they lose consciousness, fall into a permanent vegetative state, are in extreme pain, or are under medication to relieve pain. When someone becomes incompetent, it is important to the medical staff to have some idea of the course of treatment desired by the patient. If this is written in a living will, then the physicians have some direction to guide them. If the incompetent patient's wishes are not known, a *surrogate*, or *proxy* decision maker is recognized. This is someone, usually a family member or close friend, who can be trusted to represent accurately the desires of the patient. Some living wills contain a *durable power of attorney* for health care, which designates someone to act as a proxy in the event that the person becomes incompetent to make medical decisions.

THE CASE FOR ACTIVE EUTHANASIA

The most prominent spokespersons for legalizing active euthanasia are Derek Humphry, Founder of the Hemlock Society, English philosopher Glanville Williams, Catholic ethicist Daniel Maguire, and philosopher James Rachels of the University of Alabama. Rachels's presentation of the case for euthanasia is the most widely read and influential one, and any discussion of this issue must take his arguments into account.[3]

Rachels's case revolves around four principal arguments discussed below.

The Argument from Mercy

Faced with the options of passive euthanasia, in which the terminally ill patient is allowed to die painfully and slowly, and that of ending it quickly and painlessly through active euthanasia, Rachels concludes that by far the most merciful choice is to stop needless suffering. After all, one of the principal aims of medicine is the alleviation of suffering, and we have no hesitations about relieving the suffering of animals when they are approaching death. Although he does not argue strongly from the analogy with animals, he does raise the question of why we are more merciful to animals than to similarly suffering human beings. Even for a Christian, the Golden Rule would seem to support this general argument. This is significant for Rachels since Christian denominations actively oppose active euthanasia. Since most people would not like to be subjected to needless suffering at the end of life, Rachels suggests that a person should "do unto others" as he would have them do unto him.

He illustrates this with the 1974 Johns Hopkins Down's Syndrome case, the first well-publicized case of infanticide. In this case, a child born with Down's syndrome also suffered from an intestinal blockage that prevented digestion. Although the necessary surgery to correct the blockage was relatively simple, the parents refused to authorize it and the child was allowed to die, essentially of starvation, over a period of close to two weeks. The pain and anguish experienced by all the parties involved, the child, the parents, and the hospital staff, are not difficult to imagine. Of the three options available, aggressive treatment to correct the blockage (which unfortunately was not seriously considered an option by the parents), passive euthanasia, that is, allowing the child to die, and active euthanasia, Rachels has little doubt that the staff and parents chose the least merciful one. It is rare that people allow animals to die in this fashion, and it seems inconsistent with the principles of respect and mercy for persons to deny them active euthanasia in cases like this.

Rachels uses this case to illustrate the moral superiority of active over passive euthanasia. He is not commenting on the morality of the parents' choice to refuse to authorize the intestinal surgery. However, many others who have commented on this case suggest that the parents chose the least moral option. In this case, aggressive treatment is the only moral option since the child had a reasonable prospect for a relatively normal and functional life, as is true for many children born with Down's syndrome. From a biblical perspective that holds life to have immeasurable value regardless of birth defects, both passive and active euthanasia would be immoral options, because the child's handicap can be considered the ultimate reason for his death. Had the child not been born with Down's syndrome, the parents would likely have consented to the necessary surgery. Those considerations aside, the case is a helpful illustration of Rachels's point, that active euthanasia can be more merciful than simply allowing someone to die.

In response to this argument, the number of cases in which suffering prior to death is so severe that it cannot be controlled is actually very small, although they do occur from time to time. It is not good methodology to make public policy on the basis of such a small number of cases. In addition, under the law of double effect, it is morally justifiable to prescribe a sufficient dosage of medication to relieve the pain even if one of the possible side effects is the death of the patient. This law states that an unintended but foreseen negative consequence of a specific action does not necessarily make that action immoral. Here the intent is critical. If the intent is simply to end the patient's life quickly and quietly, then that constitutes active euthanasia, and is directly killing the patient. However, if the intent is actually to relieve pain (although not permanently), and the patient dies as a result of the amount of medication necessary to do that, that is something quite different, and may be justifiable as an unintended, although foreseen, consequence of an intended action.

The Argument from Utility

Rachels's second argument is from utility; that is, in cases where he considers active euthanasia justifiable, he believes it promotes the greatest good for the greatest number. Since the benefits clearly outweigh the harms, it is the most moral option to pursue. Consider the benefits of administering active euthanasia in these cases. The patient's suffering is ended, the high cost of expensive terminal medical care is avoided, the family can grieve appropriately and get on with their lives, and the medical staff can avoid the stress and anguish of an unnecessarily protracted dying process. This is a situation in which everyone involved benefits. But before the weighting of consequences is finished, one must also consider the impact on the public at large. Does it also produce a balance of good consequences in society in general, especially as it relates to future terminally ill patients who might be coerced into consenting to active euthanasia? Other negative consequences will be outlined in the arguments against active euthanasia. In addition, this argument assumes the adequacy of utilitarian moral reasoning. However, deontological arguments such as the sanctity of life and the prohibition against killing innocent people should also be considered, which Rachels seems to neglect.

The Bare Difference Argument: Killing and Letting Die

The next two arguments are the heart of Rachels's position. In the Bare Difference argument, he assumes the morality of passive euthanasia and argues that killing a patient and allowing him to die have no significant moral difference. In making this parallel, he does not contest the distinction that in the former the disease kills the patient and in the latter the physician does. He does contest the idea that the role of the physician is different in a morally significant way. Proponents of passive euthanasia frequently argue that the doctor does nothing to prevent the natural course of the disease. But according to Rachels, that is not to say that the doctor does nothing at all; in fact, he does something very important, since he allows the patient to die. He is clearly unwilling to say that an act of omission is equivalent to doing nothing in this case. The result is the same. In addition, he maintains that the intent of the person is irrelevant to the morality of the action. It only reveals the character of the person doing the action.

He uses an illustration of the nephew in the bathtub to argue for the absence of a distinction between killing and allowing to die. In this case, a young boy's uncle stands to inherit a fortune if his nephew meets an untimely demise. In one scenario, the uncle comes into the bathroom and actively drowns the boy in the bathtub by holding his head under the water. In the other, he walks into the bathroom just after the boy has hit his head on the faucet and is unconscious under the water. The uncle does nothing, allowing the boy to die. Clearly there is no morally significant difference in the uncle's actions, nor in the results of his actions. Rachels applies this analogy to end-of-life decisions, and concludes that there is no significant moral difference between physicians' killing a patient through active euthanasia and allowing them to die in passive euthanasia.

This analogy has been the object of a great deal of criticism. The response of many opponents of active euthanasia is that analogies like this are valid only for analogous cases.[4] Since the actions of the uncle in both scenarios is so morally outrageous, and cannot be justified, it should not be surprising that other fine distinctions (especially ones about the intent of the moral actor) necessary in the medical setting are obscured in this blatant example. This is an example of what is called the "sledgehammer effect,"[5] in which analogies mask essential distinctions when the analogy is transferred to another setting. For example, if I mixed persimmon juice into two glasses of wine, one white and one red, no one would be able to taste the difference because the persimmon juice would be overpowering and the subtle differences between the two wines would be effectively masked.

However, the most significant criticism leveled at this argument is its inadequate analysis of a moral act. A moral act is more than simply the means used to accomplish the end. Intent is a critical component and at times the only determiner of the morality of an act. For example, consider the difference between a gift and a bribe. Here the intent determines the morality of two otherwise identical acts. It would be inaccurate to say that two people who offered money to the same man, but for vastly different reasons, did the same thing. A gift and a bribe are two fundamentally different actions, and the only difference between them is the intent of the moral actor.

We can make the same criticism of Rachels's illustration of Jack and Jill visiting their sick grandmother.[6] Jack goes to visit his grandmother out of good intentions, simply to show kindness to her. On the other hand, Jill has ulterior motives relating to her grandmother's considerable estate. Although on the surface they acted the same, their motives were clearly different. Rachels would argue that different intent only reveals the different character of Jack and Jill. But here it seems clear that they did two fundamentally different acts. Whereas Jack visited a sick and elderly woman to cheer her up, Jill visited her to secure a place in her grandmother's will. Intent makes all the difference in determining the morality of an act.

Or take for example, two men, Smith and Jones.[7] Smith hates his football coach for demoting him to second-string quarterback and ruining his chances for a pro football career. On the other hand, Jones is in hypnosis therapy to cure his lack of assertiveness. While under hypnosis, he is instructed to hit the first person he sees wearing a red shirt, who happens to be Smith's football coach walking down the street. A few minutes earlier, Smith had stormed into his coach's office and vented his anger at him by hitting him. In hitting the coach, these two men did the same thing. But did they commit the same moral act? One could argue that since Jones was under hypnosis, his action was morally neutral. Because the intent of the two men was very different, in moral terms, they performed two different moral actions.

Rachels insists that intent only reveals the character of the *moral actor*, the technical term for the person performing the act. But certainly character is the tendency to act in certain ways and in certain situations. Character is linked inseparably to actions that demonstrate it. Otherwise, it is unclear how character can be known at all, if intent is separate from the act itself. It seems that either actions and intentions are linked, in which case this part of Rachels's argument fails, or intent cannot reveal character, as Rachels and most ethicists insist it does. Thus, to separate intent from the inherent morality of an action is both difficult and unwise. Intent clearly does make a significant moral difference in the distinction between killing and allowing to die. Although the result is the same, the intent is critical in justifying passive euthanasia and raising questions about the legitimacy of active euthanasia.

The Distinction Between Biological and Biographical Life

Rachels distinguishes between a person's biological life, or physical existence, and one's biographical life, or the aspects of one's life that make it meaningful. This is another key distinction for Rachels, one that must be maintained while the previous one between active and passive euthanasia must be denied in his defense of active euthanasia.

One's biographical life is the sum total of one's goals, dreams, aspirations, accomplishments, and human relationships. These things form the narrative of one's life. According to Rachels, modern medicine has enabled one to exist biologically while the person's biographical life has ended. He suggests that persons who are in a permanent vegetative state or who are in such intense suffering with death imminent have lost their biographical life. Thus they essentially exist only as a body, and have lost the essence of what makes them a person. This is what separates human beings from animals. Although one implication of this distinction is that animals do have some sort of biographical life, only human beings can have a coherent, whole, biographical life. This implies that certain handicapped newborns, certain elderly persons, and persons who have suffered permanent severe brain damage, for example, have lost their biographical life, and have only biological life, or corporeal existence. Since biographical life gives human beings their distinctive value, Rachels reasons that when that has been lost, what is essential about personhood has been lost, or more accurately, it has died. Thus, concerns about killing persons by active euthanasia are minimized, thus deflecting much of the sanctity of life criticism of his position.

He uses the well-known "Dax's case" to illustrate this distinction. After Dax ("Donnie") Cowart was burned in a gas pipeline explosion (see case #2 in the introduction to this chapter), Rachels suggests that he lost much, if not all, of his capacity for biographical life. Those priorities that were most important to him were now impossible for him to pursue. Thus, not only should Dax have been allowed to refuse the painful burn treatment, but at his request he should have been allowed to have active euthanasia administered, if such were a possibility.

Dax's case is probably not the best example for Rachels to use to illustrate this distinction, since Dax clearly recovered his biographical life through the course of treatment. He married, went to law school, and set up a legal practice in his hometown, with a focus on protecting the rights of patients wishing to refuse medical treatment. The irony of this case is that Dax not only regained his biographical life, but one of its significant goals revolves around this very distinction. For Dax and others to defend the right to die, they must maintain the distinction between biological and biographical life. Yet Dax's own experience of recovering his biographical life indicates that this distinction cannot be upheld as clearly as one would like. This makes Rachels's use of Dax's case somewhat self-defeating.

In response to this distinction, many would argue that biographical life, far from rendering biological life morally irrelevant, rather presupposes it. The notion of *substance* first put forth by Aristotle and expanded by Thomas Aquinas, is helpful here. The capacity to have biographical life is grounded in a person being of a specific kind, namely, a human being. A human being has an essence that is capable of constructing those necessary elements of biographical life. In other words, a thing possesses certain qualities because it is a thing of a particular kind. For example, my two-year-old son cannot yet speak in coherent sentences. But because of his being of a specific kind, or having the essence of humanness, he will develop that quality as a manifestation of membership in the kind, *Homo sapiens*. The possibility of a coherent, full, biographical life is grounded in biological life, both of which are part of the essence of being human. Thus, personhood is not lost when the ability to exercise its capacities is lost. Losing the use of my arm is not the same thing as having it amputated.

A second criticism of this distinction is that it leads to a subjective view of biographical life.[8] For Rachels, it seems that biographical life is independent of any normative standards of validity; that is, one's biographical life is meaningful simply because it is one's own, and no one can make any normative judgment about the value of one's biographical life. But surely some biographical lives are dehumanizing and inconsistent with being human. For example, suppose that a woman had as her primary goal in life to be the best prostitute she could be and specialized in providing sadomasochistic sex for her clients. Or consider a person whose life goal was to be the most effective administrator of torture in his country. We would certainly insist that the biographical lives constructed around those aspirations would be inconsistent with membership in the human community, and that they would devalue someone's life rather than give it value. Yet Rachels's insistence on biographical life being that which gives value to life has nothing in it that keeps biographical life from demeaning life as well as contributing positively to it.

A third criticism extends this point. If biographical life is that which gives life its value and when it is gone, essentially only a body exists, then what is to prevent us from stripping the "person" of all his rights? If biographical life gives life its value, then that would seem to be the basis for all other rights. But if biographical life is lost, it would seem that the person has lost all other rights, too. Could we then bury the "person" and treat the person like a corpse? Can we take organs with consent of next of kin? Can we experiment on the person, again with appropriate proxy consent? If the essentials of one's life and one's rights are tied up with biographical life, and if that is lost, there does not seem to be any consistent way of preventing any of the above scenarios, as long as they are done with appropriate respect for the dead. One could even argue that if rights have been lost with biographical life, not even consent would be necessary for active euthanasia. Opponents of active euthanasia suggest that this move from voluntary to involuntary euthanasia, which is performed without the patient's consent, and at times without the patient's knowledge (called *crypthanasia*), is already happening in parts of Europe. Thus it does not surprise them that this biographical-biological life distinction is problematic and could lead to abuses in its administration.

THE CASE AGAINST ACTIVE EUTHANASIA

Opponents of active euthanasia reject the biographical-biological life distinction and uphold the moral difference between killing and allowing to die, and they conclude that active euthanasia is killing an innocent person and thus it violates both Western social and Judeo-Christian prohibitions on killing innocent people. The following are other arguments that supplement this principal deontological point.

It Is Playing God

Human beings should not assume a prerogative that belongs exclusively to God, namely, the taking of innocent life. Commonly the argument is made that one should not intervene in the natural processes of death. But if applied consistently, that would eliminate almost all medical intervention. The creation mandate that gave man dominion over the earth (Gen. 1:28–29) surely includes the ability to control the human body and the forces of creation that war against it because of the curse of sin (3:13–16). Since medical practice is used as an intervention in the natural process, enabling one to more fully have dominion over creation, it justifies medicine as a part of that dominion, and therefore medicine is practiced with God's blessing. The clearer way to state the argument is that some prerogatives in life are only God's, and the direct taking of life is one of them.[9] Modern medicine does not play God when intervening to prevent death, but only when it actively takes an innocent human life. Of course, this argument is limited to people who presuppose God's existence.

Suffering May Be Redemptive

This is a specifically Christian notion, advanced particularly in Catholic circles. A significant part of the biblical explanation and justification of the existence of suffering (the technical term for this is a *theodicy*, literally, the "justification of God" in the face of the reality of suffering) is that suffering has a redemptive element to it. People grow and mature out of hardship, and God uses the process as a chisel to chip away the rough edges of a person's character (Rom. 5:3–5; 2 Cor. 4:16–17; James 1:2–4). Suffering further equips the believer to be a source of comfort to others who experience hardship.

This argument has limits when applied to medicine, however. As Rachels indicates, if this argument were applied consistently, it would preclude any medical treatment that alleviates suffering. Just because suffering produces a beneficial result in the believer's life, it does not follow that the medical profession should not work to reduce the amount of unnecessary suffering experienced by individuals. In addition, this argument has limits when applied to end-of-life medical decisions, because some suffering occurs when death is so imminent that it is difficult to see how it could be redemptive for the patient unless suffering has redemptive value in eternity. These are the only cases in which proponents suggest active euthanasia.

Misdiagnoses Are Possible, and Cures for Diseases Are Possible

Imposing active euthanasia leaves no opportunity to correct a misdiagnosis. The number of terminal illness cases in which active euthanasia could be contemplated and in which a diagnosis could be mistaken are quite rare. However, some individuals have made remarkable recoveries from what doctors thought was a terminal illness. In 1984, Sidney Hook, the American educator and philosopher, requested that doctors remove all life support from him. He was suffering from a stroke, pleurisy, and violent hiccups that prevented him from taking food orally. The doctors refused, suggesting that such a decision was premature. Within one month, he was out of the hospital and within six months, he had resumed his writing, publishing several articles and another book in the following two years.[10] As striking as cases like these are, it should be noted that the doctors acted appropriately. The cases in which people come back from imminent death are actually quite rare, although it is undeniable that they do occur periodically.

Active Euthanasia Will Likely Move from Voluntary to Involuntary Euthanasia

This is a principal concern for most opponents of active euthanasia. It is not hard to see how family pressure and mounting medical bills that eat away at the patient's estate could coerce one into consenting to ending one's life, not because the patient was tired of living but because others were tired of the patient living. The pressure to do one's "duty to die and get out of the way," as the former governor of Colorado Richard Lamm regrettably stated, could be subtle yet significant. This sentiment will only grow as the baby boomers enter their retirement years in record numbers over the next thirty years and pressures to reduce the cost of medical care increase dramatically.

Already we see evidence that this movement is occurring. The de Terp home killings in the Netherlands gave rise to the term *crypthanasia*, in which elderly nursing home residents were administered active euthanasia without their knowledge or consent.[11] In 1988 four nurses killed some fifty residents in an Austrian nursing home. Even though these may be extreme cases, they offer further evidence that the possibility of coerced involuntary active euthanasia is real and could easily lead to growing fears among the elderly about their long-term care.

Further concerns about heading down the "slippery slope" are voiced by those who fear that euthanasia will not be restricted to the terminally ill. Rather, it will be extended to people with varying quality of life circumstances. Opponents fear that candidates for euthanasia will include the nonterminally ill, such as people with Alzheimer's disease or other degenerative brain diseases, the severely mentally retarded, and handicapped newborns.

The slippery slope arguments that are frequently brought to bear on this issue often invoke the parallel to the Nazi euthanasia experience in World War II. Although society is rightly fearful of anything that would reproduce the Nazi experiments, it is important to realize what the Nazi experience does *not* teach us about our current situation.[12] It does not indicate that a practice that began out of mercy will move toward more corrupt ends, since the Nazi experience did not begin out of mercy. It does not indicate that euthanasia for the terminally ill will be extended to other handicapped people, since the Nazi experience did not begin with the terminally ill. It does not indicate that voluntary euthanasia will move toward involuntary (although many believe that a distinction will be difficult to maintain if it is legalized), since the Nazi experience did not begin with voluntary euthanasia. The Nazi program started near the *bottom* of the slippery slope and does not illustrate the movement that many opponents believe it does. However, two important parallels in the thinking behind the Nazi experience serve as cautions for us. They are the concept of the life not worth living and the separation of personhood and its attendant rights from biological life. Both are being heard increasingly in the active euthanasia debate.

Prohibition of Active Euthanasia Will Enable the Law to Stay Out of the Medical Setting[13]

Traditionally the courts have steered clear of intervening in and regulating medical matters. This has generally been left to the medical profession's self-policing efforts. It is debatable whether this can continue to be the case if active euthanasia is a live option for physicians. It is more likely that there will be greater demands for oversight and legal procedures as the courts will be more aware of the possibility for abuse and more sensitive to protecting the public from it.

Prohibition of Active Euthanasia Will Humanize the Ending Edge of Life[14]

With the possibility of active euthanasia, it is not difficult to imagine a scenario in which care for the elderly would greatly diminish. Rather than helping society to develop more compassionate ways to usher someone into his death, active euthanasia would encourage the neglect of the elderly and terminally ill.

Prohibition of Active Euthanasia Will Create a Safer Context for End-of-Life Decisions[15]

Knowing that one could not be coerced into submitting to active euthanasia will create a more secure setting in which patients can deal with their medical choices at the end of life. This prohibition would keep the elderly from developing unnecessary fears about euthanasia as they enter into long-term care. Evidence from the Netherlands supports the reality of these fears, even though the Dutch are generally positive toward active euthanasia.

PASSIVE EUTHANASIA: WITHDRAWAL OF NUTRITION AND HYDRATION

A closely related and highly controversial issue is the legitimacy of withdrawing medically provided food and water from patients who are in a permanent vegetative state. Patients in a permanent vegetative state are those who have lost all higher brain function, while the only part of the brain that continues to function is the brain stem, which controls the person's involuntary activities such as breathing, heartbeat, and digestion. A person in this condition is likely to live to a relatively advanced age, as long as food and water are provided.

Legal Background of Withdrawing Nutrition and Hydration

Although the Supreme Court denied the request of Nancy Cruzan's family to have nutrition and hydration withdrawn, the 1990 landmark case of *Cruzan v. Missouri Department of Health*[16] nevertheless opened the door for patients to request in advance that this treatment be withdrawn, or not even started, should they enter into a permanent vegetative state (PVS). The Court's decision contained three important elements:

1. Medically provided nutrition and hydration can be removed with clear and convincing evidence of the patient's wishes.
2. Nutrition and hydration so provided qualifies as legitimate medical treatment.
3. There is a place for substituted judgment of a proxy decision maker.

The Court rightly affirmed that no constitutional rights were being violated in their decision to keep Nancy on artificially provided nutrition and hydration. The Court rejected the claim of the family that it would be a benefit to them if support were withdrawn from her. Instead the Court focused their decision solely on the welfare of the patient. In addition, they affirmed that even though people do not tend to talk formally about end-of-life decisions, their requirement of clear and convincing evidence of the patient's wishes prior to removal of the feeding tubes was neither burdensome nor unreasonable, since these are life and death decisions at hand. Without making any comment on the ethics or the wisdom of the Missouri law, they affirmed that the state was within their constitutional limits to have a restrictive law in this area. The Justices insisted that it is a protection, not a denial, of a person's rights for states to insist that clear directions be given when life and death medical decisions are being considered.

After the Supreme Court decision, the Cruzans returned to a lower court with additional evidence from Nancy's roommates and coworkers that she did not desire to be kept alive artificially. The lower court then allowed the feeding tubes to be removed, satisfied that the clear and convincing requirement of the Court had been met. She died within two weeks of the removal of the feeding tubes in early January 1991.

In a similar case in Massachusetts,[17] the court allowed the tubes to be removed, and the process was completed without appeal to any higher court. The Massachusetts court allowed more latitude for the substituted judgment of a proxy decision maker, although they did require that evidence be presented confirming the patient's desire. How this case would have fared before the Supreme

Court is unclear since the evidence presented to the court by the patient's family and friends resembles that presented by the Cruzans to the Supreme Court.

The Massachusetts court reasoned that the removal of nutrition and hydration did not violate any of three key state interests. First, it did not violate the integrity of the medical profession, since physicians were not actually being asked to violate their code of ethics or the Hippocratic Oath. In other words, they were not killing a person, they were simply acknowledging the request of the patient to terminate a particular type of medical treatment. Second, it did not violate the state's interest in the protection and preservation of life, since the court ruled that the state's interest is at stake only when the disease or condition is curable, and that the protection of life included more than simply preserving corporeal existence, thereby making the distinction between biographical and biological life. Third, it did not violate the state's interest in the prevention of suicide, since they reasoned that the patient's condition was the ultimate cause of his death, not the removal of feeding tubes. Had it not been for his massive head injuries, he would never have been in a condition requiring artificial feeding.

Arguments for Withdrawal of Nutrition and Hydration

A *permanent vegetative state* (PVS) defined as the loss of all mental activity, including feeling, thought, emotion, and self-awareness.[18] According to the consensus of neurologists, the PVS patient cannot feel pain and has no capacity for anything except involuntary activity. The brain stem is the only part of the brain that is still functioning; all higher brain function is lost. However, the person in this state is not dead in any sense. Most people would be uncomfortable with treating the PVS patient like a corpse and subjecting the person either to burial or taking their organs as a donation. Thus, the person still has all the essential elements of personhood. All that is lost is the ability to exercise them. Simply because a person has lost the ability to exercise the key functions of personhood, it does not follow that they have lost the essence of it. To say that I have lost the use of my leg is not the same thing as having lost it. In addition, although they cannot experience harm (again, the neurological consensus is that they are not able to experience any sensation, including pain), it does not follow that they cannot be harmed, since treating them as a corpse or a premature organ donor would clearly harm them. Had someone amputated Nancy Cruzan's leg prior to her death, she would certainly have been harmed, although unable to experience it as such.

Recent discussion by evangelicals on this issue has focused on the PVS patient's loss of personhood and the image of God, linking both to performing the functions involved with God's image instead of the essence of it.[19] This functional rather than essential view of personhood and the image of God in human beings is not only unwise and potentially dangerous, but it is unnecessary with regard to this issue. The discussion of the personhood of the PVS patient is irrelevant, since medically provided nutrition and hydration are legitimate forms of medical treatment that a patient has the right to refuse. If one admits that this is indeed genuine medical treatment, and if one allows some place for substituted judgment, then removal of nutrition and hydration can be ethically justified apart from any considerations of the personhood of the PVS patient.

The reason for this is that medically provided nutrition and hydration is medical treatment. One of the most helpful aspects of the Cruzan decision was the clear reasoning provided by the Justices on this issue. Once one allows for the general right to refuse life-sustaining medical treatment, a right that is becoming more established in our society, then the heart of the issue is whether nutrition and hydration qualify as medical treatment that a patient has the right to refuse.

The term *medically provided nutrition and hydration* is used intentionally to underscore the technological nature of it. This is a strong parallel to the respirator insofar as medical technology is performing an essential bodily function that the body, through injury or disease, can no longer perform itself. Certainly, air to breathe is as basic a human need as food and water. Yet very few question the morality of removing a respirator under certain conditions, since it is considered legitimate medical treatment.

In most cases, a minor surgical procedure, a gastrotomy, in which the feeding tube is inserted directly into the wall of the stomach, initiates artificial feeding. Like most other medical procedures, it carries with it certain risks and side effects, namely, infection. Use of the nasogastric tube, the other method of feeding, is considered highly invasive (and called so in the Massachusetts court case above), and carries with it the risk of pneumonia. Like every other medical procedure, it must be performed by licensed medical personnel and is usually done in a licensed medical facility, normally a hospital. Finally, and not insignificantly, artificial feeding is considered by most health insurance companies as medical treatment. Most insurers will cover it as legitimate medical treatment, despite the cost-cutting emphasis in their industry.

An additional argument in favor of allowing withdrawal of nutrition and hydration is based on the long-term welfare of future patients. If physicians know that there will be great legal difficulty in removing nutrition and hydration from PVS patients, they will likely be more cautious in initiating it with other patients. This could minimize the amount of time that family members and health care professionals have available to make sound and informed treatment decisions. Also, it may work to deny artificially provided nutrition and hydration to patients who, in hindsight, might have benefited from it.

Arguments Against Withdrawal of Nutrition and Hydration

People who have opposed removing nutrition and hydration have focused their position around four principal arguments. First, they maintain that nutrition and hydration are necessary to preserve patient dignity in the dying process. But it should be noted that many PVS patients are not actually in the process of dying, but could live in a PVS on artificial feeding for many years. Also, once it is removed, it is not difficult to keep the patient looking comfortable (even though they cannot experience comfort or discomfort) by periodically applying ice chips to the face and lips.

Second, nutrition and hydration is considered ordinary treatment and thus should be provided. This comes out of the distinction between ordinary and extraordinary treatment, the former always being mandatory and the latter being optional. Rather than a predetermined distinction, many are more comfortable with the distinction between obligatory and optional treatment. There are cases in which the denial of extraordinary treatment would clearly be unjustifiable and times when ordinary treatment could be withheld. For instance, antibiotics to ward off pneumonia (traditionally, the dying person's friend) in a patient who is at the last stages of a terminal illness, would not be mandatory, since it would only be prolonging an imminent death, yet would fall under the category of ordinary treatment. Although there is a presumption for treatment, even for nutrition and hydration, whether it is obligatory or optional depends on the circumstances, and these terms are not to be used as a predetermined distinction that applies regardless of the patient's situation.

Third, withdrawing nutrition and hydration amounts to starving a patient to death, something that is inhumane and not worthy of a community that cares for the dying. Although there are clearly cases in which nutrition and hydration should be provided, withdrawing them, or refusing to initiate them, does not constitute starving someone to death any more than the removal of a respirator constitutes suffocating someone to death. Even though the person is not terminally ill, it is the injury suffered that is responsible for the patient being in the present condition. Were it not for the injury (or sometimes a disease, but in most cases, a traumatic head injury), the patient would be able to feed themselves orally. The injury caused the condition, and had food and water not been artificially provided initially or had not been available, the patient would have died relatively soon and the death would have been seen as a result of the injury. Thus, parallel to the removal of other types of medical treatment, the injury is the ultimate cause of the patient's death.

Fourth, the most commonly heard argument against withdrawal is that food and water symbolize basic human care for the dying, and that we don't dare neglect it for what it will say about our care for them.[20] It parallels the "cup of water" administered to the dying by a loved one or family member. This symbolism is built on the assumed parallel between medically provided and nonmedically provided nutrition and hydration. In reality, there is very little similarity. Loved ones of the patient are sometimes involved in the process, but not in the actual feeding. In most cases it occurs in sterile hospitals, done by hospital personnel who have no connection to the patient. Some would suggest that it is indeed symbolic, but of something different. It is symbolic of someone being held hostage to medical technology, likely against their wishes. It may even be symbolic of something further, such as exile from the human community. Life in a PVS can be seen as the modern equivalent of exile, a punishment that was considered worse than death, in which the person was cut off from loved ones and died alone.[21]

Conditions for Justification

For many bioethicists, the removal of nutrition and hydration is ethically justifiable for the PVS patient. However, they admit that specific conditions must be met before the removal can be allowed.

1. If it is medically determined that the patient cannot absorb nutrients, then any attempt at feeding will be futile, and food and water may be removed. Also, it is not morally obligatory for a physician to initiate feeding.
2. If it is determined that feeding produces a calculus of burden over benefit, then artificial feeding may be withdrawn. This does not hold so much with the PVS person as with other types of patients that need tube feeding, such as those suffering from severe dementia, for whom the invasive nature of the tube may be a greater burden than benefit.
3. If there is no reasonable hope of benefit to the patient in regaining consciousness, then artificial feeding may be withdrawn. It should be admitted that the notion of benefit to the PVS patient is normally the equivalent of improvement, specifically toward recovery of mental capabilities.
4. If the patient has left some sort of written directive stating no desire to be artificially fed should he or she end up in a PVS, or if a proxy presents clear and convincing evidence that this is the desire of the patient, then artificial feeding may be withdrawn.

Thus the institutional procedure would look something like this:

1. Determine if the patient is capable of absorbing food and fluids.
2. Assuming the patient is incompetent, determine if the patient's wishes are known. Specifically, are they in writing?
3. If not, determine if there is a qualified proxy decision maker available. If so, to what extent does the proxy know the wishes of the patient? What evidence does the proxy have of the patient's desire?
4. If the evidence is unclear, it may be possible to refer to the hospital's ethics committee for their input. If not, and if the evidence is not clear, then the presumption is to treat until a time when evidence of the patient's wishes to reject this treatment are presented.

Although there is still some debate on this issue, the majority of bioethicists hold that it is ethically permissible to withdraw medically provided nutrition and hydration from the PVS patient. The rationale for this is that the right to refuse life-sustaining treatment in general is well established in our society, and this clearly falls under the heading of medical treatment. It is not necessary for patient dignity and comfort, nor is it symbolic of basic human care. The Supreme Court's insistence on clear and convincing evidence of patient desire to refuse this treatment is a necessary safeguard in a life and death decision-making area.

CONCLUSION

The issues surrounding end-of-life medical decisions and euthanasia will likely become more complex as medical technology continues to develop, increasingly enabling medicine to extend people's life span. Although one should be cautious about any separation of biological life and personhood (or biographical life, according to Rachels), one should be equally wary about utilizing scarce and very expensive medical resources on treatment that is futile. To many pro-life advocates, the sanctity of life involves more than simply postponing an imminent death. All life is valuable to God, regardless of its quality, and the biblical commands against killing innocent people should make the society and particularly the Christian community very cautious about supporting active euthanasia, as merciful as it may seem. However, that does not mean that the sanctity-of-life principle demands that every patient indefinitely receive the most aggressive treatment available. In many cases treatment clearly is no longer helpful to the patient, is no longer desired by the patient, and is more burdensome than beneficial to the patient. Although death is rightly to be resisted through reasonable medical means, the Christian's eternal destiny is beyond death. In that sense, death for a Christian is by definition a "good death," because that is when the Christian is ushered into God's presence in eternal life.

FOR FURTHER READING

Gomez, Carlos, M.D. *Regulating Death: Euthanasia and the Case of the Netherlands*. New York: Free Press, 1991.

Lynn, Joanne, ed. *By No Extraordinary Means*. Bloomington, Ind.: Indiana University Press, 1986.

Moreland, J. P., and Norman L. Geisler. *The Life and Death Debate: Moral Issues of Our Time*. New York: Praeger, 1990.

Rachels, James. *The End of Life*. New York: Oxford University Press, 1986.

Wennberg, Robert N. *Terminal Choices: Euthanasia, Suicide and the Right to Die*. Grand Rapids: Eerdmans, 1989.

NOTES

[1]Carlos Gomez, M.D., *Regulating Death: Euthanasia and the Case of the Netherlands* (New York: Free Press, 1991).

[2]Paul Ramsey, "The Indignity of 'Death With Dignity,'" *Hastings Center Report* 2 (May 1974): 47–62.

[3]James Rachels, *The End of Life* (New York: Oxford University Press, 1986).

[4]Tom L. Beauchamp, "A Reply to Rachels on Active and Passive Euthanasia," in *Contemporary Issues in Bioethics*, ed. Tom L. Beauchamp and LeRoy Walters (Belmont, Calif.: Wadsworth, 1989), 336–45.

[5]J. P. Moreland, "James Rachels and the Active Euthanasia Debate," *Journal of the Evangelical Theological Society* 31 (March 1988): 89.

[6]Rachels, *The End of Life*, 93–94.

[7]I am indebted to my colleague Dr. J. P. Moreland for this illustration. See Moreland, "James Rachels and the Active Euthanasia Debate," 89–90.

[8]Ibid., 87–88.

[9]There are exceptions to this general principle. Killing in self-defense, killing of legitimate combatants in a just war, and capital punishment are allowed by biblical principles and have been recognized by Christian tradition. Of course, Christian pacifists dispute each of these exceptions.

[10]This account is taken from Beth Spring and Ed Larson, *Euthanasia: Spiritual, Medical and Legal Issues in Terminal Health Care* (Portland, Ore.: Multnomah Press, 1988), 12–13.

[11]Richard Fenigsen, "A Case Against Dutch Euthanasia," *Hastings Center Report Special Supplement* (January/February 1989): 24–26.

[12]Robert N. Wennberg, *Terminal Choices: Euthanasia, Suicide and the Right to Die* (Grand Rapids: Eerdmans, 1989), 214–20.

[13]Susan Wolf, "Holding the Line on Euthanasia," *Hastings Center Report,* Special Supplement (January/February 1989): 13.

[14]Ibid., 14–15.

[15]Ibid., 15.

[16]See case #3 in the opening paragraphs of this chapter. For the Supreme Court's decision in this landmark case, see *Cruzan v. Missouri Department of Health*, 110 S.Ct. 2481 (1990).

[17]*Brophy v. New England Sinai Hospital, Inc.*, 398 Mass. 417, 497 N.E. 626 (1986).

[18]This standard definition is taken from The President's Commission for the Study of Ethical Problems in Medicine and Biomedical and Behavioral Research, *Deciding to Forego Life-Sustaining Treatment* (Washington, D.C.: U.S. Government Printing Office, March 1983), 174–75.

[19]See, for example, Wennberg, *Terminal Choices*, 158–62.

[20]Gilbert Meilander, "On Removing Food and Water: Against the Stream," *Hastings Center Report* 14 (December 1984): 11–13.

[21]Lawrence J. Schneiderman, "Exile and PVS," *Hastings Center Report* 20 (May/June 1990): 5.

9

CAPITAL PUNISHMENT

On April 21, 1992, Robert Alton Harris was executed in the gas chamber at the San Quentin Federal Penitentiary located outside of San Francisco, California. He had been convicted of first-degree murder and had exhausted the lengthy appeals process that is customarily granted to those who have received the death penalty. A stay of execution was signed by the governor just minutes before midnight on the day he was to be sent to the gas chamber, only prolonging the process and the anticipation of death for Harris. The next day at midnight, there was no order from the governor forthcoming, and he entered the chamber, breathed in the poisonous gases, and died at twenty minutes past midnight.

During the time immediately preceding Harris's execution, crowds were gathered outside the prison. Some were there for curiosity's sake and quite a large group of the media were there covering the event. But other groups were assembled to make statements about the morality of the death penalty. As would be expected, both advocates and opponents of capital punishment were present. The advocates claimed that Harris was getting what he deserved, that the demands of justice were about to be satisfied. Opponents protested that capital punishment was a barbaric practice, out of place in the modern world and unconstitutional as cruel and inhuman punishment.

Interestingly, Christians were found on both sides of the issue, and each group held up signs and placards with biblical references on them. The advocates of the death penalty cited Old Testament passages that spoke of the principle of "life for life" and held that condemned murderers should justly receive death as a consequence of their actions. On the other hand, opponents of capital punishment cited teachings of Jesus with emphasis on mercy, the fact that vengeance belongs to the Lord, and the sacredness of human life. These opposing opinions illustrate that the Christian community mirrors the same debate about the death penalty that exists in society as a whole.

Imagine a situation in which you were a member of a jury that was hearing a murder case. The jury has already convicted the person of first-degree murder. You now proceed to the sentencing phase of the trial. Here you must decide if the crime committed warrants the death penalty. In most states, carefully defined conditions, such as the heinousness of the crime or multiple murders, are necessary for a death sentence. You were likely questioned by the attorneys about your view of the death penalty prior to being selected for the jury. Neither the prosecution nor the defense had reservations about your view. But now that it is time to actually make a decision that may result in the death of another person, you are seriously reconsidering your view. Imagine further that the prosecution's lawyer, who is pushing for the death penalty in this case, tells you in his closing argument that the Bible supports the idea of capital punishment and that you should vote accordingly. How will you vote as a jury member? Is the prosecutor correct in his assertion that the Bible supports the death penalty?

The United States is one of the few industrialized countries that still retains capital punishment. Most countries in Europe have prohibited it, while it remains in force in some Asian countries. Many Third World countries and Islamic republics apply the death penalty for a variety of crimes, not just for murder. For example, drug trafficking warrants the death penalty in countries such as Singapore and Malaysia. The latest polls in America indicate that the majority favors the death penalty in principle; that is, most Americans oppose abolishing all capital punishment as many European nations have done.

The United States Supreme Court has issued two significant decisions concerning capital punishment. The first was the case of *Furman v. Georgia* (1972), in which the Court ruled that capital punishment as currently administered in the state of Georgia violated the Eighth Amendment against cruel and inhuman punishment. In *Gregg v. Georgia* (1976), the Court upheld a death sentence for murder but made sure that juries had careful guidelines to follow in determining the appropriateness of the death sentence. After these two cases, thirty-five states enacted new laws authorizing the death penalty for certain crimes. In 1974, in the wake of growing international terrorism, Congress legislated the death penalty for murder in airline hijacking cases.

Those who oppose the death penalty are known as *abolitionists*, since they favor abolishing death sentences. Although they may disagree about the particulars of some of their arguments, all abolitionists agree that the death penalty is never morally justifiable. Those who favor capital punishment are called *retentionists*, since they favor retaining the death penalty. Not all retentionists, however, agree on the particular circumstances that justify capital punishment or on the specific arguments for their position. Inherent in the retentionist view is the sense that capital punishment has been allowed historically and that moral reservations about its use have arisen only within the last century. Thus, capital punishment has been traditionally viewed as morally legitimate and necessary in many cultures. Only in recent modern times have objections been raised to what abolitionists call a cruel and outdated form of criminal justice. This chapter specifically addresses the question, Is capital punishment ever a morally justifiable form of criminal punishment?

While most people agree on the general morality of punishment for crime, they disagree on the primary goal of criminal punishment, whether it should be retribution, deterrence, or rehabilitation. Criminal sanctions intend to evoke a respect for the law that is necessary if society is to keep from plunging into chaos. From the biblical perspective, given the reality of humankind's nature, called "total depravity" by theologians, some kind of deterrent is necessary for people to obey the law. Further, respect for those who do abide by the law demands a penalty for those who do not.

The Eighth Amendment of the Constitution protects individuals from cruel and unusual punishment. Specifically, it provides protection from the wanton and unnecessary infliction of pain. That is the reason imprisonment is the principal form of criminal punishment administered in most of the Western world, and is why the Western justice system rejects much of the Islamic style of punishment. For example, in many Muslim countries that are ruled by Islamic law, theft is punishable by having one's hand cut off, and other crimes are punishable by public floggings. The justice system of the Western world would view such practices in violation of the Eighth Amendment. Second, the Eighth Amendment protects a person from punishment that is out of proportion to the crime committed. Finally, the Constitution protects individuals from punishment without due process of law. Historically, capital punishment has not been considered cruel and inhuman punishment because when the Bill of Rights was written in 1789, every state allowed the death penalty. Its constitutionality was not substantially challenged until the Furman case in 1972.

ARGUMENTS FOR CAPITAL PUNISHMENT

The retentionist view accepts capital punishment as appropriate under some circumstances. Advocates of this view do not favor any "across the board" view of the death penalty without careful guidelines to direct the way in which death sentences are handed down. There is a wide variety of opinion concerning the circumstances which would justify use of capital punishment, but all advocates agree that in some cases, the death penalty not only can, but should be used. The arguments in favor of the retentionist view are:

1. Capital Punishment Expresses an Appropriate Demand for Justice in Society

When a crime occurs, especially one that involves the taking of innocent life, an imbalance is created in the social order. By design, societies are to function in an orderly fashion, otherwise there would be chaos, and society as an organized entity would cease to exist. In reality the demand for justice that is a significant part of criminal punishment is a demand that the imbalance in society created by crime be restored. Thus, the punishment inflicted must be proportionate to the crime committed, and thereby able to equalize the offense, restoring balance in society.

When a murder occurs and innocent life is taken, the only punishment that is able to equalize the crime is capital punishment. Only the death penalty can express society's moral outrage at the taking of innocent life. Justice being satisfied is especially important for a society dependent on due process of law instead of vigilantism to restore the imbalance created by crime.

This demand for justice is not inconsistent with the New Testament emphasis on showing mercy and forgiveness, and vengeance belonging to God. However, the abolitionists are likely correct in maintaining that when family members of a murder victim express a demand for justice, they are often masking a desire for revenge that does not reflect the teaching of Jesus. Nevertheless it is true that the victim's family has personally experienced the imbalance caused by crime, and thus their demand for justice may be a legitimate demand.

The problem with bringing Jesus' ethic of forgiveness to bear on the issue of the death penalty is the way in which abolitionists confuse personal and social ethics. The New Testament teachings on revenge and forgiveness are part of a personal ethic that forbids individuals from taking revenge and that requires forgiveness when wronged. But that ethic cannot be applied to the state. The responsibility of the state is to punish criminals, not to forgive them. The state may not exercise its role unjustly or indiscriminately, but God has given the state the responsibility of criminal punishment (Rom. 13:1–7; 1 Peter 4:15). The retentionists argue that the biblical emphasis on forgiveness, mercy, and revenge is irrelevant to the morality of the state-administered death penalty and has nothing to do with the state's legitimate responsibility to uphold criminal sanctions.

2. Capital Punishment Provides a Unique Deterrent Against Crime

This argument has a strong intuitive appeal, particularly since many societies around the world are perceived as becoming more chaotic with less respect for law and morality. Since the fear of death is virtually a universal phenomenon, the death penalty is an unparalleled deterrent for people considering a crime. Generally, the harsher the potential penalty, the greater the deterrent value of such a penalty. Deterrence increases with the severity of the penalty involved. Perhaps that is why drug trafficking is practically nonexistent in Singapore and Malaysia, since both countries mandate the death penalty for dealing drugs. It may also be the reason why the crime rate is much lower in societies under Islamic law than it is in the West, since in many cases Islamic law proscribes much harsher punishment than imprisonment. Of course, that is not to say that Islamic law is preferable, only that its severe punishment does act as a deterrent to crime.

A strong view of the sanctity of life is not inconsistent with advocating the death penalty when viewed from the perspective of a deterrent. If society is serious about the sanctity of life, then it will mandate the strongest possible deterrent to keep people from taking innocent life. To deny the legitimacy of the death penalty cheapens life by discounting the life of the murder victim. It is not inconsistent to be pro-life and also support the death penalty, since it provides a deterrent encouraging people to think about the consequence of taking the life of an innocent person. This is even more the case if the Bible allows for the death penalty as a part of the God-given responsibilities of the state.

It is undoubtedly true that the death penalty is not a deterrent for certain types of people—for example, someone who commits murder in a moment of uncontrollable rage. However, just because the death penalty is not a deterrent for some people does not mean that it is not effective for others. Exceptions, therefore, should not undermine the general rule.[1] Although the prospect of the death sentence cannot deter all murderers, that does not mean that it is unable to deter any murderers.

Although most people have a strong intuitive belief in the deterrent power of capital punishment, abolitionists will point out that statistically, there is no relationship between capital punishment and the murder rate. In fact, the murder rate is lower in Europe in countries that have abolished the death penalty. The murder rate is very complex and is influenced by many factors other than the deterrent force that the death penalty contributes (such as the socioeconomic background of the perpetrator), which makes it difficult to determine the deterrent effect of capital punishment. Thus, substantial debate surrounds the subject of the effectiveness of the death penalty as a deterrent.

For the sake of argument, let's assume that the ability of the death penalty to deter murderers is questionable. Who should get the benefit of the doubt— the potential victims or the convicted murderers? The obligation would clearly be to the potential victims instead of to convicted murderers. Thus, in light of the ambiguity of the ability of the death penalty to deter killers, society should retain the death penalty rather than unnecessarily risk the lives of potential murder victims who may die if a potentially effective deterrent is abolished.

3. The Cost of a Life Term in Prison Is Far Greater Than the Cost of the Appeals Process

Without a doubt much expense is incurred by the long appeals process that usually accompanies a death sentence. But that expense needs to be compared with the costs of adequately caring for prison inmates for the rest of their lives. The cost of housing, feeding, security, and health care, particularly as the inmate ages and requires more extensive care, easily exceeds the legal fees and court costs borne by taxpayers during any appeals process. It costs approximately $30,000 annually to provide for the needs of the average death row inmate. Assuming an average of thirty years spent in prison, taxpayers will spend about $900,000 per inmate who is serving a life sentence.

The average cost of an appeal for an inmate on death row runs about $500,000 in legal fees and various other court costs. While some appeals cost more, some cost much less, so one needs to be careful when calculating the actual costs. Some critics of the death penalty have figured the cost of the appeals process by taking the total amount spent on the appeals of all death-row inmates in a particular state, and dividing it by the number of people who have actually been executed. This results in a greatly inflated cost of appeals per inmate that likely exceeds the actual cost incurred by a specific death-sentence appeal. When calculated on the basis of total dollars spent per individual, the cost of life imprisonment is much greater than the cost of appealing a death sentence. Of course, the debate over capital punishment involves much more than the "bottom line," but the argument frequently advanced by abolitionists, that the death penalty is very expensive due to the exhaustive appeals that are normally pursued, needs to be compared with the actual costs associated with a life term in prison.

4. Capital Punishment Is Not Cruel and Unusual Punishment

The Eighth Amendment in the Bill of Rights prohibits cruel and unusual punishment, normally taken to mean punishment that inflicts pain in a wanton and unnecessary manner, as well as punishment that is disproportionate to the crime committed. Critics of the death penalty argue that it is inherently cruel and unusual punishment, yet it is administered in a way that does not involve wanton infliction of pain. In fact, it can be essentially a painless death. There is no reason the death penalty cannot be administered by lethal injection of drugs, in the same way that active euthanasia is performed. Although I do not advocate active euthanasia,[2] it is significant that its advocates commonly refer to it as a merciful process, in which a patient is painlessly put out of misery. If that can be done medically for a terminally ill patient as an act of mercy, then surely the death penalty can be administered in the same way. Thus, in response to the argument that the death sentence is cruel and unusual punishment, we maintain that it can be accomplished in a way that is neither cruel nor unusual.

Abolitionists cannot argue that the death sentence is out of proportion to the crime committed. It is not unreasonable to demand the life of a person who has taken another's life by first-degree murder. This is not to suggest that the principle of "life for life" should be followed in all crimes in which an innocent life is taken. However, in cases where someone is convicted of first-degree murder and the criteria for the death penalty are met, such as the crime being particularly heinous, the notion that the life of the murderer be exchanged for the life of the innocent victim does not constitute punishment that is out of proportion to the crime. In fact, a good case can probably be made for a life sentence being out of proportion to the crime of murder in some cases, since it would be too light a sentence.

When compared to the alternatives, the death penalty, when quickly and painlessly administered, may actually be less cruel and unusual than serving a life term in a maximum security prison. The indignities and harsh conditions of some prisons can also be considered cruel and unusual punishment. Thus, if abolitionists are concerned about the death penalty being cruel and unusual, to be consistent, they should object to a life term in prison due to its conditions.

ARGUMENTS AGAINST CAPITAL PUNISHMENT

The abolitionist view is that capital punishment is not justifiable under any circumstances. No crime, however heinous, and no view of criminal punishment can be adequate grounds for sentencing anyone to death. Here are the most common arguments used to support the abolitionist position:

1. The Death Penalty Undermines the Dignity of Persons Made in the Image of God and Cheapens Human Life

This argument suggests that the death penalty is inconsistent with Western civilization's evolving standards of decency and respect for human beings. Thus, by definition, capital punishment constitutes cruel and inhuman punishment. While the death penalty has had a long history, that history is for the most part in a barbaric past, with criminal punishment being motivated by the uncivilized desire for revenge. Most other modern nations have seen the inconsistency of capital punishment with civilized thought and have abolished the practice. In a society that so values human life, it seems inconsistent for a person to be against abortion and for the death penalty.

For the Christian, God's call is certainly to be consistently pro-life, to be concerned about life after it emerges from the womb, too. To put someone to death for any crime is an ironic way of teaching respect for human life. This is especially the case since the death penalty is given to convicted murderers, who themselves have wantonly disregarded the value of human life. If the state wants to teach a lesson about the sanctity of life, the death penalty is surely an odd way of doing it. In fact, the cold and calculating way in which this kind of judicial killing is done may even make it worse than a crime of passion. It would seem to put the state in the position of saying to its citizens, "Do what I say, not what I do." The state should not compound one wrong (the crime committed) by committing another (putting the criminal to death).

Being consistently pro-life means acknowledging that the taking of human life is a prerogative that belongs only to God. It is not something that can be done by any human being, even one acting on behalf of God. The Old Testament allowance of the death penalty is part of life under the Law for the nation of Israel. Since the church is God's chosen instrument to work out his rule today, it is no longer subject to the civil law of Old Testament Israel, and neither is civil society. Thus, all the parts of the Law that allow and even mandate the death penalty cannot be directly applied to society today.

2. Mistakes Are Irreversible

Although the Western judicial system frequently works well and justice is served, it is undeniable that miscarriages of justice do occasionally occur. Innocent people are sometimes wrongly convicted and sent to prison. In some cases, innocent people who maintained their innocence throughout their trial and appeals process have been executed. In other cases, convictions have been overturned, leaving the judicial system to acknowledge that injustices were done. When mistakes are made, the state can compensate wrongly convicted persons and release them from prison. But if the court makes a mistake in a death penalty case, nothing can be done for the person who was wrongly put to death—the state cannot bring people back to life. The death penalty has no room for second thoughts or for correcting mistakes that are an inevitable part of an imperfect judicial system. Capital punishment leaves no room for the kind of mistakes that are a well-documented part of the Western system of justice.

3. Reform Becomes Impossible

The death penalty removes the prospect of rehabilitation that could lead to an individual again becoming a productive member of society. In some cases, with the process of appealing a death sentence taking as long as it does, a convicted murderer could be a very different person at the execution date than at the date of sentencing. A person could be put to death despite being rehabilitated during the period of time spent on death row. While many criminals do not change while in prison, some clearly do, even some who are awaiting a death sentence.

For example, Paul Crump was convicted of murder in 1955 and given the death penalty. While he was in prison awaiting execution, the prison received a new warden who instituted a series of reforms aimed at the possibility of rehabilitation. It created an environment in which Crump began to change. He learned to read and write and eventually began to write material for publication. He started taking interest in his fellow prisoners and was entrusted with progressively more responsibility over them. Over a period of seven years, his change was so dramatic that the warden testified that he had no qualms about putting Crump back on the streets again, and to execute him would be wasting a changed and productive life. In 1962, the governor of Illinois commuted Crump's death sentence to life imprisonment without parole.[3]

For the Christian, reform includes the prospect of someone coming to faith in Christ while serving a life sentence, of being redeemed and having hope not only of a changed life, but also of eternal life. The death penalty removes the possibility of someone becoming reconciled to God. Since one of the primary missions of the Christian is to be an agent of reconciliation, working to bring people into a saving relationship with God (2 Cor. 5:17–21), it would seem that support of the death penalty is inconsistent with that goal.

4. Death Sentences Are Usually Accompanied by Long and Expensive Appeals

The reason for this is to insure that no mistakes are made. As a result, the appeals process normally takes from five to seven years, and costs hundreds of thousands of dollars. It creates backlogs in the appeals courts, since approximately half of the appeals heard in the courts in which the death penalty is legal, involve death-penalty appeals. In many cases, the requests for appeals hearings are requested up until the "eleventh hour," just prior to a person's execution. It would be much simpler and more cost-effective to eliminate the death penalty in favor of life sentences without the possibility of parole.

5. The Way in Which the Death Penalty Is Applied Has Inequities

Statistics demonstrate that the overwhelming majority of convicted criminals who receive death sentences are minority men, particularly blacks, who come from the lower socioeconomic classes. Rarely do whites or middle- or upper-class individuals receive the death penalty. Thus, capital punishment is unjust, discriminatory, and actually oppresses the most disadvantaged groups in society.

6. The Demand for "Justice" Is Inconsistent with Jesus' Ethic of Forgiveness and Redemption

This is not to say that society does not hold people accountable for their crimes. But the cry for "justice," which in many cases is only a facade for revenge, is inconsistent with Jesus' ethic in the Gospels and Paul's statement that vengeance belongs only to the Lord (Rom. 12:19). Significantly, the cry for "justice" is most often made by surviving family members of the slain victim. In many of these cases the family members have clearly confused justice with revenge, having little compassion for the person condemned to die. Putting someone to death cannot bring the victim back to life or compensate the family in any significant way. In reality, this emphasis on "justice" is an expression of the primitive and uncivilized desire for revenge, which is inconsistent not only with the message of the gospel, but also with the humane standards of civilized societies.

BIBLICAL TEACHING ON CAPITAL PUNISHMENT

Now that the various arguments for and against the death penalty have been outlined, the question of the contributions of Scripture to the issue must be considered. Which view, the abolitionist or the retentionist, is more consistent with the biblical teaching, and how does Scripture help to evaluate the validity of the different arguments? Once you come to a position that reflects the biblical teaching, you can then use the arguments for the chosen position to buttress the perspective of Scripture. These other arguments are important when talking about the death penalty with someone who does not accept the authority of Scripture. You must appeal to something in addition to the biblical teaching in order to make a persuasive case to that person. Of course, all of the arguments for the position that is selected must be consistent with Scripture, and it may be that on some of the arguments the Bible is silent.

On capital punishment in general, the Bible is certainly not silent. The Old Testament law in Exodus and Deuteronomy contains most of the references to capital punishment in the Bible, but references and allusions to the death penalty are also scattered throughout the New Testament. The Old Testament prescribed the death penalty for a variety of crimes. The crimes that merited capital punishment included:[4]

1. Murder (Ex. 21:12–14)[5]
2. Cursing or killing one's parent (Ex. 21:15;[6] Lev. 20:9)[7]
3. Kidnapping (Ex. 21:16; Deut. 24:7)[8]
4. Adultery (Lev. 20:10–21; Deut. 22:22)
5. Incest (Lev. 20:11–12, 14)
6. Bestiality (Ex. 22:19; Lev. 20:15–16)
7. Sodomy or homosexual sexual relations (Lev. 20:13)
8. Premarital sexual promiscuity (Deut. 22:20–21)
9. Rape of an engaged virgin (Deut. 22:23–27)[9]
10. Witchcraft (Ex. 22:18)
11. Offering human sacrifice (Lev. 20:2)
12. Offering sacrifice or worship to a false god (Ex. 22:20; Deut. 13:6–11)
13. Blasphemy (Lev. 24:11–14, 16, 23)
14. Violating the Sabbath (Ex. 35:2)
15. Showing contempt for the court (Deut. 17:8–13)

Compared to other cultures in the ancient Near East, the Old Testament actually limited the number of offenses for which capital punishment was mandated. Except for showing contempt for the court, the capital offenses can be organized around three general classes of violations: (1) violations against the sanctity of life (nos. 1–3 above); (2) violations against the source of life, primarily sexual sins (nos. 4–9); and (3) violations against the purity of the worship of God (nos. 10–14). What these have in common is that they are violations against the sacredness of life, whether directly, as in the case of murder, or indirectly, as in the case of sexual sin (sins regarding the source of life) and the purity of worship (sins against the Creator of life).

The degree to which the death penalty was actually carried out for each of these offenses is not clear from the historical accounts of the Old Testament. For example, the actual penalty for the nation of Israel for their centuries of idolatry was not death, but seventy years of exile in Babylon. The Historical Books and the Prophets contain little information on how the death penalty was administered.[10] Although the Old Testament includes scattered examples of people who received capital punishment in accordance with the guidelines of the Law, it does not provide a thorough sense of how consistently the nation of Israel followed through on the prescribed penalties for many crimes. Of course, this may simply reflect Israel's disobedience, in their unwillingness to follow the sanctions laid down by the Law.

Ironically, in the case of condemned prisoner Robert Alton Harris, many of the proponents of capital punishment carried placards citing some of these Old Testament passages that support the death penalty. Many retentionists use these texts in the Mosaic Law to support their position. But there are significant theological questions about the relevance of the Old Testament law to moral questions today. Simply because the death penalty was widely prescribed in the Law, it does not follow that the death penalty should be prescribed for civil society today. Most advocates of capital punishment recognize some limits on how far to use Mosaic Law in support of their view. For example, most retentionists only favor the death penalty for murder under certain circumstances. They do not favor the death penalty for the wide variety of crimes for which it was prescribed in the Law, such as adultery, idolatry, a rebellious child, or children that curse their parents. The retentionist who appeals to the Mosaic Law must do so consistently and support capital punishment for the crimes laid out in the Law.

The retentionist will respond that he does not support capital punishment for all the crimes mentioned in the Law. But the Old Testament texts do give solid support for the principle of the death penalty. The details of the Law may or may not be relevant to the present day, but the Law does support the idea of the death penalty. Even though one might admit that not all the details of the Law are directly, personally applicable, one must admit that at the level of broad, general principles, the Law is certainly relevant for today. For example, believers no longer offer thanksgiving offerings as the Law prescribed. But the principle of being thankful to God for his blessings and publicly expressing thanks is clearly relevant and mandatory today. Or consider the example of the Day of Atonement (Lev. 16). While the church no longer celebrates this festival, one of its underlying principles—the necessity of confessing sin—is surely applicable and mandatory today.

Interpretive caution is called for when analyzing the place of the Old Testament law for the church. This has been the subject of great debate since the beginning of the church in the New Testament era. Most evangelicals agree that the church is no longer under the Mosaic Law as a rule of life in the same way that Israel was during Old Testament times. The books of Romans, Galatians, and Hebrews all testify that the church is no longer under the Law, since its function was only that of a "tutor" to lead people to Christ (Gal. 3:24; see also Rom. 6:14–15; Heb. 10:1). The Law consisted of three parts: the moral law (Ten Commandments), the ceremonial law (laws concerning Israel's religious rituals), and the civil law (laws for maintaining order and justice in civil society). The New Testament clearly teaches that the church no longer needs the ceremonial law, since the coming of Christ revolutionized the believer's relationship with God. For example, the sacrifices are neither necessary or appropriate, because of the once-for-all sacrifice of Christ. Neither is the church under the civil law, because God deals with the church differently than he did with Old Testament Israel. The church is not "one nation under God" like Israel was. Instead the church is a transnational, transcultural, transgenerational body of believers in Jesus Christ that is not limited by ethnic or national boundaries.

Israel under the Law was a theocracy, or a society in which the law of God was automatically the law of the land. In Old Testament Israel, the people did not vote on the laws to which they were to be subject. No legislative body made the laws, and no executive branch enforced them. People could not change the laws that God had given to Moses on Mount Sinai by "constitutional amendments" or ballot initiatives. The law of God was automatically and unquestionably the law of the land. The reason for this was to make Israel a "kingdom of priests and a holy nation" (Ex. 19:6) by setting up a model society that would corporately bear witness to the reality of God. However, with the coming of Christ, the theocracy ended. The emphasis in the New Testament was on the church as a multinational body that would go out and bring the Gospel to different cultures, penetrating them and fulfilling Jesus' mandate to be the salt of the earth and the light of the world (Matt. 5:13–16).

Debate continues over the relevance of the Law today, specifically the death penalty. A growing number of thoughtful evangelicals known as the "theonomists," "Christian reconstructionists," or "dominion theologians" advocate reconstructing civil society along the guidelines of Old Testament law, and they favor the death penalty for more crimes than simply murder. Most of the critics of the reconstructionists have argued that they do not pay sufficient attention to the distinction between Israel under the Mosaic Law and the church in the present age. The critics maintain that the reconstructionists cannot sustain their system in view of the New Testament emphasis on the church not being under the Law.

Regardless of the debate on the specifics of Mosaic Law for today, most agree that the general principles that undergird the Law are relevant for today and need to be taken seriously. Of course, abolitionists and retentionists will disagree about whether capital punishment is a specific part of the Law or one of its more general principles. The principle that underlies the idea of capital punishment is the sanctity of life made in the image of God. Whether the death penalty accompanies that principle is at the heart of the debate between those who want to abolish and those who want to retain capital punishment.

One passage of Scripture prior to the Mosaic Law that links the sanctity of life and the death penalty is Genesis 9:6, which says, "Whoever sheds the blood of man, by man shall his blood be shed; for in the image of God has God made man." The general principle is "life for life" and the support for it is drawn from the overarching theological truth of man and woman being made in God's image. It is not drawn from any cultural traditions that can be subject to change. The reason that the life-for-life principle is important is that it is based on the unchanging truth of God creating human beings in his own image. The Law expanded the crimes for which the death penalty was mandated, but almost all of that expanded list can be subsumed under the heading of crimes against the sanctity of life in one form or another. The limits on the specifics of the Law rule out applying the death penalty for any crimes other than the taking of innocent life. The life-for-life principle and its link to the image of God in human beings would seem to support the retentionist argument that the sacredness of life necessitates the strongest deterrent—loss of one's own life for taking an innocent life.

The New Testament makes scant reference to the death penalty. Clearly it was in use during the time of Jesus (see John 7:53–8:11). Romans 13:4 perhaps makes the clearest reference to capital punishment when Paul states that the responsibility of civil government is to maintain civil order as God's servant. Believers and unbelievers alike are to fear the civil authorities in the case of wrongdoing, since "he [the one in authority] does not bear the sword for nothing." Retentionists will argue that Paul assumed the legitimacy of the death penalty as a part of the role of God-ordained government. Abolitionists will counter by suggesting that Paul also assumed the legitimacy of slavery, yet no one considers slavery as a moral option for today. The use of the term *sword* evokes some debate, but it is probably a figure of speech. It may be a metaphor for punishment and law enforcement in general and not necessarily capital punishment. But it may also be a figure of speech for the death penalty, since the sword was normally used as a weapon of death, and was likely seen as such by the first-century readers of the book of Romans.

Even if one accepts the life-for-life principle, one must admit that Scripture places significant limits on its application. There are some notable exceptions to the life-for-life principle. For example, the first two murderers recorded in biblical history, Cain and Lamech (Gen. 4), were not given the death penalty. Cities of refuge were established in places throughout the land of Israel to provide sanctuary for those who were guilty of manslaughter, or accidental killings. The person who committed manslaughter could flee to one of these cities and be free from any retribution. In these cases, a life was not required in exchange for the one that was taken (Num. 35:6–29). In addition, taking the life of combatants in war is clearly justified in the Old Testament, as is evident from the numerous wars in which Israel was engaged at God's specific direction. Thus, the life-for-life principle was not meant to be applied generally, but within limits laid down by the Law.

One important limit on the administration of capital punishment is described in Numbers 35:30, which says, "Anyone who kills a person is to be put to death as a murderer only on the testimony of witnesses. But no one is to be put to death on the testimony of only one witness." This part of the Law prevented someone from being put to death on the basis of circumstantial evidence alone. The term translated "witness" literally means an eyewitness. Thus, it took two eyewitnesses of a murder to justify use of the death penalty. Since this passage comes at the end of the long section concerning the cities of refuge, the term "anyone who kills a person" must be limited to someone who commits murder. The person who commits manslaughter is included in Numbers 35:30. The general principle that is important in this verse is that the judicial system must have a high degree of certainty about the guilt of the murderer. Circumstantial evidence and a single eyewitness are insufficient by themselves. Even the testimony of an eyewitness must be corroborated, and the Law was careful to insure that no one could be put to death on the basis of one eyewitness who might have ulterior motives for testifying against the accused. Circumstantial evidence leaves room for doubt, and two eyewitnesses were necessary to insure that eyewitness testimony was corroborated before someone could be put to death for murder. Thus, the degree of certainty required for the use of the death penalty exceeded that of the "reasonable doubt" standard that is used throughout the Western legal system today.

If this principle is applied consistently to capital murder cases today, one would have to admit that the majority of people on death row have been sentenced to death in a way that is not consistent with biblical guidelines. While circumstantial evidence is handled in a more sophisticated way today and is probably more reliable in assessing guilt than in the ancient world, some people on death row were convicted and sentenced without even one eyewitness of the crime, not to mention a second eyewitness to corroborate the account. Of course, this higher standard should not undermine the tradition of reasonable doubt in securing convictions. But if advocates of the death penalty desire to administer capital punishment consistently with biblical guidelines, then we must reconsider the cases of many inmates who now sit on death row.

CONCLUSION

Both the abolitionist and retentionist have good arguments to support their positions. However, it would seem that the weight of Scripture favors allowing the death penalty as long as the absolute certainty of guilt is established. Whether or not one believes in capital punishment in certain cases, what is needed is a sense of compassion for the criminal, the victim, and the victim's family. Often compassion and the hope of redemption for the convicted criminal are overlooked in the retentionist's demand for justice. The demand for justice can too easily become a demand for vengeance and retribution, actions that belong only to God. Also, the victim and the victim's family can too easily be forgotten by the abolitionist. In a desire to protect the rights of the criminal, the abolitionist may too easily forget the life-shattering damage done by the criminal's actions. Thus, Scripture commands compassion for both parties. But Scripture also reminds us of the truth that actions do have consequences. Thus the debate continues, asking the question, Should the act of murder have consequences that include the death penalty?

FOR FURTHER READING

Bedau, Hugo Adam. *The Death Penalty in America.* New York: Oxford University Press, 1992.

Vanden Haag, Ernest, and John P. Conrad. *The Death Penalty: A Debate.* New York: Plenum Press, 1983.

Black, Charles L., Jr. *Capital Punishment: The Inevitability of Caprice and Mistake.* Rev. ed. New York: Norton, 1981.

NOTES

[1]Also, a life sentence is not an effective deterrent for other types of criminals, including people who commit a murder while serving a life sentence, terrorists, and other forms of revolutionaries, as well as professional killers. This fact supports retention of the death penalty as the only adequate deterrent for some types of people.

[2]See chapter 8 for a detailed discussion of the morality of active euthanasia.

[3]Ronald Bailey, "Facing Death: A New Life Too Late," *Life* (27 July 1962): 28–29.

[4]This list is taken from R. J. Rushdoony, *The Institutes of Biblical Law* (n.p., The Craig Press, 1973), 235.

[5]The death penalty was not prescribed for accidental killing, or manslaughter.

[6]The term for "attacking" or "striking" one's parent refers to striking with a mortal blow and is the equivalent of killing one's parent.

[7]Related to this is the command that the incorrigibly delinquent, criminally rebellious child be stoned to death. See Deuteronomy 21:18–21.

⁸It appears from these two texts that the main reason for kidnapping was not to exact a ransom, but to sell the person into slavery or to keep the person as a slave.

⁹The reason that this specific crime carries the death penalty is due to the way in which betrothal was viewed as the essential equivalent of marriage in the ancient world. Thus, to have sexual relations with an engaged person was the virtual equivalent of adultery and carried the same penalty.

¹⁰One of the few references to the death penalty occurs in Ezekiel 18:12–13, where the crimes of murder, adultery, oppression of the poor, keeping a pledge, idolatry, and usury are mentioned as deserving the death penalty. However, it is not clear from this passage if the person is to die from a judicial verdict of capital punishment or if a premature death is one of the anticipated consequences of a lifestyle characterized by these things.

10

SEXUAL ETHICS

In April 1984, *Time* magazine boldly declared that "the sexual revolution is over!"[1] With the onslaught of AIDS producing widespread fears about casual sex, a new era of sexual restraint had been proclaimed. Yet one wonders if the sexual revolution that burst onto the scene in the sixties with such passion was actually over, or if the changes in values had simply become more entrenched in society and less publicized. If the sexual revolution was over, why are sexually transmitted diseases and unwanted pregnancies, especially among teenagers, now at an all-time high? Why are there more abortions being performed today than in any other period since it became legal in 1973? Why are reports out of the nation's junior high and high schools indicating that the average age of a person's first sexual encounter is getting younger and younger, even as young as age 13? Why do further studies show that the great majority of teenagers have been sexually active long before graduation from high school? Careless, promiscuous sex is on the decline due to fear of AIDS, but there are few signs of a return to the biblical concept of sex within monogamous marriage. Rather, it seems that many of the values of the sexual revolution have entered the mainstream of society's way of thinking about sex. Even among Christian couples contemplating marriage, abstinence until marriage is considered somewhat outdated, and it cannot be assumed that committed Christian couples are not sleeping together.

Imagine that you are a pastor in a local church who is conducting a premarital counseling workshop for engaged couples and couples considering marriage. The topic for discussion this evening is the sexual relationship in marriage. Part of your agenda is to present the case for abstinence prior to marriage. How would you do that—both biblically and with other supporting reasons that are not dependent on the Bible for those in your group who may not recognize the Bible's authority? In this chapter, we will give you some direction for leading such a discussion. We will explore the biblical teaching on sex by outlining the key texts of Scripture that address the subject. We will then apply that teaching to the two most controversial areas in Christian sexual ethics—homosexuality and premarital sex.

BIBLICAL TEACHING ON SEXUAL RELATIONSHIPS

Much to the surprise of people who have never read the Bible carefully, there is a wealth of material in Scripture that addresses the sexual relationship. God did not appear to be bashful or embarrassed when he spoke about sex in his Word, and his teaching is both clear about the need for restraint and explicit about the passion of sex when expressed within the proper parameters. Central biblical passages include Genesis 2:18–25, where the notions of sex and marriage are both introduced; Leviticus 18, a listing of illicit sexual relationships; the Song of Solomon, which passionately celebrates sex in marriage; 1 Corinthians 5–6, which addresses the sexual excesses of the church in Corinth; and selected statements in the Epistles that encourage avoiding sexual immorality.[2]

Genesis

In Genesis 1–2, there is a critical link between the man and woman in the context of marriage and the sexual relationship that will eventually result in the procreation of children. Though there are two creation accounts in Genesis 1–2, they are complementary and not contradictory. Genesis 1 provides the broad overview of creation. Genesis 2 views the most important aspects of creation in more detail— the creation of man and woman and their relationship to each other and to God.

In Genesis 2:18–25, both marriage and sexual relations are instituted. Thus, this account actually fits into the broader overview of Genesis 1. It occurs after the divine initiative in 1:26 to create mankind and prior to the command to the newly formed couple in 1:28 to begin procreating and populating the earth. The first command given to them is the command to reproduce in 1:28, clearly a result of their becoming "one flesh" in 2:24.

Most scholars believe Genesis 2:24 to be the first reference to the institution of marriage. There are various reasons for this. First, the way that this text is quoted in other places in the New Testament makes it clear that it was originally intended for married couples (Matt. 19:5; Eph. 5:31).[3] Second, the term *leave* is used to suggest that a man and woman who will be intimately related (as the term *cleave* suggests) are to separate from their families of origin and begin a new family unit of their own—contrary to ancient Near Eastern cultural practice in which the bride moved in with the groom and his family. Third, the concept of one flesh clearly involves a sexual unity (though not limited to that), and throughout the Scripture it is evident that sexual relations are restricted to the setting of marriage. Thus, it would appear that 2:24 is where marriage as a divine institution begins.

Placing the more specific account of the creation of male and female and the subsequent institution of marriage back into the broader context of the creation in Genesis 1:26, the command to procreate, which presumes sexual relationships, is thus given to Adam and Eve in the context of their leaving, cleaving, and becoming one flesh—in the context of marriage. This sets the precedent for heterosexual marriage and sexual relationships for the purpose of procreation within that setting. Though it does not suggest that every male and female must be joined in marriage, it does indicate that marriage is to be between male and female, and that only in marriage are sexual relationships and procreation to occur. In other words, God has established sex and procreation to be restricted to heterosexual couples in marriage. There is continuity between God's creation of the family in Genesis 1–2, sexual expression, and the command to procreate within that context.[4] This structure of the family seems to be basic to God's creative design, however extended the family became due to cultural and economic factors.

The term *one flesh* is widely considered to refer to sexual oneness. Since the Hebrew term *basar*, translated "flesh" is used, it appears to emphasize the physical side of the married couple's relationship. Though it certainly also refers to a spiritual and emotional oneness experienced by couples, had the author wanted to stress that and downplay the sexual aspect, he could have used the term *nephesh*, translated "soul." Whatever else it signifies, the use of *basar* clearly involves the sexual relationship. Since it is linked with the terms *leave* and *cleave* in the passage that institutes marriage, it makes sense to say that the Bible intends sex within the bounds of marriage. When Genesis 2:24 is cited in both Matthew 19:5 and Ephesians 5:31, it is clear that the original design for the one flesh relationship of sex was intended for marriage, since both contexts indicate that married couples are in view.

The Seventh Commandment, "You shall not commit adultery" (Ex. 20:14; Deut. 5:18), was designed to protect this creation ideal for family life that was instituted in Genesis 1–2. Though adultery (sex between a married person and someone other than his or her spouse) does not encompass all the prohibited sexual relationships in Scripture, it is central since it involves breaking the intimate one flesh connection with one's spouse. Most cultures around the world have some moral rules to protect the family, and a prohibition against adultery is widely recognized since it breaks the sacred covenant of marriage. The prophets bring out this aspect of adultery by routinely comparing Israel's spiritual breach of covenant with God in their idolatry to the violation of the marriage covenant that occurred when adultery was committed. Just as individuals broke a marriage covenant with their partners when guilty of adultery, so Israel was guilty of spiritual adultery when, through idolatry, they broke their spiritual covenant with God. The irony of the adultery imagery to describe Israel's spiritual condition was that often idolatry did involve adultery. Religious prostitution was a regular part of idolatrous worship in the ancient world and was part of its appeal. So the prophets were correct both literally and figuratively to describe Israel's idolatry as spiritual adultery (see, for example, Jer. 3:6–10; Hos. 1–3).

Leviticus

There were other places in the Old Testament Law that were designed to safeguard this creation model of the family. For example, the prohibitions against illicit sexual relations assumed that the creation model for sex within marriage was normative and functioned to preserve the family from breakdown. In the sexual code in Leviticus 18, every sexual relationship except that between a heterosexual couple in marriage is prohibited. All forms of incest (sex with a relative), homosexuality, adultery, cultic prostitution, premarital sex and even bestiality (sex with an animal) are forbidden. Though there is no specific reason given for these prohibitions in Leviticus 18, it is clear that these violate the normative structure of the family that is rooted in creation. Keeping the creation ideal of the family intact and free from influences that would undermine it was considered central to the preservation of Israel as a society set apart as God's holy nation (Ex. 19:6).

Song of Solomon

In contrast to the Law, which stresses sexual prohibitions, the Song of Solomon celebrates the beauty of sex in marriage.[5] Throughout the Song there are exquisite descriptions of the lover and his beloved bride, particularly in 4:1–10, where Solomon describes the body of his bride in passionate detail prior to the consummation of their marriage (see also Song 5:10–16; 7:1–9). The imagery for sexual enjoyment is vivid and includes things like the choicest foods, drinks and spices, and water from the freshest springs and fountains (4:11–5:1). It is seen as a sensual delight, entirely blessed by God and encouraged to be enjoyed.

However, there is restraint in the premarital period in 1:1–3:5. During courtship, there is a normal and natural longing and deep desire for the other person, but restraint is required even though it is difficult. It is further significant that the book progresses in a rough chronological order. The book can be divided into four major sections: courtship (1:1–3:5), marriage and consummation (3:6–5:1), conflict (5:2–6:3), and reconciliation (6:4–8:14). Restraint is exercised during courtship (2:7, 3:5) and sex is not fully enjoyed until after the wedding procession (3:6–7) and ceremony (3:11). The book appears to assume that sex is to be enjoyed only within the parameters of marriage.

New Testament

The New Testament consistently appeals for the believer to avoid sexual immorality. For example, in 1 Thessalonians 4:3, Paul equates avoiding sexual immorality with the will of God for the believer, one of the few occasions in which it is stated that directly. Similarly, the believer is to avoid even the hint of immorality since it is inconsistent with his or her position as one of God's people (Eph. 5:3). Sexual immorality is seen as a part of the old life of the believer (Col. 3:5), and they are discouraged from associating with those who boast in such immorality (1 Cor. 5:9). Marriage is to be kept pure, particularly in the sexual expression (Heb. 13:4). Sexual immorality is also included in many of the "vice lists"—lists of specific sins that the believer is to avoid (Matt. 15:19; Mark 7:21–23; 1 Cor. 6:9–11; Gal. 5:19–21; Rev. 21:8).

First Corinthians 5–6 is one of the New Testament texts that develops its teaching in more detail, presumably because the church at Corinth was having significant problems with sexual immorality in the church. They seemed to be proud of their accommodation to the sexual morality of the Corinthian culture (1 Cor. 5:1–2), and it appears that many in the church came to faith in Christ from a background of immorality (1 Cor. 6:9–11). Paul rebuked both their incestuous relationships and the pride that accompanied it (1 Cor. 5:1–13). Then in 6:12–20, he laid some theological groundwork for his admonition for sexual purity.

Paul gives three theologically grounded reasons the believer should avoid sexual immorality. First, God the Father will raise the body to immortality at his second coming (1 Cor. 6:14). Because of this, the body is important and should be treated with as much care as the soul. With this point, Paul is combating a view that dominated the Greek culture of the day—that the soul was all that mattered about a person. There were for the Greeks, therefore, two options for the body: either the person could severely discipline the body in order to keep it from interfering with the soul's development (also known as asceticism), or he or she could do with one's body whatever one desired (hedonism), since the body was of no consequence to the soul. The Corinthian culture had clearly chosen the latter option, and sexual license was commonplace as a result. Paul is suggesting that there is as much of a future for a person's body as there is for his or her soul. Thus, a person's body is to be maintained with the utmost purity and care since God will redeem it at Christ's second coming.

A second reason for sexual purity is that believers are one with Christ the Son (6:15–17). Since believers are "members of Christ" (6:15) and one with him, the believer should never become one with someone other than his or her spouse. This is especially true if, in sexual immorality, the believer is actually participating in idolatry through religious prostitution, as was the case in Corinth (6:16). Not only does immorality result in breaking the one-flesh relationship with one's spouse, it also violates a person's relationship with Christ by joining him to the person with whom one has sex.

A third reason Paul gives for avoiding sexual immorality is that the believer's body is the temple of the Holy Spirit (6:19). Thus, it is to be revered and cared for, not abused or used in any way that would compromise a person's testimony for Christ. Ultimately, the body does not belong to the believer since it has been purchased by God at the cost of his Son's death. Therefore, the believer does not have the right to do with his or her body whatever he or she desires. The believer's body belongs to God and is to be used to honor him, chiefly by avoiding sexual immorality (6:19–20).

In 1 Corinthians 6:12–20, sexual immorality is prohibited because it violates the believer's relationship with all three members of the Trinity. God the Father will raise the body (6:14), thus it is to be considered sacred. The believer is one with Christ the Son (6:15), and thus should not join a part of him sexually to someone other than one's spouse. The believer is also a temple of the Holy Spirit (6:19), and thus the body is to be used for his honor. The way Paul outlines this passage shows that sexual immorality, apart from damaging a person's witness for Christ, also violates the essence of a person's relationship with Christ.

HOMOSEXUALITY

Imagine that you are sitting on a panel discussion, perhaps even on a program like *Donahue* or *Oprah Winfrey,* and you are representing the Christian community in the discussion. Others on the panel include a militant gay rights activist and a Christian homosexual couple who claim that their homosexual lifestyle is consistent with Scripture. They are attending a branch of the Metropolitan Church of Christ, a denomination of gay churches, and are genuinely trying to grow in their faith. Your position is that homosexuality is not a valid lifestyle and you must defend it both to the Christian couple and to the militant gay activist who cares little about what the Bible says. When the microphone comes to you for you to present your position, what will you say? With what arguments will you defend your view?

There are more than 800 congregations in the Metropolitan Church of Christ today. This shows that many homosexuals care increasingly about the spiritual side of life and what the Bible teaches about their lifestyle. More and more books are being written that attempt to harmonize homosexuality and biblical teaching. Objections to the traditional Christian opposition to homosexuality are now coming from within the Christian community as well as from more militant gay activist groups. The church, therefore, must respond to both groups if its position on homosexuality is to have credibility.

The Two Sides

In the debate over homosexuality, there are two clear positions that often are presented as extremes with a good deal of rhetoric. The traditional Christian position is that homosexuality is a sinful, perverse deviation from God's created order. Purely and simply it is a choice. It is a perversion from which the person who is suffering from it must be healed, either miraculously or through the longer term processes of prayer, spiritual growth, and therapy. Homosexuality ultimately issues from a demonic source, and the Bible unequivocally condemns both the desire for someone of the same sex and any physical expression of that desire.

By contrast, the advocates of homosexuality affirm that it is natural for that person, and thus a part of the natural order that is ordained by God. It is not a choice but a genetic predisposition. Homosexual relationships can be loving expressions of commitment, though advocates admit that this is not always the case either in homosexual or heterosexual relationships. Any emphasis on healing the homosexual is a waste of time since the attraction for the same sex, once developed, is irreversible. Far from being of a demonic source, homosexuality is seen as God's gift for relationships in the same way as heterosexual relationships. Rather than believing that the Bible condemns every instance of homosexuality, they see selective condemnation of particularly perverse homosexuality, similar to the way the Bible would condemn perverse heterosexuality. They claim that the Bible is actually silent on homosexual relationships that are loving and committed expressions of care.

Defining the Term Homosexual

The term *homosexual* can mean many things. Exactly what kind of person is in view with the label "homosexual"? First, it can refer to a true homosexual, one whose sexual preference has been inverted and who only prefers members of the same sex. This is what most people mean by the term, yet it constitutes only about 5 percent of the total persons to whom the term homosexual may apply. The latest studies indicate that only 1 or 2 percent of the total adult population are homosexual by sexual inversion. Most of the militant gay activists fit into this category. Second, it can refer to someone who is bisexual—someone who has an interchangeable sexual preference.

Third, it can refer to someone called a situational homosexual. This person has had some homosexual experience, but does not have a predominant homosexual orientation. He or she has experienced homosexuality in some form, however limited. For example, a relationally needy person will sometimes use a homosexual affair to meet his or her needs for affirmation and love. Here the sexual attraction is not the controlling factor, but the person acts out his or her neediness in a homosexual relationship. The person is attracted to another person because his or her needs are being met, not because of the person's gender. A second example is in the preteenage exploration of one's sexuality. Some of that experimentation may take place with another member of the same sex. This is not particularly uncommon; studies show that up to 30 percent of adolescents have experimented in some way with a person of the same sex.

Myths About Homosexuality

These categories help dispel some of the myths of homosexuality, the first of which proposes that all homosexuals are effeminate. Though many homosexuals are readily identifiable, many are not, and there is nothing in their public lives that would outwardly indicate their homosexuality.

A second myth is that all homosexuals are promiscuous perverts that go from bath house orgies to gay bar restrooms to other one-night stands in search of sexual pleasure. Though it is true that the average homosexual has had a relatively high number of sexual partners, to characterize all homosexuals as perverts is certainly unfair. There are also loving, supportive, and committed homosexual relationships.

A third myth asserts that homosexuality is always a chosen way of life. It may actually be learned developmentally and therefore be neither hereditary nor chosen. Adjustment to the homosexual subculture is often difficult, though for many homosexuals that community may be the first place they have felt accepted without having to hide their homosexuality. Many homosexuals want desperately to fit into the heterosexual culture. A widespread homosexual fantasy is to be heterosexual and happily married with children.

A final myth is that homosexuality occurs only in the more artistic professions. Though there may be a disproportionate percentage of homosexuals in those professions as opposed to the rest of society, homosexuality cuts across most cultural boundaries. It is found even in such "masculine" circles as the National Football League.

Causes of Homosexuality

How does a person acquire a disposition toward homosexuality? No single, specific cause can be pinpointed with any precision, and there is currently great debate about the evidence for a genetic link. The gay community clearly hopes that some genetic predisposition will be found by researchers working on the Human Genome Project. This project is sponsored by the National Institutes of Health and is attempting to map the entire human genetic code, searching for all available genetic links to disease and behavior.

There do seem to be certain developmental factors that many homosexuals have in common, indicating that a homosexual orientation may be learned rather than chosen. These factors apply primarily to male homosexuality, and not female homosexuality, or lesbianism. First, there is the combination of an angry or absent father and a close bonding and/or domineering mother. This is especially a factor if the boy becomes an emotional substitute "husband" for his mother. Second, the boy does not enter the "boy becoming man" social processes with pleasure. He either does not participate or, if he does, he does not enjoy it, and for that reason is derided by his peers. (Another way to put this is that the boy does not have available outlets to release aggression, as through sports, for example.) Finally, the boy's introduction to his sexuality is a crucial factor. Two critical key questions are, With whom was he introduced to sex? and Was it pleasurable? If he was introduced to sex with a male who enjoyed it, that may contribute toward a homosexual orientation.

Though homosexuality is a diverse phenomenon and there is no clear pattern for its development, there may be some common elements that help pinpoint the way in which it developed.

Biblical Response to Homosexuality

With that background, one can go to the Bible with compassion and some understanding of the phenomena of homosexuality. In the Old Testament, homosexuality is unequivocally condemned. Homosexual sex is prohibited in the Law and is called an abomination (Lev. 18:22; 20:13). However, of all the illicit sexual relations listed in Leviticus 18, homosexuality is not singled out as being any different or more worthy of condemnation than other sexual sins. God's attitude toward homosexuality is dramatically portrayed in the judgment on Sodom and Gomorrah (Gen. 19). Though homosexuality is not the only thing that contributed to their destruction, it was certainly a major factor. When the prophet Ezekiel draws the parallel between the nation of Israel under judgment for their idolatry and the judgment of Sodom and Gomorrah, he includes among the sins of Sodom the "detestable things," using the same term as in Leviticus 18 to describe homosexual acts. During the idolatrous times of the Judges, a parallel to Sodom and Gomorrah is recorded. Both occurrences contain requests for homosexual gang rape, a clear perversion, even according to homosexuals who hold that the Bible allows wholesome homosexual relationships. It is not fair to characterize all homosexuals as sex-starved individuals who want to have gang rape with male visitors. But it is also not fair to conclude that nonperverted homosexual sex is justifiable simply because these two narratives describe degenerate perverts. The law condemned all homosexual sex and does not distinguish between perverted and wholesome homosexual relationships.

The central New Testament passage that addresses homosexuality is Romans 1:24–27. It is set in the context of the condemnation of those who reject God as revealed in creation or through natural law. It is part of Paul's broader argument for the universality of sin and judgment, setting the need for the believer to be justified by faith in Christ's atoning death on the cross, as outlined in Romans 4–5. Those who reject the available knowledge of God and choose instead to worship the Greek and Roman idols have lifestyle consequences that they cannot avoid. One of these consequences is homosexual behavior. Paul implicitly appeals to the natural order of creation to condemn homosexual behavior (Rom. 1:27). Male and female were created with an innate tendency toward

207

opposite sex attraction, but because of sin, the human race developed the potential for homosexuality. This potential is often realized when certain developmental factors are present. Because of the reality of sin, every person has the potential for homosexuality in the same way that we have the potential for any other kind of sin that the Bible describes.

The reference to homosexuality in this passage has been interpreted in a variety of ways. First, it has been taken to refer to homosexual male religious prostitutes in idolatrous worship ceremonies. Therefore, idolatry, not homosexual relations, is condemned. This is parallel to the description of homosexuality in Deuteronomy 23:17–18, where religious prostitution of all types is condemned. Since idolatry is in the immediate context of the condemnation of homosexual sex, this adds strength to this view.

A second view is that Paul is condemning true heterosexuals who are engaging in homosexual acts. This view comes out of Paul's emphasis on homosexuality as being unnatural. Many homosexuals, however, argue that their orientation is natural for them. An example of homosexuality that is not natural would be true heterosexuals who perform homosexual acts.

A third view is that Paul is condemning perverse expressions of homosexuality as opposed to the loving, committed relationships that are possible for homosexuals. Thus Paul's condemnation would be parallel to the way he would condemn heterosexuals for perverse expressions of their sexual identity.

A fourth view is that Paul intended to condemn all homosexual behavior. Paul's appeal to a universal truth about sexual relations linked to the order of creation prevents someone from seeing this passage limited to only certain kinds of homosexual behavior and from seeing Paul as culturally outdated in his teaching. Rather, it provides an appropriate context for a judgment on all homosexual relationships.

In applying these passages that forbid homosexuality, some suggest that it is important to make a distinction between homosexual attraction and homosexual sexual relations. There is a difference between being homoerotic, that is, being attracted to a person of the same sex, and homosexual, that is, acting sexually on that attraction. It may be helpful to see this distinction paralleled with heterosexual relationships. For a married person to be attracted to a person of the opposite sex other than his or her spouse is not sin. It becomes sin when that attraction is acted upon, either in lust, which is the process of mentally having sex with a person, or in sexual overtures. Likewise, it may be that the homosexual attraction in itself is not sin, though at variance with the order of creation. But when that attraction gives way to lust and ultimately to sexual activity, it is sin. Some argue that what the Bible condemns in homosexual relationships it also condemns in heterosexual relationships—lust and sexual involvement outside marriage. Thus the options for the Christian homosexual would be the same as for the Christian heterosexual—either abstinence or heterosexual sex in marriage. Some Christians who struggle with their sexual identity have grasped this distinction and rejected the gay lifestyle while attempting to work out issues related to their sexual identity. It may be that failure to recognize this distinction between being homoerotic and homosexual has kept the church from being a more accepting place for those struggling with their sexual orientation.

Curing Homosexuality

This above distinction may also be helpful in discussing a cure for homosexuality. It is common for gay activists to hold that cures rarely, if ever, happen. But they are using the term *cure* in a way that is not used in treating other kinds of struggles and addictions. There is a critical distinction between being cured of the behavior and cured of the impulse. To be cured in the most common psychological and medical usage is to be content apart from the specific behavior in question. For example, the alcoholic who is cured has not necessarily lost the craving for alcohol. Rather, he has learned to be content apart from drinking. The same is true for the homosexual. He or she may not be cured of the attraction for persons of the same sex, but is content apart from acting out sexually on that attraction. On this view, it is possible for someone who has developed a homosexual orientation to follow Christ and abstain from homosexual behavior in the same way that an alcoholic can follow Christ and stop drinking.

Whether or not a person accepts this distinction, it is important that the church not view homosexuals as somehow outside the boundaries of God's grace. The church needs to be a place where those struggling with their sexual identity can come and receive grace, truth, and compassion. Those who would more aggressively promote a gay rights agenda that would compel society to accept homosexuality as an equally valid lifestyle must be confronted. Most civil rights of homosexuals must be protected too. For example, it would seem unjust for homosexuals to be objects of discrimination in the workplace (though it is certainly appropriate for Christian institutions to hire in a manner consistent with their doctrine). But the aggressive gay rights agenda, which seeks for much more than simply societal tolerance of homosexuality, must be resisted.

Responding in Addition to Scripture

Crafting an argument against homosexuality that is addressed to a secular audience, such as the gay activist on the panel on which you are serving, is more difficult than interpreting the biblical teaching. Three primary arguments have been attempted. The first is a public health argument. It is based on the statistics that clearly link the transmission of AIDS to homosexual sexual activity. Proponents of this argument insist that homosexuality constitutes a threat to public health and thus it should not be embraced. While one should be honest with the statistics and admit that there is a significant link between certain types of behavior (unprotected sex, particularly homosexual sex, and intravenous drug use) and the spread of AIDS, one should also admit that AIDS has spread to the heterosexual community, although with far less incidence than in the homosexual community. Further, at best this argument would seem to support being careful about all unprotected sex—not just homosexual sex, though some suggest that homosexual sex is more likely to spread AIDS than heterosexual sex.

A second argument is a historical argument. It is based on the precedent that no civilization has ever survived the destruction of the traditional family. Homosexuality as a valid lifestyle clearly undermines the model of the family that has characterized most societies throughout the history of civilization—husband, wife, and children. Thus to ensure the best prospects for the flourishing of society, one of its major institutions, the family, should be encouraged, and any competing institutions that tend to undercut the family should be resisted. However, historical arguments, though they can be very persuasive, always have the possibility of exceptions to which the gay rights activist may appeal.

A third argument comes from the moral philosophy of Immanuel Kant, whose system was based on the categorical imperative or the principles deduced by reason alone.[6] One way in which Kant formulated his moral duties was in terms of what he called the principle of universalizability—if a certain moral rule can be comfortably made universal, then and only then is it a valid moral rule. For example, Kant held that truth telling should be a universal moral duty, because it was necessary to a functioning society. If people stopped telling the truth, then the prospect for meaningful communication in society would be slim because one could never know if he or she was being told the truth. To put it differently, what might happen if no one held to the moral rule in question? As in the case of truth telling, social relations would be severely damaged. The same kind of argument might be applied to homosexuality. What would happen if no one obeyed the moral rule that prohibited homosexuality? It is likely that procreation would decline significantly unless reproductive technologies were employed on a massive scale, and the existence of the next generation might be at stake. Of course, one must adhere to Kant's ethical system, and though there are many moral philosophers who do not, his way of fashioning moral duties has survived in the popular culture.

Making the biblical case against homosexuality persuasive to a secular audience that has little regard for biblical authority is difficult, particularly in view of the aggressive gay rights movement and a growing societal tolerance for homosexuality. But that does not mean that further attempts to make the Bible's teaching on homosexuality persuasive to the broader culture should not be undertaken.

PREMARITAL SEX AND ABSTINENCE

The general term in the New Testament that is translated "sexual immorality" is the Greek term *porneía*, from which the English word "pornography" is derived. Though at times it does refer to a more specific type of sexual immorality,[7] in general it refers to all illicit sexual relations. These are listed in Leviticus 18, as we discussed earlier, and the New Testament repeatedly urges the believer to avoid sexual immorality and thus restrict sexual expression to marriage (Eph. 5:3; Col. 3:5; 1 Thess. 4:3; Heb. 13:4). In the Song of Solomon, the various figures of speech used to describe sex also suggest that sex is reserved for marriage. Solomon compares sex to a garden, spring, and fountain, and compares his bride's virginity to a locked garden, sealed spring, and enclosed fountain (Song 4:12–5:1). Prior to his wedding night, he realizes that he cannot enjoy the fruit of her sexual garden or the water of her sexual spring and fountain. After they have consummated their marriage, he speaks of having entered the garden and tasted its choice fruits and spices. Thus the way that the sexual imagery is used in the Song of Solomon strongly suggests that full sexual enjoyment is not an option prior to the marriage ceremony.

Sexual Purity Versus Safe Sex

It is one thing to outline the biblical case for premarital sexual restraint. But it quite another to apply it consistently in a society that is inundated with sexual stimuli. Even with the growing fear of AIDS and other sexually transmitted diseases, as well as the long-standing fear of pregnancy (though less today due to the availability of abortion), practicing sexual purity is still a significant challenge. People are being encouraged to practice "safe sex" and there is a great deal of debate about how *safe* sex can actually be. Public awareness of the failure rate of many types of condoms is growing. Condoms fail to prevent sperm penetration in roughly 15 percent of all cases, and it is becoming more clear that many brands of condoms are incapable of preventing HIV transmission and fail to do so in as many as one-third of the cases. The following illustration suggests that condoms may not provide entirely safe sex. A few years ago, a professional association of approximately eight hundred sex therapists was asked if they would have sex with a partner whom they knew was infected with HIV, using only a condom for protection. None of them responded that they would. As advertised in society, safe sex may not be nearly as safe as its advocates would like the public to believe. There is even a sense that the term *safe sex* is an oxymoron. One writer put it this way:

> Consider the notion of "safe sex." Surely, the two words are ludicrously contradictory. Sex can be many things: dark, mysterious, passionate, wild, gentle, even reassuring, but it is not safe. If it is, it is not very likely to be sexy. How to abandon oneself to another, how to give your body into someone else's care and control, and remain safe? Sex is dangerous. It's supposed to be.[8]

In moving toward sexual self-control, it is important to realize that individuals are capable of controlling their sexual urges in the same way that they are capable of controlling any other desire. Abstinence is routinely dismissed as unrealistic today because adolescents are simply going to "do it." But such language is actually insulting to teenagers because it suggests that they are incapable of self-control in this area. It likens them to animals for whom sex is qualitatively different than for human beings. Individuals do have choices about sex, and the choices are more than whether or not to use adequate protection. They also have choices about whether or not to become sexually involved.

Given the way sex outside marriage is viewed in the popular culture, making the right choice to keep its full expression within the boundaries of marriage is difficult. Many people who desire to keep themselves for marriage are thus viewed as hopelessly out of date, belonging to the Victorian era of a few centuries ago. And many who desire sexual self-control are frustrated by their inability to maintain it consistently. There is a great deal of encouragement for sexual self-control in Christian circles, but not much advice on how to make it a reality. The secular culture treats abstinence as though it were not a possibility, and its main concern is with preventing pregnancy and sexually transmitted diseases.

Winning the Battle for Sexual Purity

There are a variety of things that a person can do in the battle for sexual purity. First, it is important to avoid sexually tempting situations in the same way that one should avoid other potentially morally compromising situations. Paul puts it in a simple and straightforward way when he says to "flee ... immorality" (1 Cor. 6:18). The comparison of this advice with Peter's later advice to believers to resist Satan (1 Peter 5:8) shows the power of the sexual temptation. Believers are encouraged to *resist* Satan, but to *flee* sexual temptation. This involves conscious decisions to limit one's intake of sexually stimulating media and avoid situations in which a person could end up sexually involved. This may also require some sort of accountability from a trustworthy friend to whom permission is given to ask hard questions about what is happening in one's sexual life.

A second element of sexual self-control is to realize that sex is not the glue that holds a relationship together. If anything, sex is the dessert and the main course of the meal of marriage is the emotional and spiritual relationship of the couple. Sex is simply not like the media portrays it. It seems that on television or in the movies, every time a couple goes behind closed doors it is assumed that fireworks and magic result. Rarely does one get the impression that anything disappointing ever happens in the bedroom. Yet many married couples will testify that sex, particularly without emotional intimacy and commitment, is overrated. A healthy sexual relationship does not happen like spontaneous combustion. It takes work, adjustments, and communication—none of which are ever portrayed in the media. It is not unusual for the average married couple to take up to a year to initially adjust to each other sexually, and it is not uncommon for couples who have been happily married for five to ten years to say that they are just now beginning to enjoy the sexual aspect of their marriage. There are actually more conflicts about sex than about anything else in marriage except money. It is hardly the glue that keeps a relationship together, even though it is treated as such by the popular culture.

A third element in the move toward sexual self-control is to accurately assess the damage that premature sexual relations can do to a relationship. For example, when a couple gets sexually involved, the physical aspect of the relationship normally begins to dominate and can short-circuit the development of the emotional and spiritual sides of the relationship—the ones that are important for long-term sexual enjoyment. Most sexual problems in relationships are not physical, but relational in origin, and the solution has nothing to do with sexual technique. It lies with relational harmony and contentment. Couples who get sexually involved prior to marriage risk mortgaging long-term sexual development for short-term pleasure if a dominant sexual aspect of the relationship stunts emotional and spiritual growth. In addition, for many Christian couples there is a good deal of guilt involved in premarital sex, and for many couples there is often pain and frustration if the relationship does not last. There can also be a loss of objectivity about the direction of the relationship when the physical aspect is dominant since sexual involvement often communicates a greater sense of commitment than may actually exist. Finally, sex before marriage can sow seeds of mistrust. If a person cannot control his or her sexual desires before marriage, then what assurances are there that he or she can control sexual desire after marriage when the complicating factors of pregnancy and children often enter in for the first time? Control of sexual desire thus tends to build trust in one's partner that is essential to good sexual enjoyment in the long term.

Restoring Sexual Purity

Frequently in discussions of sexual morality, one's moral obligation is clear but the person is disturbed by failure to live up to that obligation. Of more interest than how to maintain sexual self-control is the question of what to do when someone sins sexually. An extension of the garden imagery for sex in the Song of Solomon is particularly helpful here in addressing a lack of sexual self-control (Song 4:12–5:1). It may be that a person has unwisely allowed someone to enter his or her garden and as a result the garden is in a state of disarray. Or worse, it may be that someone has forced himself or herself into a person's garden through rape or sexual abuse. Solomon's bride kept her garden locked until the appropriate time, but she is the ideal and many people's actual experience falls discouragingly short of that. If someone came to you and asked what to do about sexual failure, perhaps you could tell him or her something like this:

> If I were a gardener and someone had broken into my garden and overturned
> the flowers and fairly well spoiled it, I suppose I would be the best person to

go in and fix it and place things back like I wanted them. I could accept the problem and restore the garden to its original beauty. You are the garden of your Creator. He is the One who made you and He knows how you are best prepared for marriage. He can accept the problem and remake the garden. He can accept the broken flowers of your life and forgive them. And He can give you instructions for your part in the restoration of the garden.[9]

Even though physical virginity cannot be restored, it appears that emotional and spiritual virginity can be. In his forgiveness and grace, God can heal the emotional scars of past sexual promiscuity and restore a person's hope for a fulfilling sexual relationship in marriage. The individual's responsibility is not to let anyone in the garden while the divine gardener is at work restoring it. One woman who wrote to *Dear Abby* put it this way:

Dear Abby:

I was raped by a relative when I was a teenager. I spent the next five years searching desperately for love through numerous brief sexual encounters. I felt cheap and dirty and was convinced that no one could love or want me. Then I met a very special young man who convinced me that God loved me just the way I was, and that I was precious in His sight. I then let go of my burdensome past, and by accepting God's forgiveness, I started on the long road to forgiving myself. It works. Believe me.

Free and Happy

FOR FURTHER READING

White, John. *Eros Defiled*. Downers Grove, Ill.: InterVarsity Press, 1977.

Glickman, S. Craig. *A Song for Lovers*. Downers Grove, Ill.: InterVarsity Press, 1976.

Grenz, Stanley. *Sexual Ethics*. Dallas: Word, 1990.

NOTES

[1]*Time,* 12 April 1984.

[2]Paul's teaching on homosexuality in Romans 1:18–32 will be discussed in this chapter in the section on homosexuality.

[3]The exception to this is in 1 Corinthians 6:12–20, where Paul argues against sexual promiscuity on the basis of Genesis 2:24. He is not speaking to married couples here. Rather his point is limited to the one-flesh relationship that is associated with sexual intercourse, thus making promiscuity wholly inappropriate for the believer. This is magnified by the indwelling Christ in the believer, so that Christ is actually joined to the person with whom one has had an affair.

[4]This is not to say that single-parent families are any less genuine families in the sight of God, only that procreation cannot occur in that setting. Single-parent families

usually began as two-parent families and procreation occurred in the proper context. Divorce, however tragic, does not prevent the resulting single parent and children from being a legitimate family.

[5]I am assuming a more literal interpretation of the Song of Solomon and reject the allegorical interpretation that views the relationship between Solomon and his bride as symbolic of the relationship between Christ and the church. Although that comparison is certainly appropriate in the light of Ephesians 5:22–33, the consensus among recent commentators is that Solomon's primary intent was to address literal sex in a literal, heterosexual marriage. For more on this, see S. Craig Glickman, *A Song for Lovers* (Downers Grove, Ill.: InterVarsity Press, 1978).

[6]See chapter 3 for more detail on Kant's ethical system.

[7]For example, see Matthew 5:19 and 19:1–10, in which Jesus discusses divorce. There is a great deal of debate on what exactly *porneía* means in this context. Some hold that it means premarital sex, while others hold that it means adultery. Whatever one's interpretation of these difficult passages, it is clear that *porneía* is used to specify a particular type of sexual immorality.

[8]Kari Jenson Gold, "Getting Real," *First Things* 39 (January 1994): 6.

[9]Glickman, *A Song for Lovers*, 115–16.

11

THE MORALITY OF WAR

In January 1991, only a few short years after the Berlin Wall came crumbling down signifying the end of the Cold War, the United States launched an aerial attack on Iraq, in response to their invasion and occupation of the tiny emirate of Kuwait. American involvement was justified by its supporters as a moral obligation to stop the tyrant Saddam Hussein from ruthlessly overrunning Kuwait. In addition, although it was never clearly stated that this war was about Kuwait's oil, terms like the "strategic national interests" that were at stake in the conflict were interpreted by the average person on the streets to refer to stopping Iraq from taking over Kuwait's massive oil production facilities. This war was very disillusioning to many observers who were thrilled that the Cold War had ended. Because the threat of the superpowers engaging in a nuclear conflict had been minimized, many people shared a new optimism that the world was a safer place to live. But the Gulf War in 1991 and the numerous regional and racial conflicts that erupted during subsequent years have significantly tempered this optimism. The wars in the former nation of Yugoslavia—especially the protracted conflict in Bosnia—the wars in Somalia, Rwanda,[1] and the former Soviet Union are grim reminders that humankind possesses greater skill and machinery to bring death and destruction in war than at any other time in human history. Even without the threat of a nuclear nightmare, the specter of continuing war looms ominously over various continents. This provides the contemporary background for the current debate over the morality of warfare.

The Gulf War had just begun, and much debate ensued over American involvement in it. Imagine that you are sitting on a panel that is discussing the morality of the Gulf War. As a Christian, how would you assess American involvement in this conflict? Was the United States justified in exercising its overwhelming military strength against Iraq in order to liberate Kuwait and insure the free flow of oil from the Persian Gulf to the West? Or is this an example of aggressive Western military arrogance, stepping in and risking the lives of American troops in a conflict where the United States does not belong? On what basis would you make such a moral judgment? And how would you incorporate the New Testament teaching on loving one's enemies and not taking vengeance?

Others on this panel include a Christian currently serving in the military, a Catholic priest and a Protestant minister. All three have different views of the morality of war in general and the morality of the Gulf War in particular. What follows below are brief opening statements which outline the position of each participant.

A Christian Currently on Active Duty

My position is that the world is a very dangerous place today, and many of the heads of state in certain parts of the world are aggressive, ruthless tyrants. War is necessary not only to defend ourselves from them, but also to reverse the injustices they have perpetrated on other nations and peoples. I further hold that in certain cases, preventive strikes against enemies that are poised for imminent attack are also justifiable. I hold that the Gulf War was morally justifiable, and furthermore, I am irritated that we have done nothing to stop the genocide of Muslims by the Serbs in Bosnia.

The Catholic Priest

I believe that my military colleague has gone too far in defending which wars can be justified. My view is that the only wars that are justifiable are wars of self-defense. I hold to what is called the *just war theory*, which states that once aggression is visited upon a nation, the properly constituted authorities in that nation are morally justified in meeting force with force and defending its peoples from a hostile aggressor. I cannot support any aggressive use of military force. It cannot be used unless and until another country has initiated a conflict. The only wars that are morally allowable are those fought in self-defense, such as the West's efforts in defeating the Nazis in World War II. Since Iraq did not initiate aggressive military action against the United States directly, and it is debatable whether defending the flow of Persian Gulf oil is a legitimate national self-defense for which we should go to war, I have major reservations about calling the Gulf War a just war.

The Protestant Minister

I think you are both wrong and out of step with clear biblical teaching on this subject. Both Jesus and the early church were pacifists. Jesus taught his followers to "turn the other cheek," to leave vengeance to God and not to use violence in any way to accomplish any purpose. The Beatitudes tell us, "Blessed are the peacemakers," and I take that to mean that any involvement in war, either as a combatant or noncombatant, is inconsistent with that. In addition, the people who were closest to Jesus chronologically were also pacifists. The early church for about the first three centuries had nothing to do with the military. Only when Christianity became the official religion of the Roman empire and had "national interests" that needed defending did the use of violence get church sanction. Thus, not only was the Gulf War totally unjustified, I hold that all use of violence is wrong.

The morality of war affects more people than just those who serve in the military. Most consistent pacifists hold that *any* participation in war violates Jesus' command to be peacemakers. So war creates moral tension not just for the soldier or officer who is a Christian, but also for the Christian who is employed by aerospace companies that manufacture weapons for the military. During the 1980s hundreds of thousands of people worked for the defense industry in various capacities producing different components to be used in military conflict. Perhaps even a Christian involved in financing these defense industries might face moral tension. For example, a banker whose loan portfolio includes some of these defense-based companies might experience some moral conflict with Jesus' command to be a peacemaker.

WAR IN THE BIBLE

The debate over the morality of war is set against the backdrop of war in the Old Testament. Throughout the Old Testament, Israel was commanded by God to go to war. Some of these wars were designed to secure Israel's boundaries and could be called preventive strikes (2 Sam. 5:17–25; 11:1–2). Others were clearly wars of national defense, fending off the attacks of a belligerent foreign nation (1 Kings 20). But others were aggressive in nature, designed to push Israel's enemies out of the Promised Land (Josh. 6–12). Military force was one of the methods God used to help accomplish his purposes for his chosen nation Israel. What is particularly difficult about some wars in the Old Testament is that God commanded total annihilation of certain enemies because of their idolatry (Deut. 25:17–19; 1 Sam. 15:1–3).

Simply because God commanded and sanctioned Israel's wars in the Old Testament does not mean that war is justified today. Important differences distinguish Israel in Old Testament times from the believer living the present age. First, Old Testament Israel was a theocracy, literally, one nation under God, in which the law of God was the law of the land. God had a unique relationship with Israel under the Law that has never been duplicated. No nation today can say that God is commanding them to go to war in the same way that he commanded Old Testament Israel.

Second, Israel was promised the land of Canaan as a national homeland, a place in which God would fulfill the covenant he made with Abraham. One way that was done was through the Messiah coming from the lineage of Abraham. But another way was the manner in which Israel lived together as a community of God's people in the land that God had selected for them. It was a strategic plot of land, in the center of commerce and travel between the empires of Egypt and Mesopotamia, maximizing the visibility of Israel's ideal society for their unbelieving neighbors.

Third, Israel was placed in the land of Canaan because of its vulnerability to military attack. Generally, when Israel was obedient to God, they experienced peace in the land; when they were disobedient, they experienced war. The period of the Judges gives a variety of examples of this trend. In order to develop Israel's trust in God to protect them from their enemies, he placed them in a particularly vulnerable piece of land that necessitated their possession of it. No nation can say that of its relationship with God today. Thus, one should be very careful about drawing any conclusions validating military force from the Old Testament, since God is not dealing with the church or the nations today as he did with Old Testament Israel. The case for war cannot be made from the precedent in the Old Testament alone.

It is true that the New Testament reflects a spirit of pacifism. For example, the Sermon on the Mount forbids resistance or retaliation with respect to evil (Matt. 5:38–42), enjoins love for enemies (5:43–48), and blesses peacemakers, calling them sons of God (5:9). Similarly, the apostles encouraged submission to persecutors (1 Peter 4:12–19) and to civil government, even to the tyrannical Roman Empire (Rom. 13:1–7). During the first few centuries of church history, this same spirit is carried forward. No mention is made of Christians serving in the military, and the early Christian martyrs offered little resistance to their persecutors.

Critics of pacifism will suggest that there were good reasons why there were no early Christians in the military. Many of the first Christians were Jews, and to join the Roman army would have been unthinkable, as it would have been for Gentile Christians, once the Roman persecutions were begun. But more importantly, joining the Roman legions normally involved swearing an idolatrous oath of loyalty to Caesar, which the believers were clearly unwilling to do. Thus, just because there were few if any Christians serving in the military in the early days of the church, it does not necessarily follow that pacifism is the biblical teaching on war. Nor does that conclusion follow from the admonitions to avoid personal resistance and retaliation. Many advocates of the moral use of military force argue that Jesus is addressing personal relationships, not the Christian's role in society. Paul clearly sanctions the state's valid use of coercion to maintain justice and public order. If that role of the state is valid, then the critics of pacifism can argue that a believer is not prohibited from involvement with the state in its divinely ordained function. Also, neither the Gospels nor Acts have any record of soldiers being converted and then being asked to give up their profession (Luke 7:1–10). Pacifists rejoin that the state is permitted to use violence to achieve its ends, but the Christian cannot participate with the state in those instances.

MAJOR VIEWS ON THE MORALITY OF WAR

Although many fine distinctions can be made among the different positions on the morality of war, most major views essentially correspond to one of two positions. For lack of a better term, we will call the first position *pacifism*. Although there are numerous varieties of pacifism, both in secular and religious arenas, pacifists basically hold that participation in any war is never justifiable for the Christian. The primary difference between the varieties of pacifism is the definition of "participation." Some pacifists hold to what is called *nonresistance*, that is, that Christians cannot be involved in war as combatants. That is the only restriction on Christians required by the New Testament teaching on nonviolence. But other pacifists suggest that participation of any kind is never justifiable, including "behind the scenes" work that supports a war effort or national defense in peace time. This would include being employed by companies that make military weapons and support machinery.

The second major position also includes two variations of a similar theme. This group is comprised of advocates of the *just war*, who hold that participation in war can be morally acceptable under certain conditions. Again, the primary difference is one of definition, namely, the definition of "just war." Some people within this camp favor the more traditional idea of the just war, that is, war is justifiable only when it is undertaken in self-defense, when one has been the victim of aggression by an outside intruder. Others define the just war more broadly to include preventive strikes that ward off imminent attack. These people hold that this is a similar form of self-defense that only operates prior to an attack instead of solely in response to it. Those in this latter group can usually justify wars that reverse clear cases of injustice visited upon a vulnerable group or nation by a stronger aggressor.

All of these groups agree that the church must not use violence to advance its ends. Although some might debate the morality of the church defending its people and property from violent attack, they agree almost unanimously that the church cannot use force to achieve its spiritual mission. The heart of the debate concerns the legitimate role of the state in conducting warfare and the Christian's participation with the state in that role.

If representatives of each of these views were on the panel debating the morality of the Gulf War, the pacifists would oppose it unequivocally. Some debate would likely occur among more traditional just war advocates, unless the panelist holding to that view was a citizen and resident of Kuwait. Then, according to just war theory, it would be justifiable. Other Western just war theorists might argue that their nation's security was jeopardized by the prospect of its oil supply being cut off. It would also be justifiable for those who held a stronger form of the just war. The West and their Arab allies were acting to reverse a clear injustice that was visited upon vulnerable Kuwait by the much stronger aggressor, Iraq. Let's look at each of these positions and their justifications in more detail.

Pacifism

Most versions of pacifism are premised upon a strict separation of the church from the world. Violence, pacifists claim, characterizes the world's way of doing business and accomplishing its ends. As such, the Christian can have no part with the world in using force. Christ's kingdom is not of this world (John 18:36) and the Christian does not wage war with the weapons of the world (2 Cor. 10:3–4). Since the Christian's citizenship is in heaven (Phil. 1:21), and since Christians are called to be separate from the values of the world (Rom. 12:1–2), use of violence cannot be a part of the Christian's modus operandi. Some pacifists suggest that a major indicator of the advance of Christ's kingdom is the degree to which nonviolence is practiced in society.

Biblical Basis for Pacifism

Christian versions of pacifism are grounded in several central passages of Scripture. These include selections primarily from the Sermon on the Mount (Matt. 5:38–48; Luke 6:27–36), Paul's teaching on vengeance in Romans 12:19–21, and Peter's doctrine of nonresistance to persecution in 1 Peter 2:18–24. Undoubtedly, the primary text used to support most forms of pacifism is Jesus' teaching in the Sermon on the Mount. The heart of this passage as it applies to war is as follows:

> You have heard that it was said, "Eye for eye, and tooth for tooth." But I tell you, Do not resist an evil person. If someone strikes you on the right cheek, turn to him the other also.... You have heard that it was said, "Love your neighbor and hate your enemy." But I tell you: Love your enemies and pray for those who persecute you, that you may be sons of your Father in heaven. (Matthew 5:38–40, 43–45)

Jesus here is teaching nonresistance to an evil person. The circumstances are not narrowly circumscribed to exempt combatants in war. Rather that would seem to be the case in which the passage would most directly apply since in times of war, your enemies are the most intense and most clearly defined. According to pacifists, Jesus' teaching that commands believers to love their enemies is inconsistent with being a participant in war. The context also appears to be broader than simply referring to persecution. It refers to the way in which a believer is to treat enemies in war, in persecution, in business, and in the church. According to pacifists, one cannot ever justify using violence, not even in self-defense. That is not to say that the Christian is to stand by idly while being overrun by evil and evil people. They are to resist by any means that do not involve violence. These may include nonviolent ways of making their task more difficult, similar to the way in which Operation Rescue advocates make procuring an abortion more difficult, as well as prayer, love, and other spiritual means to resist evil.

A second central passage is a teaching of Paul on nonretaliation.

> If it is possible, as far as it depends on you, live at peace with everyone. Do not take revenge, my friends, but leave room for God's wrath, for it is written: "It is mine to avenge; I will repay," says the Lord. On the contrary: "If your enemy is hungry, feed him; if he is thirsty, give him something to drink. In doing this, you will heap burning coals on his head." Do not be overcome by evil, but overcome evil with good. (Romans 12:18–21)

The beginning admonition sets the context for the rest of the passage. The goal for the believer is to be at peace with everyone, while realizing that a person cannot control the two-way street that being fully at peace involves. Just because someone cannot control all aspects of being at peace with another, that does not justify the use of violence. Rather, the rest of the passage lays out the believer's response when someone is intent on being at war. The pacifist argues that both violence and retaliation are ruled out by this passage, and that the classic case of being overcome with evil would be to take revenge or act violently in response to it. This is Paul's way of stating what Jesus made clear in the Sermon on the Mount, that you are to love your enemies. Whatever that does involve, certainly it does not leave room for using violent force.

A third central text occurs specifically in the context of Christian persecution. Pacifists argue that 1 Peter 2:18–24 reinforces the nonviolent thrust of the New Testament and grounds it in the example of Christ, strongly suggesting that it is normative for the believer today. The heart of the passage is that section that refers to the nonresistant model of Jesus on the cross:

> To this [suffering] you were called, because Christ suffered for you, leaving you an example, that you should follow in his steps.... When they hurled their insults at him, he did not retaliate; when he suffered, he made no threats. Instead, he entrusted himself to him who judges justly. (1 Peter 2:21, 23)

Because nonresistance is such a significant part of the identity of Christ on the cross, and following Christ in his sacrifice is such a significant part of the Christian's lifestyle, the pacifist concludes that trusting God and using nonviolent means of resisting evil are the only appropriate responses to evil for the Christian. Thus, genuinely following Christ and participation in war are mutually exclusive. Some critics of pacifism would point out that Jesus' and Peter's teaching, if taken in the kind of absolute sense that pacifists take them, would also rule out nonviolent resistance to evil. Jesus seems to be very clear that the believer is not to resist evil, and on the cross, he did not simply avoid the use of violence with his enemies, but he did not resist at all. In the Sermon on the Mount, Jesus instructs his disciples to go the extra mile, and if someone takes your coat, let him have other parts of your clothing. This does not sound much like nonviolent resistance to evil. Rather it sounds like complete nonresistance.

Nonviolence and Nonparticipation

Most Christian pacifists would only insist on nonviolence for the Christian; that is, based on their strong view of the separation of the church from the world, one's personal ethic cannot be imposed on society and made into a social ethic. It is a social ethic only for the church, not for the culture. Thus, since the society at large does not claim to follow Christ, it cannot be expected to follow his mandate for nonviolence. Certainly they desire that such a view of war would permeate the general society, but the expectation of nonviolence is only addressed to believers in Christ. As a result, Christian pacifists generally do not suggest that the state cannot be involved in war, only that Christians cannot participate with the state when it does wage war. Some versions of secular and other religiously grounded pacifism suggest that the state should not ever go to war, but the support for these versions of nonviolence usually is based on the harm caused by the ravages of war, both to people and the environment. Those who would uphold pacifism as social policy would oppose efforts to create a strong national defense. They would also argue that the money used to support the defense effort could be and should be better spent on social programs aimed at helping the poor and other vulnerable groups in society.

Some Christian pacifists oppose more than simply participation in war as combatants. They would oppose any involvement in the war effort because of the Christian's calling to be a peacemaker (Matt. 5:9), and our role as ambassadors of reconciliation, bringing men and women back to God (2 Cor. 5:18–21). Supporters of this more extreme version of pacifism (although they would not call it more extreme, but more consistent with Jesus' teaching) suggest that it is inconsistent to be involved in any way with a system that by waging war, kills people for whom Christ died. Not only can the believer not be personally involved in the use of violence (which would rule out Christians being involved in law enforcement as well), but anything that contributes to the overall war effort is seen as on the same moral level as being a combatant. Thus the believer in Christ cannot be involved in support of the defense industry, such as working for companies that make weapons and other materials used in war. They would suggest to the other school of pacifism that forbids only combatant participation in war that they are making an artificial and somewhat ad hoc distinction between combatant and noncombatant aspects of war; that is, it seems arbitrary to allow the believer to support every other aspect of the war effort, but not to be a combatant. They hold that if they were consistent, they would realize that there is little moral difference between the direct combatant role and other indirect supporting roles.

The supporter of nonviolence, that is, the more moderate pacifist, would respond by insisting that the teaching of Jesus prohibits only the personal use of violence in resisting evil. In addition, they might respond that the more extreme pacifism leads to a position in which it is impossible to draw any meaningful lines that distinguish participation from nonparticipation in war. To prohibit the Christian from supporting the defense industry would make many jobs off-limits for the Christian. For example, consider the companies that do some business with the defense establishment, while the majority of their business is not related to the military. Rubber companies that make tires for commercial airplanes also make them for military airplanes. Can the Christian work for these firms, since separating military from nonmilitary use of the company's product would seem to be virtually impossible, or at the least, would make a Christian go to absurd lengths to be consistent with the Bible's teaching? Or consider companies that bottle water for sale. Most of their business is clearly nonmilitary use. Yet they played a very important role in supporting the troops engaged in the Gulf War in the desert. Should the Christian who owns a company that bottles water refuse to sell it to the military? Or should the Christian who works for one of these companies quit when they start selling water to the army, even though this is a small part of the company's overall business? To be consistent with this more extreme pacifism, the Christian would need to separate military from nonmilitary use. However, the more moderate pacifist would argue that this simply cannot be done in most cases, and is not necessary since the Bible only prohibits personal use of violence.

Criticism of Pacifism

The primary criticism of pacifism is not necessarily related to involvement in war, but to the use of violence in general. Imagine that your wife and children were being brutally attacked by someone who had broken into your home and intended to kill them. He is a crazed killer who has chosen your home at random, and unless you intervene personally, your family will be dead shortly. There is not enough time to call the police. What should you do? What would be most in keeping with your calling as a Christian? One response would be to attempt to disarm him and detain him until the police arrive. If that can be done, that would be the best option, although it could be argued that you still used violence in disarming him. In this case, it may be that the only way to disarm him would be to inflict some kind of bodily harm on him in order to get him to stop his murderous rampage. But what if the only way to stop him is to kill him? If you don't, your family, and likely you, will be killed.

Most people have a strong intuitive opposition to pacifism because of cases like this. Somehow they think it cannot be right or Christian to stand by and let their family be slaughtered because they are not willing to use violence when necessary. One can argue that using force is justified here because a person has a higher moral obligation to protect his family than to obey the mandate for non-violence; that is, there is a conflict between two moral absolutes, the command not to use violence and the command to protect and provide for one's family (1 Tim. 5:8). St. Augustine put it a bit differently, and in the course of church history, opened the door to legitimizing force for Christians. He held that at times, the only way that a Christian can obey the law of love is to use violence when another person is threatened with deadly force. The only way I could truly fulfill the law of love for my wife and children is to do whatever is necessary to repel their attackers, even using lethal force in response if necessary. To refuse to take such action would not be loving toward my family. Seen in this way, it is argued that the use of violence can be justified as a fulfillment of the higher law of love (Rom. 13:8; Gal. 5:14).

A further criticism of pacifism comes from the view of the state in Romans 13:1–7. There Paul suggests that the state legitimately employs force ("wields the sword") to keep public order and promote public justice. The state exercises these responsibilities under the authority of God himself. If it is legitimate under God for the state to use violence in the God-given exercise of its responsibility to protect its citizens and maintain order, and if the Christian is called to support and be involved with government in its legitimate role, then it is difficult to see why the Christian cannot be involved with the state in a role that involves the use of force. This would open the door for Christians to be involved in internal law enforcement as well as external military affairs that protect its citizens from harm, both from inside the state as well as outside it. The critic of pacifism might state this another way and accuse them of creating a double standard in too sharply distinguishing between one's personal and social ethic. The two objections listed above provide a footing for the just war theory and the use of force.

The Just War Theory

The just war tradition goes back ultimately to the time of St. Augustine but was not systematically well-developed until Catholic theologians did so in the Middle Ages. For some time it has been the dominant justification for the use of force. More recently, its adequacy has been called into question with the development of nuclear weapons capable of destroying the planet. Advocates of the classical view hold that war is justifiable under certain carefully worked out conditions, namely, when it is a response of self-defense to unprovoked aggression. Some just war advocates have taken the view a bit further and justified preventive wars, or those which anticipate aggression, and wars to reverse clear injustices visited on vulnerable nations by stronger aggressors. Both are justified as just wars, but the definition of what constitutes a just war is different.

Traditional Criteria for the Just War

Proponents of the classical just war tradition maintain that only wars of self-defense are justified. They admit that war is an atrocity, but is sometimes regrettably necessary to maintain security and justice within one's borders. Any just war must meet a series of conditions that specify when a war is just in order for a war to be engaged. They are as follows:

1. *The war in question must be prompted by a just cause*, defined as a defensive war; that is, no war of unprovoked aggression can ever be justified. Only wars that are a response to aggression already initiated are morally legitimate. Thus, after the Japanese attack on Pearl Harbor during World War II, the United States had just cause to respond to Japanese aggression by declaring war. Whether the war was entirely just depends on how well it measures up to the rest of the just war criteria, but the just cause rule is a critical one. But simply because a nation has a just cause for war, does not mean that the war can be morally justified. It must meet the rest of the criteria.

2. *The war in question must have a just intention*, that is, its intent must be to secure a fair peace for all parties involved. It cannot be undertaken with the aim of securing a peace that is to one's clear advantage, not only a peace that insures one's security. This criteria rules out wars of national revenge, economic exploitation, and ethnic cleansing. Many would argue that the Allies (except perhaps the Soviet Union) in World War II had a just intention to secure a just peace, as evidenced by the Marshall Plan to help rebuild Europe.

3. *The war in question must be engaged in as a last resort*. All diplomatic efforts to resolve the conflict must be exhausted prior to engaging in defensive war. This criteria also implies that diplomatic efforts should continue once the war is begun in an effort to settle the hostilities at the negotiating table rather than on the battlefield.

4. *The war in question must be initiated with a formal declaration by properly constituted authorities*. Warfare is the prerogative of governments, not individuals, vigilante groups, or paramilitary units operating outside legitimate government authority. A just war is declared and engaged in by the highest authority in government, and must be recognized by appropriate legislative bodies, assuming they operate in the nation in question. This criterion does not mean that individuals do not have the right of self-defense, but on the surface, it would seem to preclude wars of national liberation by paramilitary groups operating against the government.

5. *The war in question must be characterized by limited objectives*. Wars of total annihilation, unconditional surrender, or wholesale destruction of a nation's infrastructure and ability to rebuild following war, are not moral. The overriding purpose for a just war is peace, not the humiliation and economic crippling of another nation. It may be that insuring the victor's future security may involve disarming the enemy nation and crippling its offensive military capabilities, but it must not involve destruction of its potential to survive as a nation.

6. *The war in question must be conducted with proportionate means*, that is, the amount of force used must be proportionate to the threat. Only sufficient

force to repel and deter the aggressor can be justifiably used. Total destruction, perhaps by nuclear attack, is ruled out. The defending nation, in responding to the attack, must not be guilty of "burning down the barn to roast the pig." Many critics of just war theory aim their criticism right here, that any use of nuclear weapons violates this criterion, and thus any war in which nuclear weapons are engaged cannot be just. Thus, they would conclude that American attacks on Hiroshima and Nagasaki violated just war doctrine. But advocates of the bombing of these two cities could respond by saying that if conventional war had continued and an invasion of Japan had taken place, far more lives would have been lost than were lost as a result of the nuclear bombing. However, the final criterion poses even greater problems for nuclear weapons.

7. *The war in question must respect noncombatant immunity*. Only those individuals who are representing their respective governments in the military can be targeted in the course of the war. Civilians, wounded soldiers, and prisoners of war cannot be objects of attack. Since most nuclear weapons are indiscriminate in their destructive capacity, they would not be considered implements in a just war. It may be that strategic nuclear weapons will be perfected, but until then, noncombatant immunity poses significant problems for any nation's nuclear arsenal within the just war tradition. This would also rule out other weapons of mass destruction, such as chemical and biological weapons. It also raises questions about one of the strategies employed in World War II, the fire-bombing of cities both in Britain by the Nazis and in Germany by the Allies.

Responding to the Pacifist's Biblical Support

Only if a military campaign meets these seven conditions can it be termed a just war, in the traditional sense. In their attempts to justify the use of force to resist evil, Christian just war theorists must respond to the pacifist's appeal to New Testament teaching in the central passages mentioned above. The texts from the Sermon on the Mount are often interpreted as applying to the age of the kingdom,[2] or taken as an ideal morality, similar to Jesus' statement, "Be perfect, therefore, as your heavenly Father is perfect" (Matt. 5:48). Thus, they are either not intended for this present age, or not intended to be applied strictly, but like an ideal, used as a general goal at which the church is to aim. The passages from Paul (Rom. 12:19–21) and Peter (1 Peter 2:18–25) are often taken to refer to the Christian enduring persecution for faith in Christ, not military service under the authority of the state. Thus, if someone threatened to do violence to you on account of your faith, that should neither be resisted nor avenged. But those passages would not apply to someone who threatened your family with random violence or someone who invaded your nation's borders in warfare. Another way that just war theorists attempt to justify the use of force is by taking a hierarchical view of God's commands;[3] that is, one has a higher obligation to defend oneself and one's family against the imminent threat of harm, over and above the obligation to not resist evil. Whether that higher obligation, if you hold to that, justifies anything more than immediate personal or family self-defense is open to debate. Most pacifists find all of these explanations unconvincing, and one of the perceived weaknesses of the just war tradition is its inability to explain what appears to many to be the clear teaching of Jesus and the apostles advocating nonviolence.

Just war advocates defend the use of force with a set of other, more theologically grounded arguments. First, they insist that the sinfulness of people and the biblical demand for justice make the use of force necessary in society. The inhumanities against the human race in this century alone, which has surpassed any in the history of civilization, makes it apparent that force is sometimes necessary to maintain social control and to keep societies from moving toward chaos. The Christian demand both for love and justice, coupled with the depravity of people, make the use of force necessary to deter and repel aggression. Some just war advocates argue that pacifism might actually contribute to the spread of evil by not resisting it when it comes and by not deterring it before it comes. Some pacifists will grant this argument, but insist that the Christian's calling prohibits him or her from its use. The state is permitted to use force to maintain order and secure justice, but the Christian cannot participate with the state in this role. This gives rise to a second just war argument, based on the role of the state in Romans 13:1–7.

A Second Just War Argument

In this passage, Paul outlines the God-given role of the state to maintain order and justice by enforcing the law and punishing those who break it. The state is entrusted by God with maintaining social order and restraining sinful, self-interested people. The state is to be not an instrument of personal vengeance, since that prerogative belongs exclusively to God (Rom. 12:19), but rather an agent that enforces restraint on a person's pursuit of his or her self-interest. When Paul says that the state "wields the sword" in accomplishing this, at the very least this is a figure of speech for the use of force. It may even justify capital punishment, but that is not at issue here. At a minimum, the state is authorized by God to use force to maintain order and secure justice. Based on this, the just war argument is as follows:

1. The state is entrusted by God with a divinely given responsibility to wield force only as necessary to maintain social order.
2. Christians in both the Old and New Testaments were involved with the state in the exercise of this force.
3. If the state is exercising its legitimate, God-given authority by using force to maintain order, and if Christians in the Bible were involved with

the state in this role, then there is no reason Christians cannot be involved with the state today in the exercise of the same legitimate, God-given role. This is particularly true, since the Christian is called to support the state in this role, as long as the state does not command the Christian to do something that Scripture forbids. This does not mean that the believer is commanded to use force in participation with the state, only that he or she is permitted to do so if necessary.

Pacifists might respond to this argument by insisting that their view of the Christian's relationship to the state and society is different from the just war theorist. And they would be correct. To which the just war theorist would respond that their view of the Christian's involvement in society more closely reflects Jesus' teaching that the church is to be the salt of the earth and the light of the world (Matt. 5:13–16).

WHO BELIEVES WHAT

In Christian circles, the pacifist position is often held by groups of the Anabaptist and Mennonite persuasion. These groups tend to encourage a greater degree of separation from the world. They embrace the idea of the two kingdoms, the earthly and heavenly ones, with the believer being a member of the latter. For many groups this means that the church and individual believers are to have little or no political involvement, and little or no attempt to directly influence society other than by their witness, that is, the way they live together in community bearing corporate witness to the reality of Christ and his commands ordering communities. Thus, they acknowledge the legitimate role of the state in maintaining social order, but insist that the Christian cannot participate with the state in that role. The primary reason for this is their view of the clear teaching of the New Testament on nonviolence. A second reason for their separation from bringing about direct social change is their concern that the purity of the church would be compromised if it engaged in the rough and tumble world of politics and social change.

Most just war theorists have a different view of the Christian's relationship to society and social change. Coming from primarily either Reformed or Catholic traditions, they hold that the Christian is to be involved in transforming society by direct involvement with it. They hold that this is what Jesus meant by the phrases "the salt of the earth" and "the light of the world." Further, they hold that the use of other figures of speech such as yeast and leaven to describe the church's role (both have a pervasive, penetrating influence on things with which they come into contact) suggest that more direct contact with society is necessary than the Anabaptists and Mennonites hold. Thus, the basic stance of the believer toward society is quite different for the Reformed and Catholic traditions. They hold that the believer's calling is engagement with society rather than separation from it. To be sure, the believer is to be separate from the values of the world; both pacifists and just war theorists agree here. But the just war theorist approaches the Christian's relationship to society very differently than does the pacifist, and holds that their view accords more closely with Jesus' teaching. If you accept their view of the church transforming society by more direct contact and involvement with it, it clearly warrants the Christian being involved with the state as it exercises its God-given functions, even the use of force.

EXTENDING THE JUST WAR THEORY

Once you accept the basic position of the just war theory, that the Bible allows the use of force under certain conditions, then it may be difficult to stop with traditional just war doctrine. Proponents of a broader definition of what constitutes a just war argue that two extensions of just war theory follow logically. First, a preventive strike would seem to be morally acceptable. If your enemy is poised for an imminent attack and capable of dealing you a damaging blow, it makes little sense to wait until formally attacked to defend yourself. In other words, a preventive strike can still be essentially a war of self-defense, if the signs that you are in imminent danger from military attack are clear.

The classic example of a justifiable preventive strike was undertaken by Israel in the 1967 Six Day War. Their Arab enemies were virtually in place at their borders, and Israel had very reliable intelligence that its Arab neighbors were coordinating a massive offensive designed to erase the state of Israel from the map. It would have been foolish, and perhaps, suicidal, for Israel to wait until their enemies crossed their borders to respond with their own military action. It was a strike that had self-defense as its goal. One can argue that once you accept the idea of a just war of self-defense, there is no moral difference between self-defense taken *in response* to attack and self-defense taken *in anticipation* of imminent attack. The only difference is the timing, that is, when the strike for self-defense occurs. Of course, one has to be careful that preventive strikes do not become a disguise for hiding aggressive intentions toward a nation's enemies. The threat of attack must be clear and imminent in order to justify a preventive strike.

Again, if you accept the basic moral acceptability of the just war, it can be argued that another type of war follows logically. If war is justifiable to prevent or restrain the spread of evil by a hostile aggressor nation, would it not also be justifiable to use force to reverse injustices perpetrated on vulnerable nations? If it is legitimate to prevent evil from spreading to another's territory, then certainly it is legitimate to use force to reverse injustices that have already been visited on a vulnerable people. This is the way the Gulf War was justified, and the way many people argued for international intervention in the former nation of Yugoslavia, particularly to the atrocities in Bosnia, and in the recent eruptions of catastrophe in both Somalia and Rwanda.

CONCLUSION

Jesus predicted that wars and rumors of wars will be with us until his second coming. With the end of the Cold War, it may be that the threat of a global nuclear catastrophe may be less than a decade ago. But tribal and ethnic conflicts are continuing with increasing ferocity and are likely to remain for some time. As society becomes more violent and people become more fearful of being victims of violent crime, even the use of force in matters of personal self-defense is becoming an issue for more people. Thus, the questions that are at the heart of the debate over the morality of war affect people personally, beyond the decision that concerns actually going to war. Whether the Christian can use force and violence, even lethal force if necessary, goes beyond questions of war and participation in it to issues of personal safety and protection. Thus, the age-old debate between pacifists and advocates of the just war will likely remain until Christ, the Prince of Peace, returns and brings a real and lasting peace. The prophet Isaiah predicted this final, universal peace in vivid terms: "They will beat their swords into plowshares and their spears into pruning hooks. Nation will not take up sword against nation, nor will they train for war anymore" (Isa. 2:4).

FOR FURTHER READING

Clouse, Robert G., ed. *War: Four Christian Views*. 2d ed. Downers Grove, Ill.: InterVarsity Press, 1991.

Craigie, Peter. *The Problem of War in the Old Testament*. Grand Rapids: Eerdmans, 1978.

Hauerwas, Stanley. *The Peaceable Kingdom*. South Bend, Ind.: University of Notre Dame Press, 1983.

Ramsey, Paul. *The Just War: Force and Responsibility*. New York: Scribner's, 1968.

Yoder, John Howard. *The Politics of Jesus*. Grand Rapids: Eerdmans, 1972.

NOTES

[1]The cover of one issue of *Time* magazine in May 1994, describing the slaughter in Rwanda, quoted a missionary as saying, "There are no devils left in Hell; they are all in Rwanda."

[2]Many interpreters who approach the Scripture from a dispensational perspective take the Sermon on the Mount to be an ethic of the kingdom, not addressed to the church prior to Christ's second coming. See, for example, Stanley Toussaint, *Behold the King* (Portland, Ore.: Multnomah Press, 1983), for a defense of this view and a survey of the interpretive options for the Sermon on the Mount. An exception to this general trend is Herman A. Hoyt's essay, "Nonresistance," in Robert G. Clouse, *War: Four Christian Views* (Downers Grove, Ill.: InterVarsity Press, 1991), 27–57.

[3]For a brief discussion of the three main ways of viewing ethical conflicts, see chapter 2, "Christian Ethics."

12
LEGISLATING
MORALITY

Imagine that you are a representative in your state legislature, charged with the task of formulating wise and responsible laws that will be enacted across the state. You decided to run for elected office because of your Christian convictions, and now that you have been elected, you intend to represent Christ in your political office, a part of which is to introduce bills into the legislature that you think reflect Christian morality and to vote on bills in a way consistent with your convictions. What kinds of laws would you favor? To what degree should you support legislating Christian morality in a secular, pluralistic society? To what degree is it right that you bring your Christian views into the political arena? These questions are at the heart of the debate over legislating morality, especially in a culture that assumes the separation of church and state and claims pluralism as one of its foundational elements.

As a Christian, you have the responsibility to be the salt of the earth and the light of the world in whatever sphere of influence you happen to occupy. That sphere may be your home, a small business, a major university, or the state legislature. Whether that means that you can legislate biblical morality is another matter. Surely some aspects of biblical morality are appropriate for legislative efforts. Others belong in the realm of moral persuasion, not political power. Where you draw the line between what should be the object of legislative support and what should remain an area of moral persuasion is the subject of this chapter.

As a Christian lawmaker, how would your Christian morality inform your decisions on the following legislative matters?

1. A law that would restrict the availability of abortion
2. A bill that would prohibit physician-assisted suicide, or active euthanasia
3. A bill that would establish homosexual couples as legitimate married couples, entitled to all the tax and civil advantages of marriage
4. Enforcement of sodomy laws (that prohibit homosexual sexual activity) that are already on the books in several states
5. Laws that would make adultery a criminal offense
6. A bill that would prohibit the death penalty in your state
7. A law that would restrict the practice of commercial surrogate motherhood

CONNECTING THE LAW AND MORALITY

When various groups, especially religious ones, attempt to influence society, one often hears the opposition saying, "You can't legislate morality!" Whether that statement is true depends on exactly what is meant by morality. If moral beliefs, or one's worldview, is meant, then that certainly cannot be legislated. In fact, the First Amendment that guarantees freedom of religion and expression was written to keep the state out of the business of imposing beliefs on its citizens. If by morality one means a moral intent, then that also cannot be legislated. A person's genuine moral intent is changed by persuasion, not coercion, since intent has to do with one's free choices. But if by morality one means moral behavior, then that can be, and is legislated virtually every day around the world.

Most, if not all laws have some moral overtones to them. For example, even laws such as driving on the correct side of the road implies a respect for life and property. We rightly assume that the person who drives on the wrong side of the road and ignores other similar traffic laws has respect for neither life nor property. Most people hold that for laws to be valid, there must be some connection to widely shared moral principles, that is, a law that violates society's widely held principles, cannot be a valid one. Thus, in most cases there is a significant connection between law and morality.[1] The question then is, What should the relationship be between sin and the law? Or to put it another way, Which immoral behaviors should also be considered illegal?

How then should Christians who care about morality in society try to influence which behaviors should be regulated by the law? The style and manner with which Christians are involved in society are often as important as the substance of what a particular Christian group has to say. Of course, by running for elected office, a person can attempt to gain political power in order to pass one's views into law. One can use various pressure tactics, such as boycotts and lobbying to influence public officials into voting consistent with your convictions. One can use a variety of types of moral persuasion, either by appeal to a widely recognized sacred authority, such as the Ten Commandments or the Sermon on the Mount. A person could also appeal to other widely accepted forms of moral reasoning, such as general moral principles (justice, fairness, and equality), consequences (both negative and positive), or rights and liberties (freedom of expression, right to privacy, free expression, and right to life).

The manner in which the church attempts to influence which behaviors are regulated by law is important and should not detract from its stand on the issue itself or compromise its role in evangelism and discipleship in the world. That is, the church should first of all be a model community, one that in its life together bears corporate witness to being distinctive as the people of God. Second, Christians who attempt to influence moral behavior in society should be aware that using biblical language has only limited effectiveness to a secular audience. Unless Scripture is recognized as authoritative (many non-Christians recognize the moral authority of only some parts of the Bible), it is more prudent and persuasive to use arguments that are not explicitly dependent on the Bible or one's theology. Although a person must not compromise his or her theology, use of a more secular terminology and arguments is more likely to reach an audience for whom the Bible is no longer a significant source of moral authority.

THE CHANGING MEANING OF PLURALISM

But we still must ask, Which immoral behaviors should also be illegal, especially in a pluralistic society? The term *pluralism* suggests that there are a wide variety of philosophies and worldviews competing for influence in society. Pluralism and tolerance were designed to go together, because the heart of a pluralistic society is not just the presence of many different views of the world, but tolerance toward others who hold different views. For example, religious perspectives are diverse, ranging from liberal Protestantism to Catholicism to various Eastern religions. Although lacking an ostensibly religious basis, many other groups also compete for influence in society, including radical feminists, New Age believers, secularists, and radical environmentalists. Pluralism demands an open playing field in which all worldviews can compete for influence and where tolerance is one of the highest virtues. Unfortunately, the definition of pluralism has changed somewhat in recent years to mean more than simple tolerance of a variety of worldviews. Today it often implies an acceptance of all worldviews as equally valid, since they involve religious questions which many in society cannot verify as true. Moving from toleration of worldviews formerly viewed as mistaken to acceptance of them as valid is a significant shift.

Pluralistic societies need a strong view of the separation of church and state to flourish, that is, the state cannot favor or endorse any specific worldview, religious or not. As originally intended, the First Amendment that established religious freedom only prohibited the federal government from establishing state-supported and state-sanctioned churches, as had been done in Europe with disastrous results that included religious wars and harsh, religious persecutions. The First Amendment guaranteed religious freedom by prohibiting the establishment of a state church. The state was supposed to be neutral toward all religious groups. This clearly emphasized freedom of religion.

From the separation of church and state, it did not follow that the state was to be neutral or hostile toward religion in general. Many of the founding fathers who wrote parts of the Bill of Rights were very clear that a democracy needed the moral restraints and the grounding for rights that religion provided. Here is a sample of their opinions on the centrality of religion for democratic societies.[2]

Thomas Jefferson: "Can the liberties of a nation be thought secure, when we have removed their only firm basis, a conviction in the minds of the people that these liberties are the gift of God?" It seems clear that, as Jefferson wrote in the preamble to the Declaration of Independence, rights and liberties are ultimately, theologically grounded, and need religious nurture in order to be maintained. He further stated that, "religion should be regarded as a supplement to law in the government of men and as the alpha and omega of the moral law."

James Madison, writing in the government charter for the Northwest Territory, said, "Religion, morality, and knowledge, being necessary to good government and the happiness of mankind, schools and the means of learning shall forever be encouraged." Here Madison, representing Congress, is calling upon the government to promote religious and moral education, which today would be considered a violation of the separation of church and state.

George Washington, speaking in his farewell address at the end of his second presidency: "Where is the security for property, for reputation, for life, if the sense of religious obligation desert the oaths, which are the instruments of investigation in courts of justice? And let us with caution indulge the supposition that morality can be maintained without religion. Whatever may be conceded to the influence of refined education on minds of peculiar structure, reason and experience forbid us to expect that national morality can prevail in exclusion of religious principle."

Benjamin Franklin, writing in his plan for public education, said, "[history shows] the necessity of a public religion, the advantage of a religious character among private persons and the excellency of the Christian religion above all others, ancient or modern. [The great mass of men and women] have need of the motives of religion to restrain them from vice, to support their virtue, and to retain them in the practice of it until it becomes habitual."

The founding fathers never imagined a society in which the state would be neutral or hostile toward religion in general. As A. James Reichley of the Brookings Institution said, "The founders' belief in the wisdom of placing civil society within a framework of religious values formed part of their reason for enacting the free exercise clause. The First Amendment is no more neutral of the general value of religion than it is on the general value of the free exchange of ideas of an independent press. The virtually unanimous view among the founders [is] that functional separation between church and state should be maintained without threatening the support and guidance received by republican government from religion."[3] But the interpretation of the First Amendment has changed over the decades since it was first written. As originally intended it meant freedom *of* religion, but today it has come to be interpreted as freedom *from* religion. That is, religious perspectives only belong in the private sphere of one's personal life and should not be allowed to intrude on matters of public policy that concern the society as a whole. Society should be free from religion in matters that affect both religious and secular citizens. Thus, by definition, religious people should not be allowed to legislate religious morality.

The irony of this new understanding of the separation of church and state is that from the beginning of American democracy, religious groups have exercised moral influence in society and have attempted to legislate their specific moral positions. For example, the abolition of slavery, prohibition, and much of the New Deal legislation were all heavily influenced by religious groups. Only in the last twenty years, with the birth of the Religious Right, have such efforts suddenly violated the separation of church and state. Whether one agrees with everything for which the Religious Right stands, they have been the victim of an unfortunate double standard. This is only time when a religiously based morality has received widespread opposition on the basis of First Amendment violations. Most other religious persuasions have been allowed to exert considerable influence in legislating morality. For example, the Civil Rights movement in the 1960s and the Vietnam War protests had the broad support of mainline Protestant and Catholic denominations. They faced little if any opposition on First Amendment grounds. Yet when the Religious Right and conservative Catholics publicly opposed abortion or when evangelicals supported prayer in public schools, they were accused of violating the separation of church and state. This view of the First Amendment is not only inconsistently applied, but it is out of step with the original intent of the founders.[4] It cannot be used to justify excluding religious involvement in legislating morality.

IMMORALITY VERSUS ILLEGALITY: THREE VIEWS

Religious communities attempting to influence which moral behaviors are regulated by law operate within these conceptions of pluralism and the separation of church and state. Since religious groups attempting to legislate moral behavior violates neither pluralism nor the First Amendment, the question still remains, What immoral behaviors should be deemed illegal? Perhaps even more important is the question, On what basis should certain immoral behaviors be considered illegal?

Within Christian circles, three distinct positions emerge on this question: (1) the theonomists (or Christian reconstructionists); (2) the restored Christian America position; and (3) the pluralists. Both the theonomist and restored Christian America positions question the legitimacy and wisdom of the separation of church and state, while the pluralists function with that as an assumption. Adopting either the theonomist or restored Christian America positions would involve significant changes in the way society views the role of religious groups in public policy.

Theonomists

According to the theonomists, Old Testament moral and civil laws in the Pentateuch that are not specifically overridden by the New Testament are still binding for society today.[5] Certainly the ceremonial portion of the law, which included the sacrificial system and the religious festivals, have been superseded by the coming of Christ and are no longer in force. But unless the law has been specifically superseded by later parts of God's revelation, there is no reason to think that they are not still applicable, not only to the church, but also to the wider society. As one theonomist writes, "in all of its minute detail (every jot and tittle), the law of God, down to its least significant provision, should be reckoned to have an abiding validity, until and unless the Lawgiver reveals otherwise."[6]

The advocates of theonomy are very sensitive to the current moral decay in the culture and hold that God's law has always been intended for the nations, not just for Israel, and the law's continuing validity can be assumed unless there is reason to believe it has been set aside. For example, in view of the resurrection of Christ, Christians now celebrate the first day of the week as the day of rest, making the Jewish Sabbath no longer binding. The theonomists would insist that laws be enacted in accordance with Old Testament civil law. How some of these laws would be applied would be fairly simple, such as expanding the death penalty for crimes other than murder. But in other cases, it would not be so easy. For instance, Old Testament real estate laws such as the Year of Jubilee and law of redemption of property (Lev. 25) were designed for an agricultural society, not a modern industrial state. They could perhaps be used for nations undergoing land reform for the first time, but their application to the industrialized West is difficult to envision.

Restored Christian America

The second position, called a restored Christian America, has a similar spirit but with less scope. This position has both mild and strong forms. Advocates of the milder form of this view hold that the United States has regrettably abandoned its rich Christian heritage, in which Christianity exercised much influence in public policy and matters of state. Biblical values have in effect been erased from most aspects of our public life. They suggest that Christians should aggressively reintroduce Christian values into all levels of government so that the laws of the land reflect distinctively Christian teaching.[7] Similar to the theonomists, this group assumes that the law of God is designed for both believers and unbelievers, and that both groups are accountable to it. Unlike the theonomists, however, they would not advocate that the laws of the land also reflect Old Testament law.

Also, they would hold that the church is not under the law in the same way as Old Testament Israel, but that the general principles revealed in the law are still valid today, just not their specific prescriptions. They would end the separation of church and state and use both groups to enhance the welfare of all its citizens. They suggest that tremendous good comes to a society that is informed by Christian values and that America should unapologetically endorse the Christian faith as the nation's moral compass to avoid moral catastrophe in the future. They hold that the Ten Commandments and the principles of the New Testament should be the bedrock of American civil law.

Advocates of a stronger form of this second position suggest that it needs to be applied more deliberately and broadly. Using the example of Puritan New England in the seventeenth century and the National Covenant of Scotland during the same time period, this group holds that "all contemporary nations should officially declare allegiance to Jesus Christ in their public documents and devise political structures and policies that honor God and promote His justice."[8] They insist that the most significant things that Christians can do in society are not specific reforms but the general reform of the government's acknowledgment of Christ as the ultimate power over the state and the One to whom all its citizens owe their primary allegiance. Both the mild and strong views hold that the separation of church and state is not in society's best interest, and both understandably make non-Christians nervous about the protection of their rights.

Pluralists

A third view is that of the pluralists. Using the parable of the wheat and the tares as the cornerstone (Matt. 13:24–43), pluralists hold that since God tolerates the existence of the tares amidst the wheat in the age prior to the second coming of Christ, he tolerates, as should the church, a wide variety of differing worldviews in the same society. Also, they argue, since God never compels belief but allows it to be freely chosen, then part of a God-ordained state is the coexistence of many different views of the world, all legitimately competing for influence. Thus the state is less involved in legislating Christian morality than with the theonomistic or restored Christian America view.

The pluralists hold that Romans 13, perhaps the central passage of Scripture on the role of civil government, teaches that the state's role is to provide for public order and justice. For the most part, its role is not concerned with essentially private matters between consenting adults, in which no clear, tangible harm results. The primary role of the church is to use moral persuasion, not legal coercion, to bring public morality back into conformity with biblical ethics. The pluralists hold that Christian morality can only be legislated to preserve social order, protect essential civil rights, protect from clear harm, and provide for public justice. Such laws must be enforceable, and they presume the support of the general public.

APPLYING THESE VIEWS

Returning to our test case laws on which you would have to vote as a Christian legislator, each of these three groups would vote differently. Here are the specific laws on which you must decide to vote:

1. A law that would restrict the availability of abortion
2. A bill that would prohibit physician-assisted suicide, or active euthanasia
3. A bill that would establish homosexual couples as legitimate married couples, entitled to all the tax and civil advantages of marriage
4. Enforcement of sodomy laws (that prohibit homosexual sexual activity) that are already on the books in several states
5. Laws that would make adultery a criminal offense
6. A bill that would prohibit the death penalty in your state
7. A law that would restrict the practice of commercial surrogate motherhood

The theonomists would likely support the death penalty, oppose homosexual marriages, and vote into law all the other items. The advocates of restored Christian America would likely enact laws prohibiting abortion, euthanasia, and surrogate motherhood, would clearly work to defeat a bill legitimating homosexual marriages, and would generally favor the death penalty. The pluralists would likely oppose enforcement of sodomy laws and they would not support a bill that would make adultery a criminal offense. Some might even allow for surrogate motherhood and the opinion on the death penalty might be mixed. The pluralists would neither initiate nor support laws that involve matters of personal privacy, that do not involve clear harm, and that are difficult to enforce.

CONCLUSION

Regardless of the position that a person takes on legislating morality, everyone in Christian circles recognizes the importance of the church as a model moral community, faithful to God, and promoting both justice and compassion within it. The church's efforts to influence society will be futile if we fail to live by the morals that we are trying to persuade society to embrace. We must be willing to abide by those same standards that we wish to see enacted into law. For example, we must not clamor for a law prohibiting abortion if we ourselves are unwilling to carry unwanted pregnancies or support those who do make that choice. In addition, the church should clarify on what basis some forms of immorality should be made illegal and others should not. Finally, the church should be committed to high-level moral persuasion, lest it be in the awkward position of trying to enact into law those things which we are unable to persuade society to adopt. Granted, this is the explicit tactic of many special interest groups, but the church should be distinct, not only in its message, but also in the manner and style with which it attempts to influence society.

FOR FURTHER READING

Neuhaus, Richard John. *The Naked Public Square.* Grand Rapids: Eerdmans, 1983.

Smith, Gary Scott, ed. *God and Government: Four Views of the Reformation of Civil Goverment.* Phillipsburg, N.J.: Presbyterian and Reformed, 1989.

Guinness, Os. *The American Hour.* New York: Free Press, 1993.

NOTES

[1]For further reading on the relationship between law and morality, see the following works: H. L. A. Hart, *Law, Liberty and Morality* (London: Oxford University Press, 1963); Lord Devlin, *The Enforcement of Morals* (London: Oxford University Press, 1965); the debate between Hart and Harvard Law Professor Lon Fuller in Hart's, "Positivism and the Separation of Law and Morals," *Harvard Law Review* 71 (February 1958): 593–629; and Fuller, "Positivism and Fidelity to Law," *Harvard Law Review* 71 (February 1958): 630–72. The debate is summarized in Scott B. Rae, *The Ethics of Commercial Surrogate Motherhood: Brave New Families* (Westport, Conn.: Praeger, 1994), 126–29.

[2]All of the following citations are taken from A. James Reichley, *Religion in American Public Life* (Washington, D.C.: Brookings Institution, 1985), 89–106.

[3]Ibid., 113.

[4]For further detail on this important aspect of legislating morality, see Richard John Neuhaus, *The Naked Public Square* (Grand Rapids: Eerdmans, 1983).

[5]Primary advocates of theonomy include philosopher-theologians Greg L. Bahnsen (see note 6 below) and Rousas John Rushdoony and economist Gary North, founder of the Institute for Christian Economics.

[6]Greg L. Bahnsen, *Theonomy in Christian Ethics* (Phillipsburg, N.J.: Presbyterian and Reformed, 1984), 40–41.

[7]Key advocates of this position include John Whitehead and Harold O. J. Brown. Most would include the late Francis Schaeffer in this group.

[8]Gary Scott Smith, ed., *God and Politics: Four Views of the Reformation of Civil Government* (Phillipsburg, N.J.: Presbyterian and Reformed, 1989), 173.

GENERAL INDEX

SCRIPTURE INDEX

251